MAKING MEN

Making Men

Gender, Literary Authority, and Women's Writing in Caribbean Narrative

BELINDA EDMONDSON

Duke University Press   Durham and London   1999

© 1999 Duke University Press
All rights reserved
Printed in the United States of America
on acid-free paper ♾
Typeset in Sabon by Keystone Typesetting, Inc.
Library of Congress Cataloging-in-Publication
Data appear on the last printed page of this book.

A portion of chapter 4 originally appeared as
"Black Aesthetics, Feminist Aesthetics, and
Problems of Oppositional Discourse," *Cultural
Critique* 22 (fall 1992): 75–98. Reprinted by
permission of Oxford University Press.

For my parents,
Dorothea and Locksley,
with love

CONTENTS

Acknowledgments   ix

Writing the Caribbean:
Gender and Literary Authority   1

PART I
Making Men: Writing the Nation   17

1 "Race-ing" the Nation: Englishness, Blackness, and
the Discourse of Victorian Manhood   19

2 Literary Men and the English Canonical Tradition   38

3 Representing the Folk: The Crisis of Literary
Authenticity   58

PART II
Writing Women: Making the Nation   79

4 Theorizing Caribbean Feminist Aesthetics   81

5 The Novel of Revolution and the Unrepresentable
Black Woman   105

6 Return of the Native: Immigrant Women's Writing
and the Narrative of Exile   139

Notes   169
Bibliography   205
Index   221

Acknowledgments

I would like to thank the many people and institutions who have helped to make this book a reality.

The ideas for what has now become *Making Men* are heavily drawn from my doctoral dissertation in the English department at Northwestern University. Accordingly, I would like to thank the members of my dissertation committee for their helpful comments and suggestions: Françoise Lionnet, Paul Breslin, and Kenneth Warren. Also, I would like to thank the graduate school at Northwestern and the Woodrow Wilson Foundation for giving me research grants which got me started in the right direction.

I received two fellowships which allowed me to complete this manuscript in both its incarnations, in its first as a dissertation and in its second as a book. The Women's Studies Program at the University of California, Santa Barbara, provided me with the predoctoral fellowship which was invaluable in allowing me the time and space to complete the manuscript. I would also like to thank the faculty and staff of the English department at Johns Hopkins University for their assistance and camaraderie while I worked on the book as a postdoctoral Mellon Fellow there. Gabriel Miller and Wendell Holbrook, chairs of the English department and the program of African/African-American Studies at Rutgers-Newark respectively, gave me some much-needed leave from teaching, for which I thank them.

I would also like to acknowledge the assistance of particular individuals who helped with the manuscript in various ways: my editor at Duke University Press, Ken Wissoker, for his interest in my work and ability to get things moving; my colleague Barbara Foley, whose attentive reading of my dissertation produced many insightful comments and suggestions which helped me start the revision process; Jean D'Costa, whose thorough reading of the manuscript as well as the historical sources she provided are much appreciated; Antoinette Burton, who not only read parts of the manuscript but also sent along all sorts of invaluable clippings for which I can never thank her enough; Jennifer Morgan and Mary Poovey, for their helpful suggestions; Richard Halpern and Supriya Nair, who kindly sent me their own essays and works-in-progress; Faith Smith, for her indefatigable tracking of citations at any time of day or night, as well as her intellectual rigor in all our discussions; and, most of all, my family, just for being there. All of these people were instrumental in helping me to finish this book, and their contributions simply cannot be measured.

WRITING THE CARIBBEAN:
GENDER AND LITERARY AUTHORITY

The idea for this project grew out of my observation of two apparently unrelated phenomena in literature of the English-speaking Caribbean. The first was an ongoing fascination on my part with what I can only describe as the Victorian sensibilities of Caribbean writers who are otherwise described as nationalist, modernist, and engaged in the revolutionary project of defining the Caribbean nation in the new era of Caribbean independence. The primarily male writers in this category — C. L. R. James, V. S. Naipaul, George Lamming, Derek Walcott — are centrally concerned with the question of how to represent Caribbean national identity, and though they (most noticeably Naipaul) sometimes come to different conclusions, the manner in which they structure the relationship of *writing* and nation formation is remarkably similar. For example, Naipaul's narratives reveal a preoccupation with the texts of nineteenth-century English travel writers and their imperialist views on the Caribbean: he begins each chapter of *The Middle Passage*, his study of the Caribbean islands after independence, with a quote from either Victorian novelist Anthony Trollope's *The West Indies and the Spanish Main* (1859) or Oxford historian James Anthony Froude's notorious *The Bow of Ulysses: The English in the West Indies* (1888). Similarly, in *Beyond a Boundary*, his remarkable study of cricket and Caribbean nationalism, the Marxist James cites Trollope approvingly and tells the reader that it is the Victorian author "Thackeray, not Marx," who is most responsible for the beginnings of his Caribbean nationalist outlook.[1]

That James and Naipaul, two distinctly opposed writers in ideological terms — Naipaul is perhaps the region's most famous neoconservative, James its most famous Marxist — should find it necessary to refract the lens of their Caribbean identity through the prism of the canonical figures of Victorian England points to a structural issue of Caribbean national identity that reaches beyond the mere espousal of ideological positions. Englishness — *Victorian* Englishness, no less — is somehow important in the definition of what it means to be Caribbean, and since I take my cue from Foucault that "nation" is a *discursive* formation more so than mere allegory or imaginary construct, then the *writing* of the Caribbean is paramount in the *production* of the nation. The obsession with Victorian writers and writing that reveals itself in this primarily male West Indian canon, then, becomes a factor in the construction of the nation itself. Many of these narratives are therefore engaged in rewriting the stories of the English classics: Jean Rhys's *Wide Sargasso Sea* tells the story of the Jamaican wife of Rochester in *Jane Eyre*; Wilson Harris's *Palace of the Peacock* relies in no small measure on a memory of Conrad's *Heart of Darkness*; and of course there are the innumerable reinterpretations of Shakespeare's *The Tempest*, which usually recast Caliban as the Caribbean hero of the story, and Prospero as the colonizer/villain.[2]

My second observation is the result of my readings of recent novels authored by migrant women from the Caribbean who currently live in the United States — Michelle Cliff, Paule Marshall, and Jamaica Kincaid. At the time of these readings — the late 1980s/early 1990s — the literary criticism of these works tended to discuss them in terms of feminist theory, African American women's literature, or both.[3] Rarely were they discussed as *West Indian* writers. Consequently, these analyses always retained a disembodied quality for me, a sense that their discussion of female-authored West Indian novels had somehow leaped over their "West Indianness" so that they could be recast as part of a more universal American feminist literary tradition. Though the scholarship has now changed, and the writers are often discussed as West Indian writers, it is symptomatic of the literary establishment's desire to categorize "national" literatures into easily recognizable genres, that these writers are now *either* West Indian writers *or* African American writers, but rarely both.

In the current reassignments, female-authored West Indian narratives of this genre still are not seen to have any relation to the West Indian canon. As one scholar puts it, "These are writers who because they are U.S.-based and did not reproduce the anti-colonial text seem to have forfeited their identity as part of the Caribbean literary tradition."[4] She observes further that they are engaged in an antihegemonic discourse with the United States in the same manner that the prior generation was engaged in an antihegemonic discourse with Great Britain.

Yet my impression of the works of Marshall, Cliff, and Kincaid was similar to that of my impression of Lamming et al.: like the prior generation, the women's central concern was with the reconfiguration of the Caribbean space, on which the colonial experience has left an indelible print. Marshall explicitly thematizes the West Indian experience in many of her novels, among them *The Chosen Place, the Timeless People, Soul Clap Hands and Sing,* and *Daughters*; Cliff's *Abeng* and its sequel *No Telephone to Heaven* attempt to rewrite the twin histories of the experience — master and slave, white and black, female and male — through the life of a mulatto Jamaican girl; Kincaid's *Annie John* and its "sequel" of sorts, *Lucy,* use the ambivalent relationship between a West Indian girl and her mother as a metaphor on what it means to be a West Indian woman.

What all of these novels have in common is the thread drawn between the peculiarly *female* experience of West Indianness in the Caribbean context. The presumption upon which the texts present their female characters is that the *male* experience is already understood, has already "made its case," so to speak, which indeed it has, but it has done so through this prior West Indian literary tradition to which these female-authored texts are presumed to have no relation. Moreover, these female-authored texts, far from evincing no interest in the colonial relation, often situate the protagonist's current problems in ancient colonial history: Cliff's Clare Savage is the descendant of a nineteenth-century slaveowner, whose actions then "mark" her postcolonial identity; in Marshall's *Praisesong for the Widow* the African American protagonist Avey has flashbacks to her slave ancestors, whose spirit is reincarnated in the West Indians she meets during a cruise; and in Kincaid's *Annie John,* Annie gets into trouble for mocking the image of Christopher Columbus during a classroom lesson on Columbus's "discovery" of the islands.[5]

Most importantly, the female-authored migrant texts consistently reproduce the same concern with images of West Indians — or lack thereof — in the English literary canon. Lucy wins a prize for the proper elocution of Wordsworth's poem, "Daffodils,"[6] and imagines herself to possess any one of the names of the Brontë sisters, whose names are infinitely preferable to her own; in Marshall's *The Chosen Place*, the protagonist Merle Kimbona loses her job as a schoolteacher because she insists on teaching black revolutionary history to the island children rather than the English history that has been mandated for them;[7] Marshall's short story "Brazil" reconsiders the use of Caliban as a symbol of Caribbean independence; and Clare Savage, Cliff's protagonist in *Abeng* and *No Telephone to Heaven*, ponders the meaning of origins in *Jane Eyre* and *Great Expectations*. If the United States has replaced Britain as the hegemonic presence in these texts, it certainly does not show in their intertextual moments.

This continuing fascination with the English canon cannot be explained merely by the application of African American or mainstream feminist approaches. The earlier example of the critical approaches to the novels of Jean Rhys is instructive of the dangers of exclusionary readings. Feminist readings could only see their "purely" feminist sensibilities, and did not consider questions of geographic *space*, or *race*, questions which are crucial to the understanding of Rhys's specificity as a white West Indian woman writer.[8] Race probably has something to do with that oversight—as Alice Walker has noted, white feminist critics often excuse their oversight of black women's texts on the terms that they have no "experience" of black culture.[9] Conversely, Rhys's status as a white female writer possibly overrode considerations of her *minority* status in her country of origin, Dominica. Like Naipaul and James, Rhys has an ongoing preoccupation with the modes of Victorian discourse, but as a woman writer this reveals itself in different ways. For instance, Froude's *The Bow of Ulysses* makes a small but crucial appearance in her short story, "The Day They Burned the Books," which I discuss in detail in chapter 6. Froude's book is "saved" from destruction at the hands of a black West Indian woman because of its commercial value, while other books, particularly those by English women writers like Christina Rossetti, are burned.

One feminist reading of this gesture contends that the black woman has internalized the oppressive values against which she rebels because she reserves special ire for books written by women.[10] Perhaps so, but considered from the vantage point of the Caribbean, Christina Rossetti's Englishness overdetermines her femaleness; consequently, there can be no question of a common female experience between the two. Moreover, Froude's text has commercial value precisely because *West In-*

dians still value it. Its significance as a cultural marker is embodied in the West Indian woman's ongoing confrontation with England and Englishness that has consigned her to the margins of Froude's master text. Destruction solves nothing: "saving" the book implies its ongoing dialectical relationship as a Victorian "master" text to Caribbean national identity.

It is only by returning Caribbean women's texts to their cultural points of origin that the textual pieces that have fallen in between the cracks of European and American literary theory start to emerge as definitive to their structure as a whole. The Caribbean-American women writers have clearly read the English canon, but more importantly they have read it in the same *context* as the West Indian literary "old guard." The intertextual moment revealed in their narratives is at one remove from another moment of engagement in the male-authored texts. In that remove is a wellspring of issues about the place of the West Indian author in relation to this canonical tradition: does it *mean* the same thing for West Indian women to read Milton et al. as it does West Indian men? Does their similar preoccupation reveal a similar desire for similar kinds of literary authority?

My contention is that the terms of writing "West Indian" novels for the male writers of the pre- and post-independence English-speaking Caribbean are founded on the interpellated meanings of manhood and cultural authority that have been passed on to them from British intellectual discourse of the nineteenth century. These are the terms of writing which Caribbean-American women writers must address yet revise in order to mark the "West Indianness" of their own texts. The tropistic relationship between nineteenth-century Englishness and twentieth-century West Indianness has structured the meaning of "authorship" and "nation" in anglophone Caribbean discourse such that what is now recognized as West Indian oppositional discourse to Britain is still marked by a utilization of a specifically English vision of what constitutes intellectual production. That English "vision" of intellectual authority is the idea that intellectual labor is the realm of "real" men, "gentlemen," middle-class/upper-class Englishmen. For nonwhite, non-English men to make a case for self-government, they must state their case as *gentlemen*, which means they must, in essence be "made" into Englishmen. If *authorship* is marked as a specifically masculine, specifically *gentlemanly*, enterprise, and national narratives are fundamental to nation formation, then in order to engage in an insurgent Caribbean nationalism the female writer must re-vision what constitutes literary authority itself by rewriting the paradigm of the gentleman author.[11]

Since the concept of manhood is central to the thesis of this book, a word here on my use of "manhood" is necessary. I do not believe in any such essential trait as manhood or, for that matter, womanhood. Rather, I find these to be dynamic ideological categories that are played out *through* loosely biological categories. For example, I argue that the Victorians had concrete ideological beliefs that predetermined the kind of man who could accede to the manly ideal. The result was that man would usually, *but not always*, be white. The intersection of class with race in the Victorian conception of manhood created a small but significant space in which nonwhite Caribbean men could renegotiate their status as (non)men into not merely men but gentlemen. In a way, gentlemanliness *was* manhood for the Victorians, encompassing as it did an intellectual, moral, and physical ideal to which all men could aspire. Therefore, the idea that men can be "made" is an essential attribute in the English project to create native ruling classes in its nonwhite colonies.

Why a title like "Making Men" for a book that claims to be about *women* authors as much as men, if not more so? Quite simply, because I believe that the founding moment for the anxieties of Caribbean migrant women authors over literary authority can be traced back to these Victorian speculations on whether men could be "made" out of black West Indian men. The emphasis on "Making Men" in the title of the first part, and "Writing Women" in the title of the second, is meant to highlight the speciousness of the hierarchical kinds of labor associated with both groups by illustrating their connectedness as binaries of each other. Therefore, if male authors base their literary authority on intellectual labor — the project of writing the Caribbean into literary existence — then the physical labor so often associated with migrant women can also be re-imaged as a basis for women's literary authority.

I would also like to point out that I deliberately use the term "West Indian" to designate "Caribbean" in specific instances, despite its critical and historical problems, because the name is still used in the French- and English-speaking Caribbean, whose inhabitants are perceived as "West Indian," as opposed to the Spanish-speaking islands whose inhabitants are not. I submit that the different usage has created a distinction which has now become "real." Therefore, since I focus particularly on anglophone Caribbean discourse, I use West Indian interchangeably with Caribbean.

The first part of the book, "Making Men: Writing the Nation," is specifically concerned with canonical West Indian fiction and issues of masculinity which, I argue, are to be found in the twin preoccupations over West Indian identity and English cultural authority. The anxieties over West Indian identity and Englishness in these texts most often coalesced around issues of race, in particular racialist views of black and white peoples. Therefore, race is a central category in this analysis.

My first chapter, " 'Race-ing' the Nation: Englishness, Blackness, and the Discourse of Victorian Manhood," attempts to establish the intimate relation of a specifically English intellectual discourse to the production of blackness in the English-speaking Caribbean. Though a significant portion of the writers under discussion are not black, nevertheless in the Manichaean world of English political discourse, "blackness" comes to embody all that Englishness is not. Consequently, I assert that the mutually constituted meanings of Englishness and West Indianness throughout the variously authored texts are structured by this binary relation of racialized cultural essence, regardless of the race of the author.

I also wish to make a clear distinction between *Europe's* discourse about its colonies and *English* discourse on the West Indies. The latter I assert has a culturally distinct meaning, which in its turn has produced a culturally specific brand of nationalism and national identity in the English-speaking Caribbean. In other words, the way that English-speaking West Indians view blackness is in large part determined by their relationship to Englishness. For example, in nineteenth-century Cuba, African ethnic difference was often institutionalized in the government-sponsored *cabildos*, lodge-type associations where black slaves of different ethnic groups could congregate. Even as this meant that Cuba retained a high degree of African survivalisms, it also meant that black Cubans were prevented from seeing themselves as a group: they were not "black" but "Ashanti," and so forth. Compare this to the British policy, which "persecuted all African manifestations."[12] The difference in the colonial vision of how to control the black population had inevitable consequences in how that population perceived its sense of black cultural identity. (I think it more than a coincidence that the pan-Africanist, black nationalist rhetoric of the Caribbean is more likely to be found in the English- or French-speaking Caribbean than in the Spanish-speaking islands.) I assert that this difference does not *negate* the obvious similarities between the anglophone Caribbean and nonanglophone, but rather that it is important to our understanding of the contextual meaning of colonialism to explore the specificity of colonial relationships in the Caribbean.

Victorian debates on whether or not the Caribbean region was deserving of independence — or, more specifically, whether or not its inhabitants were *fit* and *capable* of "ruling" themselves — often circled around the issue of black West Indian *masculinity*. As I discuss in chapter 1, for the English the idea of nation was essentially tied to the idea of masculinity, such that Caribbean men would have to prove themselves the masculine equals of the Englishmen who currently dominated the imperial landscape. It did not help their case that black West Indian women were perceived to have the traits that Englishmen associated with men. Black men were seen as lazy and docile — though "singularly" ambitious to be scholars — while black women were described as hard workers, but loud and *aggressive*.[13] The Victorian perception of difference in black labor — black men attempting intellectual labor, however perniciously, black women performing arduous physical labor, however pathologically — is one that will undergird the way in which the intellectual "inheritance" of England will be passed on to West Indian men: that is, the question of who *ought* to be doing what will determine who *will* do what. The inversion of gender characteristics that the English imagined onto black West Indian society circumlocuted the discourse of later West Indian nationalism, such that the nationalist project became inseparable from the epistemological issue of defining West Indian manhood.

The one chink in the English imperial armor was its domestic class policies; the degraded status of blackness could be renegotiated through black men's access to the status of "gentleman" through the critical knowledge of the artifacts of English cultural archaeology. If, on the one hand, nineteenth-century English imperialism defined England as superior to its nonwhite colonies, on the other it allowed for a handful of the nonwhite "elect" to be trained in the manner of the English gentleman. These men were to pass on the tenets of Englishness to their societies in their roles as civil servants and other kinds of "go-betweens" between the colonial government and the colonial society. The black men of this class became the West Indies' first black middle class, and in them became articulated the apparently contradictory beliefs in Englishness as a transcendent category and pan-Africanism as a political ideology.

Chapter 2, "Literary Men and the English Canonical Tradition," is more specifically concerned with revealing the linking between Caribbean authorship and the English literary tradition. If, as Gauri Viswanathan asserts, "the English literary text [in the colonies] functioned as a surrogate Englishman in his highest and most perfect state,"[14] then the West Indian desire to emulate, not the *stories* of the English literary tradition but rather the *idea* of the master tradition itself, points to a desire to function as an author in relation to the West Indian text in the same way that the "surrogate Englishman" functions in relation to the English text. (I am, of course, using the term "master" here deliberately, to highlight the gendered connotations of learning and artistry in this context.) The strategic necessity of locating the West Indian author as a master of a literary tradition finds support in West Indians as ideologically varied as Naipaul and Edward Kamau Brathwaite, the historian, poet, and famous proponent of a pan-Caribbean "nation-language" which revalues African-derived creole oral languages as the basis of an authentic West Indian literature. Again, it is important to distinguish the opposing *political* positions of these authors — as always, Naipaul more or less versus the rest — from their similar assumptions about the meaning of the English literary tradition for themselves as West Indians.

Chapter 3, "Representing the Folk: The Crisis of Literary Authenticity," explores the logical consequence of the West Indian attachment to the English literary tradition described in chapter 2. The desire for national origins unsullied by colonial taint finds its object in the representation of peasant — or what I call folk — West Indian society in the nationalist genre of West Indian literature. West Indian intellectuals used the folk culture of the Caribbean as a solution to the compromised colonial tradition, from which they themselves sprang. The idea that there remains a piece of Caribbean culture largely untouched by colonial influence is a powerful ideological argument for an authentic national literary tradition. However, this positing of an authentic West Indian literary tradition as specifically un-English and un-educated engenders a crisis of authorship for the writers themselves, whose sense of authority as authors is predicated precisely on their mastery of the English educational model.

Further, the binary of "authentic folk culture" versus "inauthentic colonial culture" becomes too easily "raced," such that "authenticity," "blackness," "folk culture," and "nation" are all elided to mean the same thing. However, the reverse is not true: "Englishness" as it relates to the issue of writing does *not* become "raced," such that Brathwaite can approve of Naipaul's *A House for Mr. Biswas* solely on the terms that it emulates the English literary tradition of "strong social convention[s]."[15] Mastery of tradition, then, is not necessarily the same thing as embodying the tradition itself; the difference between the meanings of literary mastery and cultural authenticity is where the West Indian author must continuously renegotiate the two contradictory impulses of the narrative. The paradox is that the triumph of the "folk" narrative would mean the dissolution of the idea of literary mastery itself, which has been the means to effect the recovery of that authentic culture in the first place. Since "literary mastery" carries with it an implicit masculinized English status, then the competing claims of the folk also carry with them the implication that the folk is a feminized national entity, an idea profoundly disturbing if the folk culture is also the black culture. Nationalist folk writers such as Claude McKay and Una Marson attempt to bridge the gap between literary authority and the folk by using black female proto-intellectuals in *Banana Bottom* and *Pocomania*, respectively, as a bridge between the two.[16] Still, as I argue in this chapter, in both narratives, the real intellectual work of translating folk culture for the reader remains the province of the "real" intellectuals, both of whom are English gentleman archetypes.

The second part of this book, "Writing Women: Making the Nation," attempts to link the masculinist origins of West Indian literary nationalism to the search for a West Indian female subjectivity in current literatures by West Indian–American women. Just as the first part, "Making Men: Writing the Nation," attempts to align the writing of national narratives to the "making" of West Indian male subjectivity, so does the second part attempt to reverse the paradigm. The writing of immigrant women is literally "making" the West Indian nation from another direction. I also wish to draw attention to the fact that immigrant women, though immigrant, help to produce the capital of the West Indies, in the form of the obvious — by sending goods to their families "back home" — and the not-so-obvious, the production of narratives as a different kind of "cultural capital."

My deliberate choice of West Indian women writers living in the United States can be traced to Bruce King's observation that Caribbean writers who live abroad are more concerned with "old" themes and black/white divisions, while those "at home" are more concerned with local issues.[17] This interesting — if problematic — schematic suggests that the Caribbean writers "abroad" are the inheritors of the West Indian canon as it now stands. The argument that West Indian internationalism — as such it seems to be posed — is only to be found away from the Caribbean implies that the discursive parameters of the region have shifted once more so that the ancient dialogue on what it means to be West Indian must of necessity be located elsewhere besides the material place itself.

What this distinction between migrant and local writers does *not* acknowledge is that, for the most part, the male West Indian writers whose writings have come to define West Indian literature themselves wrote from *without* the Caribbean. There is hardly a canonical writer who wrote from within the region. Further, they usually described migration from the region as a *necessary prerequisite* for literary endeavor.[18] This suggests, if nothing else, that migration is, far from a contemporary phenomenon, a peculiar tradition of anglophone West Indian writers. However, the heavily female West Indian immigration[19] to the United States has fused issues of West Indian national identity to specifically *female* issues of survival, as I discuss in chapter 6, of which more in a moment.

Chapter 4, "Theorizing Caribbean Feminist Aesthetics," tries to establish a model for Caribbean female subjectivity that takes into account current formulations for black and feminist writing. Even though African American and mainstream feminist approaches to narratives by West Indian women are limited by their own cultural contexts, nevertheless it is important to note the theoretical influence African American feminist theory has had in shaping the ideas for an oppositional interpretation of a West Indian female subjectivity that is not necessarily white or male. I argue that the "problem" of masculinized literary mastery that these women writers inherit from the West Indian canonical tradition and the corresponding lack of a female West Indian literary tradition therein, is counterbalanced by their inheritance of African American feminist narratives as immigrant American subjects. The African American female narrative tradition provides a partial solution to the masculinized conception of authorship in anglophone Caribbean narrative.

The methodology of this chapter is a distinct departure from the combination of historical argument—the development of canons—and literary close readings with which I conduct my inquiry in the rest of the book. I found it necessary to "clear a space," so to speak, for a new account of the West Indian female subject. I wanted to negate the idea that the narratives of West Indian women writers—or, for that matter, West Indian male writers—can be explained in terms of an essentializing "aesthetics" model, whereby the formal properties of the text reveal the authenticity of the national/gendered/raced subject. Because the narratives of West Indian women authors have an overdetermined relationship either to black (male) aesthetics or (white) feminist aesthetics models, I wanted to disentangle the specificity of "Caribbean" and "female" from these theoretical constructs even as I show how African American feminist models of *criticism*—if not models for African American feminist *aesthetics*—can uncover important new solutions to the "problem" of reading the West Indian female-authored narrative.

Chapter 5 examines the "novel of revolution"—that is, West Indian novels about revolutions or revolutionary discourse—in the context of gender. I argue that the traditional, male-authored representations of revolution and revolutionary discourse are tied to the image of men negotiating over the "body" of the land. The men in this tableau are, on the one hand, the English colonizer, on the other, the oppositional black male subject. In between them, the body is represented as a white female figure, displacing the image of black womanhood in the text, which I further argue is unrepresentable in these revolutionary narratives because of the historically fixed meaning of black womanhood as "threatening" or "emasculating" for *both* men. The second half of the chapter concerns itself with showing how this paradigm of West Indian narrative is taken up and revised by Caribbean women writers to reveal the gendered meaning of "revolution."

In the final chapter of the book, "Return of the Native: Immigrant Women's Writing and the Narrative of Exile," I examine the meaning of the exile tradition among Caribbean writers of the prior generation and compare it to the current status of immigrant Caribbean women writers in the United States. My argument here is that "exile" is a loaded term with certain gendered connotations in the Caribbean literary tradition. Exile writing in the Caribbean carries with it the meanings associated with high modernism; that is, the feature of alienation of the intellectuals from the "homeland" is paramount. The narrative is then articulated as a way to reconcile (or reintegrate) the intellectual to "home." Modernity and tradition are thus posed as exclusionary choices. The English migration of "scholarship boys" — West Indian men who went to England on scholarships to Oxford and Cambridge, such as Brathwaite and Naipaul — produced a very different relationship to home for the educated West Indian male migrant subject than did the largely economic, heavily female migration to the United States, which produced these female writers.

This is not to say that West Indian migration to England was by any means largely of this kind: the vast majority of immigrants to England from the Caribbean were rural and poor. But the United States did not mean the same thing as did England in the West Indian imagination. With the authority of Cambridge and Oxford in the background, West Indian male writers, writing from England in self-imposed exile, gained a certain kind of literary authority by their particular negotiation of the space between home and exile. (I do not mean to imply that *all* West Indian male writers went to Cambridge and Oxford. C. L. R. James, for instance, went right to work upon arrival in England. However, the "Oxbridge" ideal of learning is clearly at the root of these writers' engagement with the Victorian models of literary authority. Since these universities were historically associated with producing a gentleman class that otherwise had no material claim to elite status, such as the clergy, the classic Oxbridge education functions as a symbol of English literary authority. Therefore I am suggesting that this particular group of men implicitly invoked this authority when they engaged in certain kinds of discussions in their narratives.)

Unlike "exile," the term "immigrant" carries with it a different, arguably feminized, status to the metropole; one associated with physical, not intellectual, labor. The place from where the "immigrant" writer speaks, therefore, cannot carry with it the same authority of intellectual tradition. Moreover, "exile" carries with it the literary authority of modernism. In this context, I explore Luce Irigaray's idea that "woman" is always in symbolic exile from "nation," such that the narratives of women returning to the Caribbean can be conceived of as an effort to reconnect at a different level. However, lest one infer that return has the romantic overtones associated with the folk narrative, I contend that the return is not about final reintegration with the home-land—which would simply repeat the maternalized objectification of woman as the body of the nation that occurs in the earlier narratives — but rather it is a way to fuse the competing claims of modernity and tradition. As such, female narratives of return offer a different valuation of the relationship between literary mastery, home, and exile.

My purpose in this study is emphatically *not* to pose the narratives of Caribbean women writers as somehow "better" or more "progressive" than those of the male-authored anglophone West Indian canon, whether or not readers come to that conclusion on their own. Indeed, Rhys has effectively been shown to hold colonialist and implicitly racist attitudes toward black people,[20] and it might be argued that Rhys's depictions of black women such as Antoinette's maid Christophine in *Wide Sargasso Sea*, far from being the empowering image of black womanhood that some critics take it to be, is a romance of black womanhood that mystifies her *disempowered* relation to the state.[21] Nor do I mean to posit that any attempt to define a black female subjectivity is, in and of itself, *de facto* an improvement upon the masculinist paradigm. For example, Jamaican cultural critic Carolyn Cooper's reading of black "dancehall queens" in Jamaican dancehall culture, fascinating and important as it is, nevertheless treads dangerously romanticized ground in assessing black working-class women's "power" solely in terms of their sexual personae within the confined space of the dancehall.[22]

What I do wish to point out is that the one has inherited the concerns of the other, and must write *within* and *against* that prior tradition in order to be engaged in the process of national definition. In so doing, the parameters of the West Indian nation space are expanded both figuratively and literally to include Brooklyn as well as Barbados, as Paule Marshall explains.[23]

Further, I have found it particularly important to explore in detail the relationship of V. S. Naipaul and Jean Rhys to a mostly black literary tradition of nation writing. Both complicate what might otherwise be seen as the easy binarisms to which my study could lead. Naipaul and Rhys both display ambivalence in their attitudes toward black people; Rhys refers obsessively to the ingratitude of black people in her private letters, yet also identifies herself as part of a black consciousness when she refers to "us black people."[24] Rhys was a white woman writing at a time when very few West Indian women were writing anything at all; her literary presence in England usefully complicates my alignment of Englishness with a black middle-class ethos and exile with masculinity. My point in discussing Rhys here is to sharpen the configuration of race, gender, and nationality that I pose in this chapter: I argue that Rhys does not derive the same "benefits" from the Englishness as do her male counterparts due to her peculiar positioning as a white West Indian woman writer.

Similarly, Naipaul's status as an East Indian–West Indian, and one of distinctly antinationalist sentiments at that, elicits a more profound evaluation of the meaning of blackness and nationalism as structuring tropes of Caribbean narrative. Naipaul disparages "Negro protest writing," yet praises the work of nationalist C. L. R. James as illustrative of "who and what *we West Indians* are" (my emphasis).[25] Like Rhys, Naipaul is simultaneously distanced *from* yet tied *to* blackness. I hope that my discussions of these two writers will expand and reinforce my thesis on the relationship between race, gender, and writing. I have attempted to lay out a theoretical model of Caribbean narrative that is not prescriptive — not *every* text will conform to the paradigm revealed here — but that instead reveals a certain dialectical relation between the historicized meaning of literary mastery and what are tagged as oppositional, nationalist narratives.

I would also like to note that I am aware that there is a new generation of immigrant English writers of Caribbean origin, such as Caryl Phillips, who as a male English–West Indian author writing novels on the Caribbean reveals his influences to be African American male-authored narratives such as *Invisible Man* and *Native Son*; consequently, he is utilizing a very different strategy of representation of the Caribbean subject than the narratives of the prior generation of male exile writers.[26] My argument here is not necessarily meant to account for *all* of the different modes of authorship, such as Phillips's, so much as to trace a very *particular* relationship between the writing of the prior generation of male writers and that of the immigrant women writers of the United States who, unlike Phillips, are often not perceived to have a relation to the canonical anticolonial West Indian narratives.

Finally, I would like to place my study both in a body of scholarship that is identified as "postcolonial" as well as within the context of scholarship on "minority" literatures in the United States. I realize that there is an ongoing problem with the conflation of postcolonial with minority in the United States; nevertheless, it is relevant and important to the aims of my study to locate this discussion in the context of both traditions of criticism, because both are intrinsic to the main categories of analysis here.

I am also well aware that there are certain scholarly hierarchies attached to these labels: "postcolonial" scholarship has been identified with the idea of "high theory" in the American academy, and as such carries with it its own implications of "literary mastery" — a strangely ironic twist for a scholarship that is meant to deconstruct the paradigm in its representation of the "third worldness" of the Third World. This is due in no small part, I think, to the fact that many postcolonial scholars are products of the iconized educational systems of Europe themselves, and thus are seen to be invested with those very gentlemanly qualities of authority that I investigate in my study. The claims for "difference" are mediated through the "high theory" discourse of the postcolonial intellectual whose validation as a spokeswoman issues from her ability to invoke "First World" intellectual models of critique. Conversely, the criticism of minority American literatures — particularly black feminist literary criticism — has often been accused of not being theoretical enough.[27] I hope that projects such as this one will ultimately help to dissolve these specious and unproductive hierarchies of knowledge and further the study of the interdependent dynamics of culture, gender, and nation in the academy.

PART I

MAKING MEN:

WRITING THE NATION

I

**"RACE-ING" THE NATION:
ENGLISHNESS, BLACKNESS, AND
THE DISCOURSE OF VICTORIAN
MANHOOD**

In various ways West Indian discourse was constituted simultaneously with nineteenth-century Victorian debates on the essence of the English nation. Initial contact between Europe and the Caribbean formulated the terms of the relationship between the modern, mappable "Old World" and the prehistoric, unmappable "New," such that the later Victorian discourse on the region was predicated on racial and gender assumptions about the geopolitical characteristics of the Caribbean instituted in this earlier discourse. The history of the relation of the anglophone Caribbean to England is, after all, in many ways the same as that of the non-English speaking nations, even as the constitution of anglophone Caribbean discourse is based on a particularly *English* notion of nation and identity. Thus, while Europeanness and Englishness are distinct categories, the two functioned simultaneously to define the Caribbean in relation to the Old World. For this reason I will be concerned with establishing a dialectical relationship between the gendered and "raced" meanings of Europeanness and Caribbeanness in the first section of this chapter, before proceeding to the more critical discussion of the connection between the meanings of Englishness and West Indianness, and their "raced" and gendered meanings therein.[1]

Mapping Difference: Europe and the Islands

When Columbus "discovered" the Americas, his letters back to Spain on what he found there, his descriptions of its geography, his assumptions about its inhabitants, defined the "New World's" relationship to the "Old." Columbus thought he had sailed to India, and hence the islands he discovered became the "West Indies," their inhabitants, Indians. Regardless of his later understanding of his mistake, the misnomers remained and fixed the Caribbean in discourse as a permanent mistake. The place did not concretely exist — indeed, *could not* exist — on its own terms: literally as well as figuratively. The West Indies, as the region was (and is still) called, was "somewhere else": not Europe, not Africa, not India. This "somewhere elseness" has become a central trope of West Indian discourse, with its attendant notion that the *space* of the West Indies is more metaphorical than it is material, and indeed, what exactly constitutes the West Indies — the Caribbean, as many prefer to call it — has always been hazy. Some of the islands — particularly the Spanish-speaking ones — are considered and analyzed as part of Latin America, and some of the countries of the Spanish Main — Belize, Guyana, in particular — are unquestionably considered by West Indians to be a part of the West Indies. The islands themselves were not really "lands," as such, but fragments of the mainland. They themselves were not even "whole."

If we cannot, then, fix the West Indies in material terms, we must address the region in cultural terms — what defines West Indianness? Indeed, it is this particular question which has forever vexed West Indian intellectuals, and has become, as I intend to argue, the central paradigm of West Indian discourse and narrative. In this section I will analyze how early European narratives of the islands established an enduring trope of "Somewhere Elseness" through a discourse of geographical "feminization." This image of the West Indian space as amorphous, sensual, and chiefly metaphorical established the terms of the discourse of Victorian England with its West Indian colonies. In particular it put into motion the assumption that the rhetoric of Englishness and civilization must be of necessity contrasted to (Caribbean) Blackness, which was not so much primitivism (such as African Blackness) as failed or lacking civilization. This relationship with Victorian England in turn affected the first generation of West Indian writers in their efforts to define West Indianness, in which geographical unreality, cultural lack, and racial inferiority all converged to define the terms of writing.

The question of what constitutes the New World — the Americas —

has always been debated. José Martí was perhaps the first intellectual leader of the colonies to define the Americas as Latin America and the Caribbean, and not the Europe-identified United States.[2] As Hortense Spillers argues, Martí's treatise on the Americas reveals that geopolitical entities are at heart not real; cultural parameters of the entire region are in constant flux, determined variously — and I would add *only* — in language.[3] The West Indies, even more than Latin America, is representable *only* as a discursive metaphor, being as it is a series of islands and the mere periphery of the so-called Mainland. Depictions of the region consequently have emphasized this feature in such a way as to associate the geography with a subordinate relationship to the Mainland (usually meaning the United States or Europe).

Margarita Zamora notes that the Columbian texts of discovery of the "Indies" are a series of "tropes of difference" which reveal a "hermeneutical strategy of feminization and eroticization that ultimately makes gender difference the determining characteristic of the sign 'the Indies'."[4] It is the *place itself*, these texts imply, which is the root cause for the feminine traits of its inhabitants, the "Indians" — their "natural" passivity, effeteness, beauty. (As we shall see, the later inhabitants — the blacks — though not perceived in quite the same eroticized and passive terms, were similarly feminized by their sensual and childlike qualities.) It is the rich beauty of the islands, the heat, and the abundance of fruit and vegetables, which have spawned lazy, sensual people. Later writings by Rousseau and others, which argued that climate and ecology had a constitutive impact on culture and character, merely continued the ideas established in the Columbian texts, except that these ideas now came to embrace the creole[5] population of the region.[6] Despite the creoles' ancestral affinities with Europe, mere whiteness was no proof against the savage and sensual influences of the hemisphere; creoles, too, were by nature now "different" (though, of course, not so different as the Indians and the blacks, whose savagery was genetic).

Benedict Anderson asks the intriguing question, "why was it precisely *creole* communities [of Latin America] that developed so early conceptions of their nation-ness — well before most of Europe?"[7] He believes the answer is to be found in the sense of a shared community of interests opposed to those of Europe, fostered by newspapers. Through this, he argues, the creoles were in effect able to reconstruct a past, perceived to be non-existent by the metropole (in that a creole was a completely new species of citizen, having none of the traditions of Europe), in order to effect a community of interests which then could act with a view of itself in essentialized terms. The early English creole community mostly regarded itself as English,[8] however, and as such Anderson's theory does not work as well in the anglophone context. Certainly white anglophone West Indians have never occupied the prominent place in the struggles for national independence to the degree that white Latin Americans have; indeed, in the anglophone Caribbean the most influential nationalists have come from the black and brown constituencies.[9] The Spanish creoles' sense that they inhabited a land with no antecedents could arguably have set the stage for a nationalist discourse which could be completely self-generated *against* the metropole. This idea is useful for the anglophone context because West Indianness, as I will argue later, is fundamentally created out of not-Englishness, in geographical as well as social terms.

According to Zamora, the Columbian texts followed the Aristotelian principle of difference: that is, deviation from the male principle in the universe constituted imperfection, and the less the offspring resembled its father the more deviant it was considered to be. Femaleness, then, was the first step toward monstrosity.[10] The region — with its lack of borders, its wild abundance — and its pretty, passive inhabitants, were natural candidates, according to European thinking of the time, for "natural slavery" or subjugation. Accordingly, Zamora concludes, in that femininity was synonymous with exploitability, the rhetorical feminization of the term "Indian" became the natural contrast to the now-masculinized term "Spaniard" — or more accurately, we might add, "European."

Thus, the European concept of "Europeanness" became tied to its geographical as well as political difference from the Islands; the West Indies were "somewhere else," but Europe was in Europe. The concept of regional identity, then, became a trophy of sorts, based on a unique relationship of domination and inflected with gendered assumptions. That is, the epistemic status of nationhood and culture literally depended upon inhabiting the dominant side of the hegemonic equation. Yet it is important to emphasize that colonies were not *merely* the oppressed "Other," but were also involved in what for lack of a better term could be called a *familial* relationship with the "Parent" country.[11] The European powers also attempted to transfer their culture, language, and political structures to these colonies, and in this exhibited a desire to recreate themselves in their colonies. Yet, at the same time the colonies were also fixed in this relation as the not-Europes instead of the "New World." This was perhaps most true of the West Indies, with its lack not only of cultural but also of geographical identity. Therefore, the question of regional identity becomes the critical factor in assessing the notion of West Indianness.

The identity of the region was often discussed in terms of the gender, familial, and, most importantly, the racial makeup of its inhabitants, and this is why the issue of the "race" of the geographical *space* of the nation is crucial to any discussion of West Indian—and indeed, any form of—nationalism. In nineteenth-century and early twentieth-century discourse, "race" and "nation" were interchangeable terms, such that one's racial affiliation bespoke, de facto, one's national affiliation, a conflation which still vexes discussions of nationalism and "national interests" today.[12] Formulated thus, every "race" of people must have a corresponding land of its own. Consequently, the issue of land ownership, and the concomitant "race-ing" of the land, becomes a permanent feature in the discussion of citizenry and independence. In the nineteenth century the whites of the Caribbean, as owners of plantations and the means of commercial production, were identified (at least materially) with the soil, and less so with the people of the region.[13] If, as Ileana Rodríguez suggests, nationalism in the Caribbean is linked to modernity, and modernity in the region is linked to *modernization* through the acquisition of and "civilization" of the land,[14] then the inability of West Indian blacks and nonwhites to "mark" the land through ownership and exchange produces a crisis of nationalist discourse. If identity depends upon material exchange, the nascent black middle class—the primary proponents of anglophone West Indian nationalism—had to "own" something other than the land or commerce in order to produce the nation in its own image. That "something," as we shall see presently, was the "purchase" of the manners, habits, and positioning of the English gentleman class through the acquisition of Victorian models of intellectual authority and knowledge. The struggle for West Indian self-definition became fundamentally tied to the use and manipulation of key ideas embedded in the actual language of Englishness itself.

Peter Hulme has suggested that the process by which the indigenous words "hurricane" and "cannibal" became blurred in the English lexicon, signifying the same ideas of savagery in reference to the West Indies, laid the groundwork for the discourse of the plantation, which "recognised only two locations, inside and outside, white and black, and which was itself to provide a central image for the class struggle of industrial Europe."[15] The "discourse of the plantation," as Hulme terms it, also became a critical component of English rhetoric, so that what came to be understood as West Indian discourse was, as I shall presently attempt to show, intimately bound up with English nineteenth-century discourse about England *as well as* about its colonies.

Race and Manhood

Thus, the region was already commodified, gendered, and placed in object relation to Europe. However, there was also a familial relationship — inasmuch as the English had properties and relatives in the region, it is important to note that the slave- and cargo-bearing ships went both ways. Englishness and blackness (blackness in its broadest sense, referring to the darkskinned subject peoples of Britain such as Africans, West Indians, East Indians) as essential qualities became fixed in the English lexicon during this period. Understanding how Victorian England perceived its West Indian colonies is critical to any discussion of the first generation of West Indian writers, because they wrote both *from* and *against* Victorian cultural tradition. In particular, the question of the individual's relationship to the community, the individual's *responsibility* to the community, and what constituted the community (that is, what constituted England), and indeed what constituted an individual, were critically laid out in Victorian discourse. All of these issues converged in the Governor Eyre controversy of the 1860s.

Governor Eyre was the governor of Jamaica at the time of the riots of 1865 in Morant Bay. Interestingly, he had come to Jamaica from Australia, where he had earned praise as a defender of the aboriginal peoples against white racism and genocide. Moreover, the white upper classes of Jamaica cordially disliked Eyre because he was not an aristocrat, though after the rebellion in Morant Bay broke out they came to regard him as the nation's savior.[16] The blacks of the area, though freed thirty years before, were being thrown off their lands because they had not paid taxes on them. This led to a confrontation at the courthouse and a subsequent insurrection in which several whites were killed. Governor Eyre promptly instituted martial law and sent British troops out to quell the disturbance. The British troops slaughtered the blacks, in the process killing a prominent brown instigator, as Eyre perceived him: George William Gordon, an educated mulatto Baptist preacher, married to a white woman, who had spoken out against the unfair, racist land laws. The incident created a furor in England, particularly among the abolitionists and other "friends of the Negro." Eyre was subsequently investigated by a specially appointed commission, but aside from having to resign was not otherwise punished.

The significance of the Governor Eyre controversy lies in the debate it engendered among Victorian intellectuals. The most famous of these was the stormy encounter between Thomas Carlyle and John Stuart Mill in "Occasional Discourse on the Nigger Question" and "The Negro Question," respectively. The issue of whether Eyre acted properly was underwritten by the subtext of how the Victorians should accommodate blacks in the new social order, and how this affected the already changing face of English class relations. As Catherine Hall observes, the key issue between the two men and their followers was the definition of proper English manhood; both offered substantially opposed notions of English manhood, but both depended on a sense of difference from women and blacks.[17] Later West Indian discourse, we shall see, was founded on an interpellation of these two differing yet fundamentally linked notions of manhood and nationhood.

Also key to the Carlyle/Mill debate are the positions they took over what roles individuals and governments should play in the running of the nation. Despite the difference in their political positions, the attitudes of both men toward political change were derived from their fundamental belief in the ability of the intellectual — the "Man-of-Letters Hero," to coin Carlyle's phrase — to make social change.[18] In his essay "On Liberty" Mill emphasizes the role of individual self-improvement and free enterprise as the means by which the nation could achieve its full potential, while Carlyle, reflecting his curious blend of authoritarian tendencies and inchoate socialist sensibilities, attacked the concept of laissez-faire capitalism as anticommunity.[19]

These two positions can be said to mark the parameters of the issue; and indeed, both contributed to the tension reflected in subsequent West Indian literature and discourse on what constitutes a community and how the individual reflects or contributes to that community. What the Carlyle/Mill positions demonstrate very clearly is that the categories of "liberal" and "conservative" ideologies were irrevocably fused to the extent that they lose meaning in the Victorian context—at least as they pertain to issues of race and colonialism—given that what we understand to be an imperialist position such as Carlyle's on the Governor Eyre case was contradicted by his liberal—radical, even—positions on domestic policy with regard to the Irish and the English working class. Or, correspondingly, when we attribute to Mill the liberal position for his defense of black West Indians this does not account for his assumption that "the liberal theses he expounded in *On Liberty* (1859) and *Representative Government* (1861) did not apply to Indians or to other 'lesser peoples'."[20]

As Patrick Brantlinger remarks, Victorian intellectuals of all ideological persuasions believed in the moral responsibility of Britain to import civilization ("identified as especially English"), whether or not they actually thought the natives would improve, and as such, imperialist ideology could attach itself just as easily to radical as to conservative attitudes.[21] The status of imperialism as a core British middle-class ethos combined with the national vision of imperialism as essentially a mission of "high moral content" to produce a national ideology that, like religion, was striking for its accessibility to *all* of Britain's citizens, and gave everyone a stake in it.[22] Moreover, Eric Williams points out in *Capitalism and Slavery* that the seemingly divergent projects of abolition and imperialism were fundamentally linked in this matter—their differences were a matter of means to a similar end; namely, the construction of an "imperishable empire of [British] arts and [British] morals, [British] literature and [British] laws."[23]

Carlyle, his vision of England bound to his conception of the "self-created" individual, reserved special contempt for abolitionists and others espousing "sentimental" views toward the naturally weak. He headed a distinguished group of intellectuals, such as Charles Dickens and Charles Kingsley (himself of West Indian ancestry), who formed the Jamaica Defense Committee to defend Eyre's actions against these sentimentalists as being not merely necessary but also furthering the cause of England and Englishness itself.

Carlyle believed that Eyre had acted in a moral, and perhaps more importantly, a "manly" fashion in quashing the blacks; indeed, morality and manliness were crucially tied for both Carlyle and Mill, though their notions of what was supposed to constitute either were fundamentally opposed. According to Carlyle, the British had "awakened nature" in the islands and in essence given the islanders themselves; therefore they were in a position to dictate the terms of governance.[24] As he saw it, the islands, "till the white European first saw them . . . were as if not yet created, their nobler elements of cinnamon, sugar, coffee . . . lying all asleep, [a]waiting the white enchanter who should say to them, Awake!"[25] This passage bears a striking resemblance to English travel writer James Anthony Froude's fulminations on the West Indies decades later, when he writes, "Below, above, around us, it was forest everywhere. . . . a land fertile as Adam's paradise, still waiting for the day when the 'barren woman shall bear children.'"[26] The West Indies here is likened to a Sleeping Beauty, who is in need of sexual initiation. And furthermore,

Before the West Indies could grow a pumpkin for any Negro, how much European heroism had to spend itself in obscure battle; to sink, in mortal agony, before the jungles, the putrescences and waste savageries could become arable, and the Devil be in some measure chained there. . . . Not a square inch of soil in those fruitful Isles, purchased by British blood, shall any Black man hold to grow pumpkins for him, except on terms that are fair toward Britain.[27]

Clearly, then, it is not the place of the black man to inhabit the role of Prince but that of the British conqueror; the black Caribbean man is, rather, a part of the "nobler elements of cinnamon [and] sugar," part of the "putrescences," "waste savageries," and "jungle" that need awakening and taming. This sexual imagery, combined with the machismo conquistador rhetoric of the above passage, further underlines the discursive feminization of the West Indies within English rhetoric. It was the white man's "touch," as it were, that made the Caribbean the Caribbean, and not the black "Quashie," as Carlyle liked to call black men. Significantly, Carlyle does not think black men are real men. ("I decidedly like poor Quashee, and find him a pretty kind of man. With a pennyworth of oil, you can make a handsome glossy thing of Quashee.")[28] Implicit in his characterization is the standard against which black men are compared: the English conqueror, who is established—through contrast to a black *lack* of masculinity—as the quintessence of what constitutes an English gentleman.

Even as black Caribbean men were feminized in Carlylean discourse on the Eyre debate, Eyre was portrayed not only as the protector of Englishwomen from the monstrous sexuality of black men but, incredibly enough, also from the brutal appetite for violence of *black women*. Apparently Eyre had reported to the Colonial Office that the women rioters in Morant Bay were more brutal and barbarous than the men, which further presented the black populace as aberrant and monstrous, given that their men were like women, and their women like men.[29] Accordingly, "large numbers of individual Englishwomen were, indeed, involved in the activities of the Eyre Defence Committee, fully supporting the manly ideal of the hero who would protect them from danger."[30]

If anything, black men were associated with physical, rather than intellectual, masculinity, as the following passage from the *Times* (London) illustrates: ". . . only the application of negro muscles to the extraction from the soil of its natural riches will give the British West Indies the career to which they are entitled. Negroes alone can work manfully in such a climate. If they do not work, they will, at all events, have to be supported."[31] The reporter then goes on to place blame for West Indian poverty at the feet of the "motherland," which "[i]n all its influence is predominant, and . . . is morally responsible." Thus were black West Indian men at once associated with a physical virility that became vital to the success of the British "career" in the region as well as with a corresponding inability to be responsible for charting their lives without the intellectual direction of the British.

What these popular opinions and Carlyle's arguments also reveal is that, for him particularly and the nation generally, the English have in effect *purchased* the West Indies, made it a commodity, by taming it: more than just the actual possession of the region, England has proved itself the better *man*, by its ability to conquer, according to Carlylean logic. As Zamora reflects, "the land itself becomes the substitute merchandise, the desirable object to be possessed."[32]

For Mill, of course, the terms of debate are different. The quality of *Englishness* itself was violated by Eyre's actions: what characterized an Englishman was his ability to be fair and allow every individual the capacity for self-improvement — in this case his poorer black brethren. Eyre, though white, had not acted as an Englishman would — or should. The blacks, though Mill implies they are not quite the equals of the

English in morals or intellect, should yet, he believed, be given a chance to prove themselves English, to rise to the level of English gentleman. A measure of the hue and cry from the Mill camp over the Eyre case concerned the execution of George William Gordon. Gordon was, they protested, a Christian gentleman, shown to be such, significantly, by his letters. He was educated and *married to a white woman* (curiously enough, this was a plus for him — an interesting commentary on the distinction between American and British perceptions of race and class). All of this was proof positive of the ability of the black man to metamorphose into, not a white man, but a *gentleman*. Herein lay the crux of the matter.

The condition of slavery, and its aftermath, the condition of blackness, were for Mill analogous to the condition of (English) womanhood (outlined in *The Subjection of Women*, his classic defense of women's rights); as Catherine Hall notes, Mill accepts both conditions as *natural*, but argues that blackness and femaleness are the result of barbarous practices of an *uncivilized* society, and such practices can be *civilized*, civilization being the possibility of individuals achieving a community through the development of a common will and purpose.[33] The critical point in this is that for Mill, as with Carlyle, it is the English gentleman as an epistemological entity which both groups must strive to become in order to achieve the desired level of civility. As such, Mill's interpretation of community and nation is predicated on a notion of manhood which is tied to Englishness. Englishness was the character, the essence of the nation itself: unchangeable, beyond improvement or decay.

For Carlyle and followers, a gentleman was essentially a man: strong willed, white, and British. For Mill and others, a gentleman was an educated Englishman with Christian moral values and aspirations. English manhood thus defined was a tense balance between physical virility — the ability to act powerfully, even violently — and the moral sensibilities of the higher evolved.[34] The question was, could blacks, so lately risen from African savagery, be in essence re-created into gentlemen? That is, into *Englishmen*? This was what the abolitionists had argued, and what Carlyle et al. had claimed to be impossible, inasmuch as the condition of blackness made gentlemanliness impossible. The West Indies constituted a sort of testing ground for nature versus nurture theories of these factions, being not-Africa and not-Europe, but Somewhere Else: mini-Africa *and* not-yet-Europe, as it were. It was only in such a place as this, which existed as much if not more in the English imagination as in geographical reality, that the English could decide whether innate black savagery could be eradicated. Haiti, for many such as Froude and novelist Anthony Trollope, was already a testament to what would happen if the blacks were left to govern themselves: cannibalism and anarchy.[35]

Indeed, in *The English in the West Indies* Froude argues that black women work harder than black men in the West Indies, and that as such, "If black suffrage is to be the rule in Jamaica, I would take it away from the men and would give it to the superior sex. They would make a tolerable nation of black amazons, and the babies would not be offered to Jumbi" (197–98). Here, again, it is *black masculinity* that is the real essence of blackness — if "savagery" is the linguistic equivalent of "blackness," then, for Froude, it is black men more so than women who are closest to the savagery of Africa and "Jumbi" — and are therefore the real crux of the debate on the West Indies.

As if confirming the worst fears of those who supported the blacks, on November 25, 1865, the liberal London paper *The Examiner* declared that the Jamaica insurrection proved that "the negroes of our West Indies, free for a generation, . . . are still, despite of generous hopes . . . barbarians of Africa who have but changed their sky."[36]

The abolitionists and other "Negro" sympathizers argued that blacks should be educated along with whites, so that their savagery could be bred out of them, and they could rise in the social hierarchy. The only way around blackness, then, became gentility. In that the social hierarchy was predicated on levels of manliness and Englishness — with aristocrats naturally attaining the highest levels of both — such a proposition held disturbing implications for class-bound Britain: what of the white poor, who were decidedly *not* gentlemen? Where would they be placed in relation to the black man? The Victorians, as Douglas Lorimer points out, reserved the responsibilities of leadership for gentlemen alone.[37] (This particular classification affected the ways in which even those colonized attempted to resist or transcend colonial power. For example, Edward Blyden, the West Indian–born Liberian educator who founded many schools in that nation, wrote letters to Prime Minister Gladstone requesting that he be sent English literature classics. It is significant, I think, that Blyden found this to be such a crucial part of his development as an African leader.)[38]

The Jamaica Defense Committee and other so-called Negro sympathizers hoped that by developing a middle-class elite of black men in the West Indies, these men would in turn act as a reforming influence upon the whole society. Inasmuch as "Negro" education, and by inference "Negro" evolution, was measured in terms of the degree to which English ways were successfully imitated, Lorimer concludes that mid-Victorian attitudes to race rested upon assumptions about differences of class rather than racialist theories of racial essence, though he emphasizes that this was to change in the late nineteenth century when the constant association of other races with inferior class status provided the foundation for scientific racism. Still, the mid-Victorian discourse on race, class, and the concept of nationhood, insofar as it was this discourse which produced the ideological climate and the rationale for later ideas, established the export-variety concept of Englishness which functions as an ideological mechanism in the colonies even today. Moreover, this notion of Englishness which evolved in the mid-nineteenth century is critical to the development of English literature as the central discipline of academia in twentieth-century England.

Englishness, Blackness, and the Discourse of West Indian Nationalism

In nineteenth-century England, the West Indies was still seen as a place where Englishness, as represented by Governor Eyre, struggled valiantly against encroaching blackness, as represented by Paul Bogle and other leaders of the Morant Bay insurrection. Englishness was still possible, still desirable, in the islands. However, by the twentieth century it was *all* West Indians, both black and white, who represented the essential inferiority of the West Indies and West Indians. Manthia Diawara defines Englishness as "the privileging of a certain use of language, literature, ideology and history of one group over populations that it subordinates to itself," and argues that the effect of Englishness as an ideology is that it "sets in motion absolute barriers between white and black, England and West Indies, civilized and primitive, and, in the process, empowers the English subject as original and disempowers the colonized subject as the copy."[39] Defined in this way, however, Englishness could just as easily be a general principle of hegemonic *racial* (rather than cultural) ideology, and indeed, Diawara goes on to state that throughout his argument he will use Englishness interchangeably with whiteness. Yet Englishness is *not* interchangeable with whiteness; it is, if anything, a particularized form of whiteness that refers not only to ascendancy over blackness but to the way in which those qualities of whiteness are arranged. Thus, Englishness is clearly superior to Americanness or Spanishness. Moreover, it is *not* available to the white West Indian precisely because of that West Indianness, for Englishness is the essence of Culture itself.[40] Consequently, as Naipaul writes, "In the French territories [the black West Indian] aimed at Frenchness, in the Dutch territories at Dutchness; in the English territories he aimed at simple whiteness and modernity, Englishness being impossible."[41]

Englishness as representative of manhood itself, that abstract, deracialized ideal of individualism, was held up for emulation to the black colonized subject. Yet the relationship of the West Indian to Englishness is crucially different from that of the African (or indeed, the East Indian) because whereas African and Indian society are understood to have had a separate life from their English legacy (indeed, preceding that legacy) the West Indies as an entity can only exist as a creation of the colonizing project: its very name proclaims its filiation.[42] The West Indies was a foreign land but was yet the issue of Europe itself. Therefore, the project of Englishness in the West Indies of necessity had to be fundamentally different in some way.

Victorian novelist Anthony Trollope, an ardent supporter of self-government for all the colonies and an Eyre supporter, reveals distinctively English notions of nationhood and race when he writes of black West Indians:

But how strange is the race of creole Negroes — of Negroes, that is , born out of Africa! They have no country of their own, yet they have not hitherto any country of their adoption. They have no language of their own, nor have they as yet any language of their adoption; for they speak their broken English as uneducated foreigners always speak a foreign language. *They have no idea of country, and no pride of race.* They have no religion of their own, and can hardly as yet be said to have, as a people, a religion by adoption. The West Indian Negro knows nothing of Africa except that it is a term of reproach. If African immigrants are put to work on the same estate with him, he will not eat with them, or drink with them, or walk with them. He will hardly work beside them, and regards himself as a creature immeasurably the superior of the newcomer.

... [The black West Indian] burns to be a scholar, puzzles himself with fine words, addicts himself to religion for the sake of appearances, and delights in aping the little graces of civilization.[43] (emphasis added)

Trollope's curiosity at the black West Indian man's "singular" ambition to be a scholar is undergirded by his belief that he is not doing what he *ought* to be doing: tilling the land. He finds the black West Indian man essentially unrepresentable as a gentleman, to be apprehended *only* in his mimicry of Englishness. West Indianness was not necessarily entirely synonymous with blackness, since the West Indian was not the original African in thought, custom, or appearance; rather, it was not-*Englishness*. Englishness is, in this way, not so much "raced" as it is "nationed," and thus its ideas are made accessible, even as a means to provide a contrast to a nascent "West Indianness." It is this idea, I believe, which is the origin of distinctively West Indian formulations of colonialism, nationalism, and racial politics.

Manthia Diawara defines blackness as a specifically modern phenomenon, originating not in Africa but the West — a liberatory principle against dominations by peoples of African descent:

For people of African descent, blackness is therefore a way of being human in the West or in areas under Western domination. It is a compelling performance against the logic of slavery and colonialism by people whose destinies have been inextricably linked to the advancement of the West, and who have therefore to learn the expressive techniques of modernity: writing, music, Christianity, and industrialization in order to become uncolonizable. . . . Blackness is therefore a way of being African in modernity. . . .[44]

Despite Diawara's claim that blackness has its origins in the West — a claim with which I agree — his subsequent definition applies more to Africa in its Old World/New World, traditional/modern dichotomy. Though, as historical categories, blackness has been associated in the West Indies with primitivism, and whiteness with modernity and "progress" (to echo Naipaul's comment above), the region's image as a geographical, historical, and cultural "blank slate" — halfway between Europe and Africa, representing neither — was the feature that made it at once the object of fascination and revulsion in the Victorian imagination because of its possibilities and impossibilities. One need only look to Victorian responses to the Haitian revolution, with its horrified descriptions of cannibalism and heathen rituals, to understand that the West Indies constituted for the Victorians a sort of testing ground for the development of civilization and culture, which required constant supervision lest its inhabitants cave in to the savage impulses of their genetic inheritance. Even Froude admits of the possibility of making an English gentleman out of a black West Indian, although the effort would require eternal vigilance. ("With the same chances and with the same treatment, I believe that distinguished men would be produced equally from *both* races.") Whiteness as the transcendent category of Englishness evolved only in the period between the late nineteenth and early twentieth century with the growth of "scientific" racialist theories, but it is not to this later development that West Indian discourse is so fundamentally linked.

Froude's writings on the West Indies caused consternation on the part of the black educated middle class, who saw their efforts toward self-government being undermined. He argued that it was not so much *economic* issues as *character* issues — that is, the issue of the character of blacks in the Caribbean — which would determine whether or not the region could be self-ruled: "The prospects of Jamaica, the prospects of all countries, depend not on sugar or on any form or degree of material wealth, but on the characters of the men and women whom they are breeding and rearing. Where there are men and women of noble nature, the rest will go well of itself: where are not, there will be no true prosperity, though the sugar hogsheads be raised from thousands into millions."[45]

Furthermore, for Froude the implementation of English-style democracy in the Caribbean depended specifically on how black *men* could imbibe the traits of "manliness":

In democracies no one man is his brother's keeper. . . . All that is insisted on is that there shall be a fair stage and that every lad shall learn the use of the weapons which will enable him to his own way. [ ], 'manliness', the most essential of all acquisitions and the hardest to cultivate, as Aristotle observed long ago, is assumed in democracies as a matter of course. Without it, the nations founder.

. . . The black man must therefore use his own exertions to raise himself to "the white man's level." But left to himself, and without the white man to lead him, he can never reach it. . . .[46]

John Jacob Thomas, a highly educated black Trinidadian of some prominence in England for his book on creole grammar, wrote a reply to Froude in the form of a book entitled, ironically, *Froudacity*.[47] Thomas's analysis of creole linguistic systems is an important milestone in West Indian discourse, in that it treats the so-called "broken English" of the creoles as an equal language in itself, a linguistic system as worthy of scientific study as English. Thomas's use of the tools of classical English philology to effect a radical equalization of African-based language provides a central paradigm of West Indian discourse.

Begun with a quotation from Shakespeare ("Why dost thou show to the apt thoughts of men the things that ARE NOT?"), *Froudacity* is nevertheless an incipient pan-Africanist text in that Thomas attempts to identify himself with the community of Africans around the diaspora, even as his response to Froude is predicated on his *own* status as a gentleman by virtue of his English education. Thomas is at pains to excuse what he perceives as his inferior literary style, acknowledging Froude to be his literary superior. He contends, however, that his literary excellence is part of Froude's dishonesty in that "[t]o secure an artistic perfection of style, he disregards all obstacles, not only those presented by the requirements of verity, but such as spring from any other kind whatsoever."[48] Thomas's concern here with *literary excellence* as a crucial component of *political* effectiveness reveals that he conceives *literary mastery* as a form of *political mastery*. The anxieties over narrative form as a *political* issue will resurface in similar fashion for West Indian writers in the twentieth century.

Thomas's text reveals a particular outrage over Froude's depictions of black men and his emphasis on their difference from English men, despite Froude's assertion that "there is no original or congenital difference between the capacity of the White and the Negro races." Thomas castigates Froude for conflating and confusing issues of race and nationality:

Does Mr. Froude's scorn of the Negroe's skin extend, inconsistently on his part, to their intelligence and feelings also? . . . Really, are we to be grateful that the colour difference should be made the basis and justification of the dastardly denials of justice, social, intellectual, and moral, which have characterized the *regime* of those who Mr. Froude boasts were left to be the representatives of Britain's morality and fair play? *Are the Negroes under the French flag not intensely French? Are the Negroes under the Spanish flag not intensely Spanish?* Wherefore are they so? It is because the French and Spanish nations, who are neither of them inferior in origin or the nobility of the part they have each played on the historic stage, have had the dignity and sense to understand the lowness of moral and intellectual consciousness implied in the subordination of questions of an imperial nature to the slaveholder's anxiety about the hue of those who are to be benefited or not in the long run. By Spain and France every loyal and law-abiding subject of the Mother Country has been a citizen deemed worthy all the rights, immunities, and privileges flowing from good and creditable citizenship.[49] (emphasis added)

While the above passage stresses the West Indian right to Englishness, in the same way that the blacks of the French and Spanish colonies have access to the nationalistic sentiment as well as the legal benefits of those cultures, the passage below emphasizes a clear pan-Africanism:

The intra-African Negro is clearly powerless to struggle successfully against personal enslavement, annexation, or volunteer forcible "protection" of his territory. What, we ask, will in the coming ages be the opinion and attitude of the *extra-African millions* . . . dispersed so widely over the globe, *apt apprentices in every conceivable department of civilized culture?* Will these men remain forever too poor, too isolated from one another for *grand racial combinations?* Or will the naturally opulent cradle of their people, too long a prey to violence and unholy greed, become at length the sacred watchword of a generation willing and able to conquer or perish under its inspiration?[50] (emphasis added)

Evincing such a remarkable notion of pan-Africanism as it does, the above passage belies the intraracial prejudice of the West Indian described by Trollope earlier in this section. More importantly, Thomas emphasizes the potential unification of the African diaspora through its ability to civilize itself (see above emphasis). The two passages taken together deconstruct conventional theories of Englishness/whiteness and blackness/West Indianness, such as Diawara's, which read the two as opposing ideologies instead of the innately fused mechanism that both are in the West Indian context. It is this apparent paradox which is the staple of West Indian discourse of the pre-independence era, and indeed for part of the post-independence era. Part of the paradox was engendered by the position of black West Indian intellectuals such as Thomas, who in effect mediated between English discursive and African-derived political systems, presenting West Indians to the English, the English to the West Indians, and West Indians to themselves.[51] Most striking is the lack of a specific geographical audience; Thomas addresses the English, the West Indians, and the diaspora all at once, understanding his audience to be rooted in all three places, which exist only discursively. These were the intellectual beginnings of West Indian nationalism.

Yet, as Patrick Bryan points out, the very genesis of West Indian nationalism—specifically marked as a product of the black intelligentsia—was a paradox.[52] On the one hand, the education of black West Indians was consciously formulated to remove them from the world of the black community in every way—social, religious, cultural, and so forth. Personal progress therefore demanded distance from their own society. On the other, it was this very distance—this ability to manipulate European culture and manners—which provided the basis for the incipient nationalism of this particular class. Thus it was that the black Jamaican scholar and nationalist Theophilus Scholes could argue, without a trace of irony, that to perceive the "civilized class" of black West Indians, who had acquired property and education, to be the same as other black communities of England and America "as though they all belong to the uncivilized class" was "arbitrary and unjust."[53] The "black" position of the late-nineteenth-century black West Indian gentleman thus is perhaps best stated by the black medical practitioner quoted in an early-twentieth-century travel narrative who describes himself as "an imperialist, a Protectionist [who] believes in God, and Jamaica and the Negro Race."[54] The peculiar alignment of race and class authority found here lays the foundation for later constructions of authorship found in twentieth-century Caribbean male-authored canonical narratives.

2

LITERARY MEN AND THE ENGLISH
CANONICAL TRADITION

. . . to write really well about a living society. . . one has simply to be an "old-fashioned" writer like Hardy, Dickens, George Eliot, or Jane Austen. This is what [V. S.] Naipaul is. . . . the black West Indian cannot really expect novels like [A House for Mr. Biswas] until he has a strong enough framework of social convention from which to operate and until his own technique is flexible and subtle enough to take advantage of it. — Edward Kamau Brathwaite, *Roots*

Thackeray, not Marx, bears the heaviest responsibility for me.
— C. L. R. James, *Beyond A Boundary*

Much of the significance of the above quotations lies in our knowledge of the writers themselves. Barbadian poet and scholar Edward Kamau Brathwaite is well known for his model of "nation-language" for the Caribbean, which argues for an African-derived indigenous discourse for the region. V. S. Naipaul, an East Indian Trinidadian, refers to himself as a British writer despite his prominent position within the anglophone Caribbean canon.[1] C. L. R. James, the Trinidadian author of *The Black Jacobins*, is best known as an early and vigorous advocate of pan-Africanism and national independence in the colonial Caribbean. In the United States and Europe, he was known for his Marxist scholarship, and indeed, *The Black Jacobins*, the first West Indian account of the Haitian revolution, is remarkable for among other things its interesting combinations of Marxist theory and black nationalism. His statement above is taken from his reflections on the origins of his anticolonial politics. Defined as either a nationalist/pan-Africanist or a Marxist, what is most often ignored is James's own emphasis, not simply on his immersion in European philosophy and literature during his

formative years, but on its continued influence on his Marxist/nation-
alist thinking.[2]

The quotations are startling because of our assumptions about the
nature of the relationship between the radical black (de)colonized subject and the metropole. Given his repudiation of what he calls "Negro
protest writing," that Naipaul's adherence to the social conventions of
the "old-fashioned" English novel should serve as Brathwaite's model
for discursive constructions of black Caribbean society is, at first
glance, certainly perplexing. So, too, was James's homage to William
Makepeace Thackeray's politically conservative *Vanity Fair* as a *politically radical* document with which he waged war against the philistine
ambitions of the nascent black West Indian bourgeoisie, of which he
was a member.

This particular alignment of Englishness, of *Victorian* Englishness,
with a radical black discourse startles only because the terms by which
Englishness and blackness construct each other are presumed to be
essentially incompatible. In this dichotomous arrangement we as readers then must choose one version of West Indianness over another:
James and Brathwaite as either black revolutionaries or Englishmen in
blackface.

In this chapter I will illustrate how nineteenth-century discussions
on the meaning and definition of the "English gentleman" as a model of
citizenry, with its corollary of the Victorian "Literary Man" as a model
of aesthetic sensibilities, are reproduced in Caribbean *literary* discourse
and narrative. In particular, it is important to contextualize what some
might consider the reactionary gentleman scholar model within the
framework of the phenomenon that we now recognize as modern,
black, pan-Africanist, West Indian nationalist discourse, which similarly has its roots in the nineteenth-century struggles of the emergent
black gentleman class.[3]

In the previous chapter I attempted to establish that the nature of the
relationship between Victorian and West Indian discourse of the nineteenth century was essentially a symbiotic one. However, critics may be
tempted to point out that while the degree of intimacy I have argued to
exist between the two may exceed traditional descriptions, this is not
an extraordinarily surprising characterization, given the historical and
economic ties between England and the West Indies. The singularity of
the relationship between Victorian and West Indian discourse lies, ulti-

mately, in its influence on twentieth-century West Indian narrative. The argument I am laying out here is more clearly revisionist, given that scholarship on West Indian literature over the past forty years or so assumes that the first wave of twentieth-century West Indian writers (those of the pre-independence and early post-independence years) wrote primarily within an oppositional, contemporary framework, and that all readings of West Indian oppositional literature of this generation should be contextualized against a background of Euro-American modernism or "folk" literature.[4] My claim is that though this literature may have been influenced to a degree by the ideas of early twentieth-century modernism, it was nevertheless responding to the articulations of classic Victorian literature, and *its* context, and should therefore be read in relation to that canon. Furthermore, current assumptions about authorship and the imaging of the West Indian nation are fundamentally derived from this earlier engagement with the English canonical tradition.

English Literature and Englishness

It has been noted that the references to the colonies in canonical Victorian fiction are so few and isolated that, as one critic puts it, "If one believes that the great Victorian novels reflected the critical problems of the society, one is forced to conclude that interest in imperialism was non-existent. . . . No one in Dickens, Thackeray, Eliot or Trollope brooded about the imperial relationship."[5] However, as we have seen, the Victorians, far from indifferent, were engaged in passionate debate over the colonies. What, then, accounts for this deficiency of representation?

First of all, we must understand that the ties between West Indian and Victorian literature are not based solely on West Indian *images* within Victorian fiction and subsequent revisions in West Indian fiction, though they do in fact play an important role, as we shall see. Rather, it is how the Victorian novel understands its society and its own role that provides the primary link between Victorian and West Indian literature. The novel enabled Victorian England to essentialize Englishness; to reify it, give it concrete form and export it, as it were. It was this vision of Englishness, encompassing both liberal and reformist critique (Dickens, Thackeray) of the society, as well as an unchanging and essential vision of English individualism, that was presented most clearly to West Indians as the epitome of what nationhood should be.

The Victorian age in England gave rise to what Carlyle refers to as the "Literary Man" in his essay, "The Hero as Man of Letters."[6] For Carlyle — and for the Victorians as a social body — the writer was indeed a masculine figure, despite the fact that literary discourse itself had become a "feminized" discourse by the mid-nineteenth century, with the rise of women writers and their appropriation of the compassionate moral voice.[7] The moral voice of the Literary Man that Carlyle outlines is *more* than the moral voice of the people; godlike, he transcends the moral order by being more moral than the social body requires. He is — for Carlyle and his age — a latter-day embodiment of the "Hero-Gods, Prophets, Poets, [and] Priests" of Western myth who "cannot any more show themselves in this world."[8] Indeed, for Carlyle and the Victorians, writing is akin to a religious vocation,[9] the "activest and noblest" of professions, the very wellspring of democracy: "Literature is our Parliament. . . . Printing, which comes necessarily out of Writing, I say often, is equivalent to Democracy: invent Writing, Democracy is inevitable. Writing brings Printing; brings universal every-day extempore Printing. . . . Whoever can speak, speaking now to the whole nation, becomes a power, a branch of government, with inalienable weight in law-making, in all acts of authority."[10]

Yet, as Mary Poovey argues, this vision of writing as the most democratic of professions was itself a myth, inasmuch as access to the world of professional letters was still determined by one's ability to write *in a certain way*, such that what counted as "publishable literature" was at least partly a function of class.[11] Therefore, on the one hand the Victorian Literary Man embodied a very modern conception of individualism and the free trade of ideas by virtue of his ability to transcend social difference through sheer talent. On the other hand his ability to compete in the free trade of ideas was predicated on the assumption that he was *like*, not different from, the others with whom he associated in the noble profession.[12] This paradox in the conception of the Literary Man was yet essential to the larger national project of constructing a national character, as Poovey explains: " . . . the work of the literary man was to make all Englishmen like each other — or, more precisely, like the literary man. This is one of the contradictions masked by the paradox of individualism: the representative (literary) man was simultaneously considered unique (a 'genius') and like every other man (interchangeable) because he made his readers in his own image."[13] It was precisely this inherent paradox in the conception of the Literary Man, this ability to embody the national character and yet to transcend it by so doing, that was to appeal to Caribbean writers of a later generation such as Naipaul and James, as I will explain presently.

The Literary Man as an embodiment of the English nation was perpetuated through creation and exportation of the English novel. Central to the utilization of the English novel as a colonial export was the rise of English as a discipline in the early twentieth century and its enduring status as the core of the educational curriculum. The importance of English for British culture was an ability to manifest the ideologies of English nationalism, as Brian Doyle describes it: "In Britain ... English has functioned to provide a substitute for any 'theory' of the national life in the form of an imponderable base from which the quality of the national life can be assessed. . . . The sense of 'Englishness' that English came to signify was apparently so free of any narrow patriotism or overtly nationalist or imperialistic politics that any debate about the meaning of the term itself was deemed unnecessary until quite recently."[14] English literature, then, became valuable not so much for what it purported to *say* about English life or society, but for representing the thing itself: culture above and beyond politics, a sort of nationalism incarnate.

How did all of this come about? In 1921 the Board of Education appointed a committee to study what changes needed to be made to the English educational system so that the board could effect "a strategy for national cultural renewal by means of a system of education led by the universities, with English as the central pedagogic instrument": English was central because of its innate "richness" and "spiritualising quality." According to Doyle, the decision of the English Association to replace the classics with English was aimed at the "nullification of any middle-class 'hatred' for learning, and for its replacement by a taste for the finer stuff of literature, and even more ambitiously, a 'quickening' of the whole spiritual nature."[15]

Furthermore, "even the teacher of English must bow before the experience of those great minds with which the works offer contact. This would allow a 'bond of sympathy' between members of society to be subjectively seated."[16] Thus, even while it was to provide cultural access to the middle class, the discipline of English was still beyond the *interpretation* of that class in that the artist is given, by the above quotation, final say in determining the basis of culture, since in this particular schema the artist transcends class and political interests. English, then, was used as a moral force in the cultural colonization of the English middle (and lower) classes.

This notion of the discipline of English as transcendent, of representing the nation at large, is particularly relevant to the shaping of the West Indian canon, inasmuch as what came to be recognized as the first body of *authentic* West Indian literature (I use the term deliberately) was predicated on a similar concept of national identity, one that, ironically enough, came to exist precisely through the West Indian's conflicted relationship to the "Motherland." As Barbadian novelist George Lamming reflects in *The Pleasures of Exile*, "No Barbadian, no Trinidadian, no St. Lucian, no islander from the West Indies sees himself as a West Indian until he encounters another islander in foreign territory. It was only when the Barbadian childhood corresponded with the Grenadian or the Guyanese childhood in important details of folk-lore, that the wider identification was arrived at. *In this sense, most West Indians of my generation were born in England*" (emphasis added).[17]

I would add an important qualifier to Lamming's assessment: the origins of West Indianness in Englishness did not require that one actually set foot in England. It was the *essence* of England that was the site of critical interaction, and this quality was present in the West Indies, through customs and laws, but most importantly, through language. The term "Bad English" in the anglophone Caribbean is much more than a pejorative: it describes a lesser state of civilization. Edward Long, the Englishman who wrote *The History of Jamaica* in 1774, describes the various stages of decay of English in the colony, from the "broken English" of the slaves to those slaves who try to "improve their language" by "catching" at words they hear from the whites and "misapplying" them. Long notes with dismay that "[t]his gibberish likewise infects many of the White Creoles, who learn it from their nurses in infancy and meet with much difficulty, as they advance in years, to shake it entirely off and express themselves with correctness."[18]

The concern with the "correct" expression of the English language reflects Long's positioning as one who can tell the difference: as an

English gentleman, he is an authority on English language. The mastery of English literature in the West Indian context is similarly predicated on the assumption of *who* is a "natural" authority on it. A good example of how this operates is to be found in Jean Rhys's short story, "Again the Antilles".[19] The story's white West Indian narrator — apparently a woman — reminisces about a stormy exchange that takes place between an English estate owner and the mulatto editor, Papa Dom,[20] of the *Dominica Herald and Leeward Islands Gazette* in the pages of that newspaper. The editor, mockingly described in terms that suggest the gentleman-manqué, is fiercely anticolonial, being "against the English, against the Island's being a Crown Colony and the Town Board's new system of drainage." In an editorial he accuses the English estate owner of tyrannical behavior. Of far more consequence, however, is the editor's declaration that the Englishman represents "the degeneracy of a stock," being "far . . . removed from the ideals of true gentility." He concludes by quoting (he thinks) Shakespeare: "*He was a very gentle, perfect knight.*" The Englishman pens a scathing rebuttal, correcting the quotation ("He was a verray parfit, gentil knyght"), and replying that the author of those lines was Chaucer, not Shakespeare, "though you cannot of course be expected to know that." He concludes that "[i]t is indeed a saddening and a dismal thing that the names of great Englishmen should be thus taken in vain by the ignorant of another race and colour." The narrator observes that the Englishman had actually written "damn niggers."[21]

As Judith Raiskin points out, the debate is actually about who has the right to read and understand English literature, and by extension, show themselves to be proper English gentlemen. For, while the Englishman shall always remain English *regardless* of whether or not he knows the correct lines of the quotation, the mulatto must *prove* himself an inheritor, by dint of education, of the English literary tradition.[22] For the West Indian man, the problem is not Englishness but the failure of the English to live up to it. For the Englishman, the West Indian can never, despite his erudition and standing in society, truly be an English gentleman, and his inaccurate rendition and attribution of the quotation is merely the result of this essential failing.

Interestingly, while the reader is given no information on the race and gender of the narrator, we assume that the narrator is the author, or an author-like figure: a white creole woman. Reading the story with this particular triangulation in mind highlights something more than the racial politics of the English canon. If we understand that the debate over who correctly reads Chaucer is more precisely a conflict over who *owns* Chaucer, the implicitly gendered nature of the incident becomes more central. The English estate owner is a gentleman because of his acquisition of property; the mulatto editor has, not material property, but rather "property" in the form of a British education and a knowledge of the English canon, and it is this property which provides him access to the English gentry, which allows him to consider himself a gentleman even as it fuels his critique of English hegemony. The white female narrator, while clearly derisive of the editor's pretensions, is a passive chronicler of the debate: she has no stake in either outcome. The conflict over the English canon is represented as a struggle between *men* over the symbols of manhood, the symbol in this case being the English canon. The meaning of Englishness is here signified as very specifically masculine, very specifically upper class. Papa Dom's challenge to the English estate owner constitutes, at this level, a nationalist West Indian challenge to Englishness itself, signified in literature, language, and land.

Victorians and Nationalists: C. L. R. James and V. S. Naipaul

Frantz Fanon argues that "the Negro in the West Indies becomes proportionately whiter — that is, he becomes closer to being a real human being — in direct ratio to his mastery of the language," but in the British colonies, as Homi Bhabha notes, "to be Anglicized is *emphatically* not to be English."[23] In the same vein, V. S. Naipaul argues that in the West Indies for blacks mere whiteness is the goal, because Englishness is out of reach. This is to be attained through education, and, as Naipaul observes, the white West Indians were never particularly interested in attaining Englishness through education: "Education was strictly for the poor; and the poor were invariably black."[24]

Yet, for black and nonwhite West Indians, it is precisely this mastery of English and Englishness which provided the mode for instituting a specifically West Indian consciousness. In the West Indies, the middle-class intellectual community which fashioned the terms for West Indian literature did not so much imitate English customs as reflect them; by virtue of their class their upbringing was in many ways fundamentally

English — that is, the Englishness of the West Indian middle class was in many ways innate.

Understanding this, let us return once more to C. L. R. James: "In reality my life up to ten had laid the powder for a war that lasted without respite for eight years, and intermittently for some time afterwards — a war between *English Puritanism, English literature and cricket, and the realism of West Indian life*. . . . I had nothing to start with but my pile of clippings about W. G. Grace and Ranjitsinhji, my *Vanity Fair* and my Puritan instincts, though as yet these were undeveloped. I fought and won."[25] By "the realism of West Indian life" James is referring to the plans of his family and teachers to make him into a member of the British-educated black middle class — from which he rebelled, paradoxically, by voraciously rereading Thackeray's *Vanity Fair* and playing impeccable cricket. For James, then, "English Puritanism, English literature and cricket" are clearly something more than an approximation of English culture, for he finds English class structures not in English cultural artifacts but rather in "the realism of West Indian life." By learning *more* Englishness than was necessary, James transformed himself from the object of English colonizing practices into a British intellectual.

Faith Smith points out that if James is indeed waging war, as he asserts, on the bourgeois colonial life, the reader has problems distinguishing between *James*'s "arsenal" (English sports clippings and novels, and what he calls his "Puritan instincts") and *their* weapons.[26] Indeed, which side *is* he on? How can he rebel against the colonial status quo by reading *more* English novels, playing *more* cricket? Yet, as James points out, it was precisely this "Englishness," the code of gentlemanly conduct, sportsmanship, and all the other attributes of a cricket player, that united the cricket players across classes and races, by providing a system through which they all became equals. The delicate balance in evidence between James's rampant individualism, as signified by his lust for *Vanity Fair*, and his nationalist instincts, signified in his participation in cricket, re-create in another sphere the paradoxes of Carlyle's Literary Man that I have earlier described.

Elsewhere in *Beyond A Boundary* James argues that to be a nationalist, one must have a nation: the African had Africa, the Asian had Asia, but the West Indian had only this "system," this code of conduct encapsulated in the play of cricket. And indeed, the West Indian cricket team, world-renowned champions, has become one of the most potent signs of Caribbean nationalism. Cricket, with its attendant "European" ideology, has given access to a common West Indianness across national and cultural lines: can *this* be oppositionality?

The apparent disjuncture between a radical black politics and an English literary bent, if a problem for many contemporary readers of James, was not perceived as problematic by James himself. In his 1959 essay, "The Artist in the Caribbean," James rejects the notion of an indigenous West Indian aesthetic tradition upon which the West Indian writer must draw. Instead, he emphasizes the essential individuality of the artistic process and argues that it is only through the individual literary work of the "great artist" that the West Indies can achieve a national consciousness:

The question around which I am circling is this: is there any medium so native to the Caribbean, so rooted in the tight association which I have made between national surroundings, historical development and artistic tradition, is there any such medium in the Caribbean from which the artist can draw that strength which makes him a supreme practitioner?

... So far as I can see, there is nothing of the kind in the Caribbean and none in sight to the extent that I, at any rate, can say anything about it. . . . *For us and for people like us there is no continuous flow such as for instance . . . Shakespeare, Milton, the Augustans, the Romantics, the Victorians, the Georgians and the revolt against them all of T. S. Eliot.* There is no Donne in our ancestry for us to rediscover and stimulate the invention of new forms and new symbols. You will remember that to clarify his own style Eliot found it necessary to launch an assault upon Milton that nearly (but not quite) toppled that master from the throne on which he had sat unchallenged for 250 years.[27] (emphasis added)

James here subscribes to the Harold Bloom model of literary convention; that is, in order to create new literature, the Oedipus-like writer must have a literary ancestor to dismantle or challenge. This is, for James, the critical problem for West Indian writers and the impetus which drives them to "exile" in England and foreign audiences. Indeed, James considered himself as much an English writer as West Indian, for, like Lamming, he found that in order to be a West Indian writer he had to leave.[28] However, James emphasizes that those he considers to be the "great English writers of the twentieth century" — Kipling, T. S. Eliot,

Henry James, Ezra Pound — are not in fact English, and this "outsiders' view" of the English language and civilization is the founding principle upon which to structure a revolutionary West Indian literature:

> . . . [W]e have the same language as the British and the outline of our civilization is based on theirs, we are in the same situation that has created the great writers of the twentieth century. We are members of this civilization and take part in it, but we come from outside. . . . I believe that at the back of the success our writers are gaining . . . is the fact that we are part of the success our writers are gaining . . . is the fact that we are part of the civilization, we can come here and live here, we can stay abroad and understand the civilization, but we don't really belong. And it is when you are outside, but can take part as a member, that you see differently from the ways they see, and you are able to write independently.[29]

Interestingly this concomitant privileging of the British tradition with "outsider," presumably "objective" status, is always made out to be V. S. Naipaul's "problem," and the reason for his anglophilia despite the fact that Lamming and James, both advocates of Caribbean aesthetics and pan-Africanism, have also described the "necessity" of exile.[30] Naipaul is regarded by nationalist-minded West Indian intellectuals as the bête noire of Caribbean discourse for his well-known views on the Third World in general and West Indian society in particular. Naipaul is especially derisive of black power movements in the region, and has little use for what he terms "Negro protest literature":

> The involvement of the Negro with the white world is one of the limitations of West Indian writing, as it is the destruction of American Negro writing. The American Negro's subject is his blackness. This cannot be the basis of any serious literature, and it has happened again and again that once the American Negro has made his statement, his profitable protest, he has nothing to say. With two or three exceptions, the West Indian writer has so far avoided the American Negro type of protest writing, but his aims have been equally propagandist: to win acceptance for his group.[31]

Yet, despite Naipaul's disavowal of "profitable [black] protest" writing, James recounts Naipaul's response to *Beyond A Boundary* this way: "I have only read half of the book so far but I want to let you know at once I am extremely glad because it lets these English people know who and what *we West Indians* are."[32] (emphasis added) It is more than mere coincidence that Naipaul should use the oppositional, nationalist "we West Indians" in his validation of James, especially since Naipaul has said that he does not consider himself West Indian at all.[33] Given Naipaul's construction of himself as a gentleman observer subject in the model of such Victorian travel writers as Trollope and Froude, whose views on the Caribbean he uses to frame his own in his travel writings on the region,[34] it is only through this discursive tradition that Naipaul can apprehend a West Indian identity which has any validity to him. And indeed, Naipaul identifies closely with James — in his review of *Boundary* he notes that despite the racial/cultural differences in their backgrounds, he has followed James's path "almost step by step" — and finds that "we have ended speaking the same language."[35] Perhaps most importantly, he concludes his essay by emphasizing that *Boundary* is "one of the finest and most finished books to come out of the West Indies, important to England, important to the West Indies. It has a further value: it gives a base and solidity to West Indian literary endeavour."[36]

The *literariness* of *Boundary*'s nationalist outlook is important to Naipaul precisely because of his own sense of the paucity of literary tradition in the English-speaking West Indies. Like James, Naipaul was drawn to the world of books as a way of transcending his society; "the noblest vocation in the world" to him, the writer was an identity Naipaul invented himself as a teenager, long before he had discovered that he had any talent for actual writing.[37] For Naipaul as for James, then, the self-fashioning of the gentleman/artist subject, with its excessive knowledge of "social convention," was a critical forerunner to the actual production of texts. For them, the Carlylean model of the Literary Man, in helping them to define their society, could enable them to *transcend* it. Still, it was not enough. Discussing his early years as an avid reader of Victorian novels, Naipaul recounts that even as he went to the books for "fantasy," he was made ever more aware of the disjuncture between the "elaborately ordered" Victorian societies and his West Indian, non-English reality:

In literature such a society was more than alien; it was excluding, it made nonsense of my fantasies and more and more, as I grew older and thought of writing myself, it made me despairingly conscious of the poverty and haphazardness of my own society. I might adapt Dickens to Trinidad; but it seemed impossible that the life I knew in Trinidad could ever be turned into a book. If landscapes do not start to be real until they have been interpreted by an artist, so, until they have been written about, societies appear to be without shape and *embarrassing*.[38]

Therefore, the process of *writing* as an author, for Naipaul, was very much different from the process of *reading*. Knowing the English canon — Naipaul studied literature at Oxford — far from strengthening his ties to a literary tradition, removed him further from it, to the point where it "did not give me the courage to do a simple thing like mentioning the name of a Port of Spain street." To write is to write from within a tradition; "the English language was mine; the tradition was not."[39] For Naipaul, then, the crisis of literary production is predicated on two fundamentally linked issues: how to represent a land that is not "real," to paint an image of a society that is embarrassingly formless and "without shape"; and how to write *as a West Indian*. Naipaul resolves his problems as a writer by, in essence, "becoming" the Victorian gentleman travel writer in his travel books on the Caribbean, Latin America, Africa, and Asia. Given that the colonial travel narrative assumes a fundamental inviolability of the subjectivity of the traveler, the subject of the travel narrative is therefore rendered more concrete in the preemptive judgment of the "civilized" and "objective" observer.[40] Naipaul prefaces his Caribbean travel narrative, *The Middle Passage*, with Froude's quotation, "There are no people [in the West Indies] in the true sense of the word, with a character and purpose of their own." Inasmuch as Naipaul has in some sense recast himself *as* Froude, it is small wonder that he should come to precisely this conclusion as well.

Ironically, Naipaul was commissioned to write the book by then-Trinidadian prime minister and pan-Africanist scholar Eric Williams, as he describes years later. This accounts in part for his own uncertainties about who was his audience, being himself West Indian yet writing as a Briton:

I knew and was glamoured by the ideas of the metropolitan traveler, the man starting from Europe. It was the only kind of model I had; but — as a colonial among colonials who were very close to me — I could not be that kind of traveler, even though I might share that traveler's education and culture and have his feeling for adventure. Especially I was aware of not having a metropolitan audience to "report back" to. The fight between my idea of the glamour of the travel-writer and the rawness of my nerves as a colonial traveling among colonials made for difficult writing. When, the traveling done, I went back to London with my notes and diaries, to do the writing, the problems were not solved.[41]

The Middle Passage thus embodies Naipaul's struggle to identify his audience and therefore himself within the triangulation of the modern Middle Passage: First World/Third World, the European travel writer who "interprets" the primitive, versus the primitive object itself. Yet his choice of authorial voice arises not merely from what might arguably be called his own anti–Third World anxieties, but also from the fact that it has long been available to him as a member of the educated emergent West Indian middle class, whose ethos is primarily and distinctly associated with the black middle-class sensibilities of J. J. Thomas, Edward Blyden, and, later, C. L. R. James.

Naipaul invokes the authoritative voice of the Victorian gentleman traveler precisely at the moment when he is engaged in the rendering of the West Indian nations as fragmented and "unreal." This nineteenth-century authorial presence becomes strikingly apparent in his fictional representations of the West Indies and West Indian writers, particularly so in his novels *The Mimic Men* and *Guerrillas*,[42] where the visions of "disorder" and "unreality" echo the words and ideas of earlier nineteenth-century travel narratives on the Caribbean.

The Mimic Men functions as an explicit allegory of the newly independent anglophone Caribbean nations. As its title suggests, Naipaul finds that independence for the West Indian nation can only be a poor imitation of England. It is a story about the failure of politics to create historical meaning for the West Indian subject or to provide definition to the West Indian space: in other words, the failure is one of perpetual unreality—the West Indies remains forever fixed as Somewhere Else. The words of the narrator, Ralph Singh, a disgraced cabinet minister from the island of Isabella who is writing his memoirs in England, reveal the fundamental premise of the narrative: "We pretended to be real, to be learning, to be preparing ourselves for life, we mimic men of the New World, one unknown corner of it, with all its reminders of the corruption that came so quickly to the new."

The movement of the narrative goes from London to the Caribbean and back to London: the Middle Passage is reversed so that the Caribbean becomes subsumed within an English frame. History starts, and ends, in the metropolis. Ralph Singh is a dandy, a "picturesque Asiatic" (taken from Froude's description of Trinidadian Indians) who is suffering from a serious crisis of personal definition. He goes to London to study and then returns to the island of Isabella to immerse himself in "revolutionary politics." Ralph's career consists of no more than a few impassioned speeches about the "dignity of indignity" before the mostly black masses, earnest discussions and parties at his home in the suburb of Crippleville (the name is an obvious allegory), and the editing of a Socialist newspaper. Events overtake him—he is not particularly responsible, but his fall is the result of the condition of existential "distress" in the society that requires political victims—and he is exiled to London permanently.

There are a few key features of the narrative that I will explore here. The trope of the shipwreck lies at the heart of Naipaul's depiction of Isabella. In a scene in the middle of the narrative, Ralph Singh witnesses the drowning of several people at the beach. The scene has a surreal, disembodied quality: the fishermen, their faces "like masks," impassively mend their nets while "[t]here in that infernal devouring element people were drowning." Watching them, Ralph imagines himself drowning, and becomes detached, "feeling only the feebleness and absurdity of any attempt to rescue those persons, already bodies, hidden in that turquoise water beyond the breakers" (108). The land is described as "a geography lesson in miniature, with time speeded up": ". . . what had once floated lightly on the waters, coming to the end of its journey at a particular moment; the home now of scores of alien creatures . . . Here the island was like a place awaiting Columbus and discovery. And what was an unmarked boy doing here, shipwrecked, chieftain of an unknown shore, awaiting rescue, awaiting the arrival of ships of curious shape to take him back to his mountains? Poor boy, poor leader" (111).

There is no order to the journey of the plant life that floats on the waters: it simply comes to the end of its journey "at a particular moment." Such is Naipaul's vision of the Caribbean islands, which float, connected to nothing, much like the early sixteenth-century view of the islands as fragments of a far-off mainland. Thus, the "alien creatures" —the African-descended slaves, the "picturesque Asiatics," the no-longer-European Europeans—can never be marked by such a space. They do not belong to it, having been shipwrecked by force of circumstance, and the Caribbean space itself is unmarked, an alien geographical entity within the space of the global map itself.

Ralph Singh's attempt to write the history of the island through his personal memoirs is, then, a way of attempting to mark the Caribbean space and its inhabitants, to indigenize them, and itself, as a West Indian narrative. The quest of West Indian writers to body the disembodied Caribbean space is in this way transferred onto the project of writing the Caribbean narrative. The trope of writing is always prevalent in Naipaul's oeuvre, and *The Mimic Men* is no exception. Ralph Singh's attempt to create meaning out of his political and personal life frames the entire set of events on the island, so that we are invited to see postcolonial politics as an attempt to order history, to write it into existence, and thereby to write the colonial subject into existence. As Ralph reflects, "To be born on an island like Isabella, an obscure New World plantation, secondhand and barbarous, was to be born to disorder." Writing, then, is a way to make order — meaning — out of disorder, out of the ambiguity that informs the Caribbean space. However, by the end of the novel Singh has reconciled himself to the fact that his narrative will never be finished; the writing of the book has become an end in itself, for Singh cannot believe in his own existence unless it is recorded (244).

The black revolutionary in *The Mimic Men*, Brown, is also writing a novel. Brown's novel is about a slave revolt:

I heard he was writing a novel about a slave. Many people knew the plot: the slave leads a revolt which is betrayed and brutally crushed; he escapes to the forest, reflects, arrives at self-disgust, and returns willingly to slavery and death. I saw a carbon of an early chapter, the second I believe. The slaves arrive from Africa; they are happy to be on land again; they dance and sing; they beg to be bought quickly. *The scene was all done in mime, as it were, and from a distance.* It was brutal and disagreeable; I didn't want to read more. I don't believe more was written. (156, emphasis added)

Like Singh's narrative, Brown's is destined to be incomplete. Endings impose order onto narrative and thereby generate meaning, but these West Indian narratives, finally, can never conclude and thereby generate meaning, because of their intrinsic nature as copies of the European master text. Brown attempts to write into existence black history and the resisting black subject, but as the above passage reveals, he can only mime history: he cannot recreate it because he cannot apprehend it. Brown is displaced from his own history through the very tools he uses; the novel form cannot accommodate the slave past, it can only burlesque it. Brown cannot master the novel because he cannot "master" the history; literary mastery and political mastery, then, have similar ends.

Another black author figure, Jimmy Ahmed, the black revolutionary in *Guerrillas*, is writing a romance with himself as hero. Significantly, he lives at Thrushcross Grange, the name of the estate of Catherine and Heathcliff in *Wuthering Heights*.[43] Jimmy Ahmed's writing of himself as the hero in a romance where the heroine is a white Englishwoman named Clarissa bespeaks the same crisis: Ahmed's project to write himself into existence can only be achieved through the frame of the Victorian novel and a gothic notion of the antihero, as the words of Clarissa, the narrator of his novel, suggest:

He's suffered so much in England, I don't believe he will want to see someone like me. Over here they see him only as a *hakwai* [half Chinese, half black], but a woman of my class can see what he really is, I can understand what all those other people in England saw in him. They say he was born in the back room of a Chinese grocery, a half black nobody . . . but I can see that he is a man of good blood . . . He's the leader they're waiting for and the day will come . . . when they will parade in the streets and offer him the crown, everybody will say then, "This man was born in the back room of a Chinese grocery, but *as Catherine said to Heathcliff, 'Your mother was an Indian princess and your father was the Emperor of China,'* we knew it all along,". . . They will see him then like a prince, with his gold color. (57, emphasis added)

The final irony is of course that the commune of the black revolutionaries in *Guerrillas* is named after the Wuthering Heights estate, which points to their fundamental imprisonment within the master discourse.

Ralph Singh, Brown, and Jimmy Ahmed are all conceived of as poor, *black* (in its larger sense) imitations of the Original Scholar. The attempts of Brown to write a European romance of slavery as well as those of Ahmed to write a Victorian novel, and indeed Singh's desire to write a political memoir that combines both his personal and political journey, all refer the reader back to the Victorian gentleman scholar, whose characteristics were embodied in writers such as Kingsley, Trollope, and particularly Froude, all of whom wrote fiction and "commentary," combining the political, social, and personal. They ordered the world for the Victorians and made sense of the colonies through the prism of their own particular status as civilized white English gentlemen, who could therefore be "objective" and "rational" about their narrative subjects. The problem with their West Indian imitators is that their imitations of the "master text" cannot *master* the text, and thus their stories degenerate into meaninglessness and are never finished.

In *The Mimic Men* Froude resurfaces yet again. An old French slave-owning family, Deschampsneufs, traces its ambiguous reputation as aristocrats who were yet "totally committed to the island in their way" to an incident in which a Deschampsneufs accompanies Froude to the mountains, where Froude discovers a naked black man washing clothes. Froude is indignant and orders the man to leave, whereupon Deschampsneufs intercedes and speaks to the man "soothingly in the French patois of the mountains," thereby saving Froude from violence. Froude "was not greatly impressed," and rounds off his chapter on Isabella with a diatribe against the French (77–78).

One is led to ponder the significance of Froude's insertion into the narrative in this particular way, until later, when Ralph Singh is invited to the Deschampsneufs home. There he is shown a "shiny and terrible" portrait of a nineteenth-century ancestor, a "lady" who was educated in Paris and lived in the house of a French count. She has an affair with the French novelist Stendhal. When she returns to the island Stendhal sends her a copy of *The Red and the Black*, with a page earmarked. The scene underlined on the page is the one in which Julien mockingly affects the tone of the French creole maid who lives in the house of his lover, Mademoiselle de la Mole — a passage that amounts to two sentences. The words of the novel are the same words that Stendhal exchanged with the Deschampsneufs lady. It is this immortalization within the classic European text that is responsible for the Deschampsneufses' aristocratic status on the island, and Ralph Singh is suitably impressed: "I felt that Mr. Deschampsneufs's story had brought the past close. It was possible to believe in the link between our island and the great world" (174). Ralph's position is supposed to reflect that of the colonized subject who has confused history with story, who is so foolish as to believe that a distorted and minuscule representation within the European canon constitutes a link with "reality."

This ironic depiction of the derivative grandeur of the Deschamps-neufs is anchored in Naipaul's obsession with the European master text, an obsession which is responsible for such "fake" identities as Deschampsneufs's and Ahmed's. Like Jimmy Ahmed, the Deschampsneufs are not real; their stature is reduced to fleeting — and scathing — references in European narratives. Their entire history has been mapped within the footnotes of European discourse, from Stendhal to Froude. Without the master texts, the family cannot exist. When Ralph asks the younger Deschampsneufs if his father's story is true, he replies: "My father would kill himself if it wasn't true . . ." (175).

Naipaul envisions West Indian history and English stories as irrevocably tied to one another. The writers in his narratives all suffer from the same illness: the impossible desire to create their history from an English story. It is this desire that produces the existential crisis, the unnarratability that marks their narratives. Hence the pivotal role of fantasy in the inner lives of his protagonists, fantasies which are externalized into delusions of political power. Political power, as a metaphor for national subjectivity, is as ephemeral as the texts the characters generate: "real" power resides elsewhere. The geographical space of the Middle Passage in the text, that Somewhere Elseness of the narrative located somewhere between London and Isabella, between reality and unreality, becomes a philosophical condition that permeates the lives of Singh and of all the other inhabitants of the island who can neither define themselves nor their context.

The narrative's metaphor of the Middle Passage — implicitly "raced" as black, with the echoes of black Africans in the cargoes of a slave ship — is an existential void which symbolizes the impossibility of reality for the Caribbean space and therefore the impossibility of representation. Naipaul's position within this space is untenable, because the Middle Passage can only be apprehended within the role of the English gentleman scholar, whose subject positioning can confer upon the Caribbean meaning, even if that meaning is a degraded relation to England: Jimmy Ahmed, Brown, and Ralph Singh must literally become English gentlemen to make sense of themselves. But even for them to write *as* white English subjects is for them to burlesque themselves by revealing the extent of their not-Englishness. Thus, within the Naipaulian narrative, the Caribbean as text denotes the impossibility of narrative *as* a *West Indian* author.

Naipaul's conflicted status as neo-Victorian gentleman author prevents his works from being critically linked to more obviously nationalist West Indian narratives. Yet, similar invocations of nineteenth-century authority are to be found in the fiction of Claude McKay and Una Marson, two black Jamaican nationalist writers whose works and views are, at first glance, diametrically opposed to the Naipaulian vision of West Indianness. The dialectical relationship between the representation of the Caribbean intellectual and the English canon is similarly configurated in overtly nationalist West Indian texts such as these, which exhibit the symptoms of canonical authority in their constructions of a specifically West Indian oppositionality. I will pursue this link in the following chapter.

REPRESENTING THE FOLK:
THE CRISIS OF LITERARY
AUTHENTICITY

Unlike the previous governments and departments of educators, unlike the businessman importing commodities, the West Indian novelist did not look out across the sea to another source. He looked in and down at what had traditionally been ignored. For the first time the West Indian peasant became other than a cheap source of labour.... It is the West Indian novel that has restored the West Indian peasant to his true and original status of personality. (emphasis added) — George Lamming, *The Pleasures of Exile*

Lamming's striking claims for the West Indian novel are predicated on an important set of assumptions. The first is that the West Indian peasant is always a metonym for the land itself; the second, that the middle class, represented in the businessman importing commodities from abroad, should be consuming, perhaps even *exporting*, this important domestic resource. Most importantly, Lamming's argument contrasts the philistine preoccupations of the other members of the West Indian middle class to the more noble exertions of the West Indian novelist to "restore" to the West Indian peasant his "true" personality. If communities exist only as they are narrativized, one can reasonably infer from the above passage that Lamming is convinced that the West Indian novel has, in effect, *made* the peasant. The commemoration of the peasant to literary tradition is made out to be a life-giving act: the literary *image* of the peasant is more "real" than the reality of the peasant himself, who presumably has been around for some time before his "discovery" by the West Indian novelist.

The importance for Lamming in discovering an indigenous resource

REPRESENTING THE FOLK 59

for literary endeavor is connected to his anxieties about the perpetually extra-national vision of the West Indian middle class, which can find no value in the products of home. Like the imported commodities that are deemed of more value precisely because they are foreign, Lamming's mission to revalue the peasant is motivated by his desire for indigenous literary origins that owe nothing to foreign literary influence. The peasant of Lamming's literary vision becomes commodified in another way; no longer cheap labor, perhaps, but a form of barter that can combat the commodity value of Englishness in the English literary text.

The West Indian fascination with the English canon has been considered mostly in its problematic aspect within modern anglophone Caribbean discourse, and not only by the nationalists. As I have discussed in chapter 2, V. S. Naipaul found that his saturation in the images of Victorian England hindered him from apprehending the realities of his own West Indian society. From another ideological angle but nevertheless to the same end, Edward Brathwaite has described Jamaican school children whose ideas of reality are so steeped in English novels that they can no longer distinguish between their reality and those of the novels; he cites as evidence one child who writes an essay wherein the snow falls on the cane fields. C. L. R. James recounts a similar problem with one of his first efforts at writing, which turned out to be an imitation of an English author simply transferred to the context of Trinidad.[1]

If, as Bryan tells us, admittance to the West Indian middle class of the nineteenth and early twentieth centuries depended literally on the acquisition of Victorian manners and morals, then the final stage of independence logically should be, according to the thinking of West Indian intellectuals, a throwing off of these signs of colonization and a return to an apparently authentic West Indian culture.[2] However, in order to do so, the middle class first had to recognize working class, rural peasant culture as separate and distinct from their own — as somehow more indigenous to the region. This authentic culture came thus to be identified to a great extent with the suppressed and vilified African-based customs of peasant society, such that blackness became reified into a structuring oppositional ideology, the antithesis of Englishness.

The intellectual's argument that black Caribbean culture constitutes the basis of an indigenous literary tradition is, as I will argue, the basis of a certain anxiety in West Indian discourse on the question of race and authenticity. Indeed, much of what has now become West Indian canonical literature has been concerned specifically with this return to the "real" Caribbean; that is, the African-based culture of the uneducated (meaning not formally educated), often rural, folk or peasant societies of the region.[3] The idea of a "return" itself engenders a crisis of contradiction; on one level the idea signifies the intellectual's return to and re*valuing* of black, peasant origins, a necessary step in the revolutionary movement toward independence. On another, a return to peasant origins also suggests a return to a point in history where black people did not have the opportunity to represent themselves, nor to offer a critique of colonial rule. If the return to peasant origins is a movement *backwards* in historical time, it might perceptually be conceived as a move backwards in *political* terms. It is for strategic political reasons, after all, that the black peasantry's traditional reverence for education has such enduring power. A return to authentic Caribbeanness, therefore, must fulfill two contradictory principles: it must posit folk culture as whole and unsullied by the taint of colonial hegemony — a prelapsarian image of the nation — *even as* it must contain a critique of colonial domination in its very essence.

The impulse to return to "real" Caribbean culture can be linked to a larger thematic of "re-masculinization," if you will, of the Caribbean space, that occurs in Caribbean narrative. If, as we have seen, the marking of the Caribbean through ownership and "taming" of the land was identified in European discourse as a specifically masculine enterprise that in turn defined European masculinity, then the institution of a specifically Caribbean agency which could "mark" the land was also conceived of, explicitly and implicitly, as a competing "masculine" enterprise. Lamming's vision of the West Indian novel "restoring" the peasant to life evokes the similar visioning of the West Indies by Carlyle and the Victorian intellectuals, who liken the region to a sleeping beauty who must be "awakened" by the touch of the English conqueror (see my discussion in chapter 1).

The paradox of this enterprise lies in the fact that the defining of the land space has involved two intertwined components. On the one hand is posed the masculine figure, a combination of conqueror, colonialist, and travel writer. He owns the landspace, defines its parameters, inscribes it in writing. On the other hand is posed the femininized figure of the land itself, which is defined/owned/written upon. The female figure is posited as the nostalgic essence of Caribbean culture, to be "restored" to its rightful place; the male figure stands in for the newly politicized Caribbean, which will enact the restoration. For the Caribbean writer the dilemma is to occupy both sides of the equation: to be the owner and the owned, the writer and the land, the masculine and the feminine. This dilemma is resolved in the erection of Shakespeare's Caliban as the symbol of, on the one hand, political opposition to colonial rule — often signified through physical violence — and on the other, a precolonial West Indian world, the Edenic essence of West Indianness, of which more later.[4] For the purposes of my argument here, suffice it to say that the desire for recovery of the "real" Caribbean is fundamentally linked to this larger discursive project of masculine agency.

In the following discussion I intend to lay out some of the more well-known arguments for the Caribbean folk novel in order to display the inherent contradictions that arise in the distinctions between the categories of "peasant" and "writer," "race" and "community." I will argue that the innate dissonances between these categories give rise to a crisis, of sorts, over the issue of authenticity in Caribbean narrative. I will interrogate the assumptions of Lamming's and Brathwaite's claims for what *ought* to constitute the West Indian folk novel, with a view to validating *my* claim that both base their views on a similar conflation of Victorian perceptions of literary mastery and black nationalist oppositional discourse. From there, I will illustrate a similar principle evident in the works of two early West Indian writers who were similarly invested in representing peasant society: Claude McKay and Una Marson.

Caribbean Aesthetics and the Question of Race

Perhaps it is a truism that the societies that are the most unsure of what and who they are — what defines their *natio* — are usually the ones most concerned with the question of authentic culture. If, as Benedict Anderson asserts, nationalism is always an "imagining" of the nation's past, then in the West Indian situation the past is to be uncovered in the present: that is, since there is no effective past that does *not* include the Europeans (the Caribbean of the indigenous peoples is, in a sense, not really the "West Indies," the very name which, as I have noted previously, is predicated on the European intervention), then the imagined community of the nation must reside in that portion of it least influenced by colonialism: the folk, or peasantry.

Bruce King defines nationalism as "an urban movement which identifies with the rural areas as a source of authenticity, finding in the 'folk' the attitudes, beliefs, customs and language to create a sense of national unity among people who have other loyalties. Nationalism aims at . . . rejection of cosmopolitan upper classes, intellectuals and others likely to be influenced by foreign ideas."[5] Applied to the West Indian context, this definition suggests that it is the very promulgators of this return to authenticity who are themselves the intellectuals most "likely to be influenced by foreign ideas."

One of these "foreign ideas," however, may be the very idea of the folk itself. Timothy Brennan argues that the concepts of "folk character" and "national language" originate in the nationalism of English Romanticism, which utilized the peasantry for political expediency. Further, he notes that the rise of European nationalism coincides with the formation of the novel and believes nationalism to be responsible for the "largely illusory" divisions of literature into distinct "national literatures."[6] Looked at from this perspective, the Caribbean quest for authenticity as a means to define the nation can arguably be linked yet further still to a prior English nationalist literary discourse. If the basis of authenticity for the English-speaking Caribbean nationalists is the African-based rural culture of the area, how would it translate into the literary form?

The work of Edward Kamau Brathwaite, the Barbadian poet-scholar and foremost proponent of an African-based Caribbean aesthetic, has formed the basis of much of West Indian discussion on the subject. West Indian intellectuals for the past four decades have been wrestling with the notion of a Caribbean aesthetic and have spent considerable time debating the criteria for judging "West Indianness." The urgency to establish a Caribbean aesthetic is not surprising, considering the radical political and social implications of such a concept for a Third World, postcolonial society. Yet, even as much of West Indian discourse on the subject seeks to establish a regional/cultural identity against what is perceived as an imposed European culture,[7] and despite the heavy influence of negritude in political and indeed social theories of the period, the narrative form has remained essentially the same as its European and American counterparts, as Guyanese writer Wilson Harris complains.[8]

The impetus for a Caribbean aesthetic has similarly political motives in its striving to uncover an authentic and therefore liberating African-based culture from the stifling confines of European mores and structures. Yet discussions of an authentic Caribbean aesthetic often fall into a sort of orthodoxy of blackness. A case in point: Brathwaite approvingly cites Jamaican scholar and author Sylvia Wynter's call for the West Indian writer to focus on the "anonymous mass of our people" who have "absolutely no documented history at all," even as he notes that she herself has not yet been able to capture that authentically Caribbean "form" in which to do so. However, he adds, she is working her way toward it, moving as she has from "Marxist overtones and citations" to "African culture."[9] (The distinction being made here is noteworthy.) Elsewhere, he denies Jean Rhys admittance to the West Indian canon on the basis that her writing does not adhere to an African-derived worldview, arguing that her novels are more English than they are Caribbean.[10] At this juncture of Caribbean literary politics in the early to mid-1970s, to be Caribbean was to be in protest to Europe, and to be opposed to Europe was to be black: as Brathwaite remarks of white authors in the hispanophone Caribbean, "The literary expression which came out of these white creoles (and mulattoes) was black based; they recognized that the only form of expression which could be used as a protest, or an authentic *alter/native* . . . was ex-African."[11]

Brathwaite's remarks embody the basic tenets of the Caribbean aesthetics as they have been thus far defined: black, working-class culture is the "authentic" culture of the Caribbean, and "authentic" Caribbean writing must utilize the creole languages and exhibit principles of orality among other things. This is particularly ironic, inasmuch as most Caribbean writers are from the logocentric middle class and familiar mostly at a distance with working-class oral black culture.

An interesting parallel to Brathwaite's position is Lamming's, who as I have discussed identifies the West Indian novel's chief recognizable characteristic as "the peasant feel."[12] He argues that the contemporary West Indian novel has more of an affinity with Shakespeare's drama than the contemporary English novel with, interestingly, its "present exercises in anger." (44) Lamming essentially posits the Caribbean writer as the natural heir to Shakespeare's legacy, as opposed to the contemporary English writer, who no longer understands the relationship between society and the novel: "For [Caribbean] prose is, really, the people's speech, the organic music of the earth. Shakespeare knew that music, and lived at a time when it permeated society. But things have changed beyond belief in England. For the young English novelist, there are really no people." (45)

It would seem that, for Lamming, "anger" and "the peasant feel" are mutually exclusive categories. Yet one might assume that "anger" is not an uncommon feature of oppositional narratives, and indeed elsewhere Lamming argues that violence is an inevitable part of the postcolonial nationbuilding experience:

I believe that it is against all experience that a history which held men together in that way can come to an end in a cordial manner. . . . That horror and that brutality have a price, which has to be paid by the man who inflicted it — just as the man who suffered it has to find a way of exorcising that demon. It seems to me that there is almost a therapeutic need for a certain kind of violence in the breaking. There cannot be a parting of the ways. There has to be a smashing.[13]

What, then, is the relationship between Lamming's belief in the inevitability — necessity, even — of anger and violence in the decolonizing process and his critique of anger as a literary device? Given the above sentiments, Lamming's choice of Shakespeare as the writer whose works most closely resemble the nascent West Indian novel form suggest that, for him, the English tradition which Shakespeare represents is in itself the *real* revolutionary idea for the Caribbean, as opposed to contemporary English writing which reveals, in his view, a lack of communal consciousness. As such, for the Caribbean nationalist writer modernity is precisely that revelation of "traditional" society which the European counterpart shuns. The writer must presumably be "objective" and without "anger," and the novel shall essentially *become* the society.[14]

Significantly, Lamming complains that "white"[15] Jamaican writer, John Hearne, does not exhibit "the peasant feel" in his portrayals of the Jamaican agricultural middle class: "Hearne is a first-class technician, almost perfect within the limitation of conventional story-telling; but the work is weakened, for the language is not being *used*, and the Novel as a form is not really being *utilised*. His novels suggest that he has a dread of being identified with the land at a peasant level . . . He is not an example of that instinct and root impulse which return the better West Indian writers back to the soil."[16]

Thus the "root" sensibilities will, *de facto*, transform the novel structure, take charge of it, and shape it into a paradigm of West Indian narrative. The novel form and the "return to the soil" are, for Lamming, essentially the same thing: the novel *becomes* the soil in that it defines the actual, geographic national space, and in this way, the West Indian novelist is able to possess what is not actually in his possession. That Hearne has "a dread of being identified with the land" is implicitly critiqued as a political stance: identification with the land means, here, identification with the laborers of the land as opposed to the owners of it: with, in other words, blackness. The land itself, once identified with white ownership and power, is now racially re-inscribed so that it is associated with a black Caribbean history of slavery, labor, and distance from the European models of culture.[17]

If these descriptions of an anglophone Caribbean aesthetic sound prescriptive, there is also good reason to identify any definition of West Indianness with blackness. The facts are that taken as a whole, blacks are a majority in the region, and as Jamaican scholar Rex Nettleford points out, other racial groups in the region — Chinese, Indian, Portuguese, Syrian, Amerindian — are assimilated into the Euro-African cultural ethos of the region.[18] Given the strong influence of Afro-Caribbean culture, how can any Caribbean cultural theory be "too black"? Perhaps it is the angle of this critique, which presupposes that black history in the Caribbean is divorced from that of the East Indian, Chinese, or other nationalities brought into plantation colonies to replace slave labor and keep wages low. Or it may lie in the suspicion that black cultural theories, while they have done much in the way of political empowerment, have also functioned to simplify complex political allegiances within Caribbean society and without. Yet the racial/cultural mix of the Caribbean has always been used to disguise the political fact of a black majority (Jamaica's motto, "Out of Many, One People," used ostensibly as a symbol of racial harmony, functions instead to de-emphasize the undesirable image of a 90 percent black majority), and in this context the emphasis on African cultural roots is particularly appealing. The reality of nonblack power in the West Indies operated — and to a large extent continues to operate — in inverse proportion to its influence on West Indian discourse.

Black power was embraced by young Jamaicans and Trinidadians in the late 1960s for the "task of restoring to the black man his manhood, his dignity, and gaining for him real ownership in the society which was supposed to be his own," according to Nettleford.[19] (The emphasis on "manhood" is significant.) Yet, of "Black Power" he cautions that

> For Jamaica the danger probably lies in the fact that the capitalization of the first letters of these two now powerful words threatens to take the whole phenomenon of black identity and consciousness out of the ambience of Jamaican life into the mainstream of what some people may regard as yet another vulgar 'ism'. Moreover, the subsequent embrace by Jamaicans of the American importation may serve to blur the fact of the continuity of this search among the uprooted in Jamaica for self-sufficiency and self-respect. More damning perhaps for some of the Jamaican advocates is that they, like the reactionaries they berate, continue in colonial fashion to look *outside* of the society for ideas and for original thinking.[20]

Thus, theories of blackness which emanate from a European notion of whiteness are somehow more indigenous to the region, one might reason, than the "American importation" of black power ideology.

Furthermore, Caribbean literary theories of "West Indianness," which rate a work according to its degree of "blackness," are particularly contradictory when it comes to theorizing a harmony between the race of the author and the "race" of the writing. As we have seen above, Brathwaite excludes Jean Rhys's *Wide Sargasso Sea* from "West Indianness" because it does not emphasize the blackness of the Caribbean; naturally one is led to suspect that Rhys's status as an expatriate white West Indian, and one of ambivalent political and racial beliefs at that,[21] de facto prevents her from being able to write, with this prescription, a West Indian novel. Brathwaite similarly dismisses white Dominican Phyllis Allfrey's *Orchid House* (a novel about white West Indian society) as a "brilliant but irrelevant novel within the West Indian context." So far, simple enough. However, Brathwaite argues that Jamaican author Roger Mais's novel *Brother Man* qualifies as a "black novel" because of its insights into the urban black Jamaican ghetto experience and the "jazz" qualities it utilizes to do so.[22] Brathwaite attempts to use jazz as the basis of a West Indian poetics, and argues that jazz, with its improvisatory and unfixed modes of expression, is the music of protest; it provides the perfect model of opposition, creolization (a hybrid of black American and white American impulses), and blackness. Furthermore, "[j]azz is a new world negro form of expression that *has* received study, recognition and a certain measure of acceptance."[23] Interestingly, in this particular essay Brathwaite has little use for indigenous musical forms such as calypso and ska, remarking that they *"are concerned with protest only incidentally*. They are essentially collective forms, ridiculing individualism, singing the praises of eccentricity . . . a communal, almost tribal form. There is no suggestion of alienation, no note of chaos in calypso" (emphasis added).

Here we find several reversals of conventional "folk novel" theory. For one, the reliance on a foreign, not an indigenous, art form to provide the basis of an indigenous aesthetic implies that blackness — foreign or otherwise — is interchangeable and that moreover First World articulations of blackness are preferable because of their "acceptance" by — or familiarity to — metropolitan critics. Second, the privileging of the individual who shall articulate the community over the collective operates in distinct counterpoint to pan-Africanist theories which seek to negate or subsume the presence of the intellectual or the artist in the expression of the collective. Third, "chaos" and "alienation," hallmarks of European modernism, are asserted to be fundamental to the West Indian condition. In African nationalist theories, the Western-educated intellectual is alienated from his/her community through language and education, and seeks re-entry; in African American nationalist theories, the black individual is alienated from the wider white society; but in the West Indian, Brathwaite implies, alienation is an intrinsic feature that must be retained even as communal "folk" culture must be celebrated.

Brathwaite's paradoxical equation is emphasized yet further still by his views on the works of V. S. Naipaul, who as we have seen earlier is especially derisive of black power movements in the region. Yet Brathwaite cites Naipaul as a West Indian writer *par excellence*. Of Naipaul's *A House for Mr. Biswas* Brathwaite concludes that inasmuch as the novel is about a *"minority* East Indian group," "there was a very real chance that *A House for Mr. Biswas* could have turned out to be, like Phyllis Allfrey's novel, brilliant yet irrelevant within the West Indian context." However, since Mr. Biswas is an outsider trying to establish his identity within the group, "Naipaul was able to create a situation *which is recognizable to us all.* . . . Biswas becomes a kind of timeless figure—a sort of Everyman."[24]

This statement reflects a curious negotiation of various ideologies and beliefs. First, it grounds its critique in the view that Naipaul's writing is "minority literature"; at the time of Brathwaite's essay (1971), the number of East Indians and blacks in Trinidad was almost equal, and today the East Indians are a slight majority.

Second, it implies that works about white West Indians lie outside the creole continuum because they do not engage black culture. This would appear to contradict a founding principle of Caribbean creolization theory: that is, the idea that black Caribbean culture can speak for all ethnic groups in the region because of their collective grounding in Euro-African cultural norms. Curiously enough, the Indian writer— the noncreole, "foreigner" in the black-white equation of power—is able to write the West Indian novel because his ancestors were not a party to colonization, whereas, according to Brathwaite, the white creole is unable to precisely because hers were.

Three, it privileges marginal status—"us all" presumably is West Indians, and in particular nonwhite West Indians, since the "white" experience is understood to be at the center of discourse and, paradoxically, invisible because it is the absent presence against which the structure defines itself.

Fourth, it understands that the goal of West Indian literature is "universal" appeal, which again would seem to contradict the aspiration of Caribbean aesthetics to reflect the *particularities*, not the universalities, of West Indian experience. But on closer inspection, Brathwaite's simultaneous reading of universality and "Otherness" particularity in the "Everyman" appeal of *Biswas* makes sense if we read it as a call to the ideal of oppositionality *combined* with an understanding of a communal essence—that is, "West Indianness" itself—that stands in relation, but is separate from, that oppositionality. Thus Brathwaite attempts to reconcile the political necessities of Caribbean aesthetic ideology with Caribbean cultural ideology, the two of which are not particularly synonymous.

Perhaps more interesting than Brathwaite's admiration of Naipaul is his critique of attempts by black nationalist writers such as Wynter and

Lamming to use creole language and forms in their novels. He argues that the "folk rhythms" of these middle-class writers are influenced not by West Indian society but by the modernist experiments of Lawrence, Faulkner, and Hemingway and are as such the sign of their rejection of Caribbean society.[25] He concludes that their efforts to capture West Indian reality are unsuccessful, stating that ". . . to write really well about a living society . . . one has simply to be an 'old-fashioned' writer like *Hardy, Dickens, George Eliot, or Jane Austen. This is what Naipaul is. . . . the black West Indian cannot really expect novels like Biswas until he has a strong enough framework of social convention* from which to operate and until his own technique is flexible and subtle enough to take advantage of it."[26] (emphasis added)

As detailed in the previous chapter, Brathwaite's position on Naipaul is emblematic of that of other West Indian scholars who dislike him, condemn him, and generally agonize over him, but nevertheless admit him without hesitation into the West Indian canon. ("Despite his horror of being claimed, we West Indians are proud of Naipaul, and that is his enigmatic fate as well," says no less a West Indian icon than Nobel laureate Derek Walcott.)[27] No one denies his "West Indianness" — no one, that is, except Naipaul himself.[28] And it is precisely his adherence to forms of "social convention," to, amazingly enough, the "old-fashioned" English novel, which admits him. Moreover, the reference to Naipaul's "strong . . . framework of social convention" alludes precisely to his East Indian and Hindu cultural origins that are supposed to *exclude* him from participation in creole society. Yet, as I have already argued, Naipaul is taking advantage of a specifically *black*, middle-class ethos to write in the conventions of the English novel. Brathwaite, like Lamming and his citation of Shakespeare, implicitly defines the creole Caribbean as without tradition, such that the writing from within a set of traditions *about* tradition is, in itself, a revolutionary act of West Indian consciousness. The apparent contradictions of a black Caribbean literary model which seeks to include improvisatory jazz models alongside the social conventions of Jane Austen et al. make sense only in the context of the contradictions of West Indian blackness. Though Brathwaite emphasizes that he is "trying to outline an alternative to the English Romantic/Victorian cultural tradition which still operates among us,"[29] the distinction is, in light of his various positions outlined above, much like James's distinction between his Puritan instincts and the realities of the colonial status quo: hopelessly enmeshed.

Nationalism and the Folk Narrative:
Claude McKay and Una Marson

Before Brathwaite and Lamming wrote their prescriptions for the folk novel, the first West Indian writer to be associated with this genre was Claude McKay, whose novel, *Banana Bottom*, is a mainstay of the West Indian canon. McKay, who grew up at the end of Queen Victoria's reign, was simultaneously a part of the emergent black middle-class peasantry in Jamaica and, later in life, a famous artist of the Harlem Renaissance whose novels dwelt on the lives of the poor blacks of Harlem.[30] McKay's use of primitivism in his Harlem novels — that is, the idealized representation of black folk life used in contrast to the sterility of the modern world — very clearly set the stage for his representation of the black Jamaican peasantry in *Banana Bottom*, his final novel. *Banana Bottom* deals at length with the issues of Englishness, blackness, and the alienation of the black middle class from its peasant origins; as such it is of particular importance to our discussion here.

The novel's protagonist, Bita Plant, is an educated black woman who comes back to her poor rural Jamaican community after years spent getting an education in Britain. (Her name, "Plant," is suggestive of the larger aims of the narrative to return Bita to the soil, to "plant" her back into the landscape.) Bita rejects her British education, and with it all possibility of ascending the social ladder, by marrying her father's drayman, Jubban. The novel's pastoral format suggests a sort of idealization of Jamaica's poor rural population, and the author's nonjudgmental discussion of "illegitimate" children, concubinage, and Obeah practices as part of the everyday scenery is in itself a radical shift in consciousness that sees these things not according to (presumably) European moral notions of right and wrong, but simply as events.

The black middle class here is mostly marginalized, or else ridiculed and dismissed as a hypocritical imitation of English society. Herald Newton Day, Bita's middle-class fiancé, is the only other two-dimensional black middle-class character in the novel besides Bita herself. As a black man who has received a white man's education through the missionaries, Newton Day has learned to despise his own people. In contrast, Bita is validated chiefly through her decision to renounce her English education and middle-class status to return — via marriage to Jubban — to what is posited here as "real" culture: "She became contemptuous of everything — the plan of her education and the way of existence at the mission, and her eye wandering to the photograph of her English college over her bed, she suddenly took and ripped it from its frame, tore the thing up and trampled the pieces under her feet. . . ."[31]

Ironically, it is Bita's education that has allowed her to see the falsity of the European colonial system. Bita's heightened consciousness is the result not only of her education but of her friend, Squire Gensir, a British expatriat, with whom, as a fellow product of British education, she has her only intellectual conversations throughout the narrative.[32] It is not quite a meeting of equals, however, for Squire Gensir is in the peculiar position of having to explain Bita's culture to her:

"I think some of our famous European fables have their origin in Africa. Even the mumbo-jumbo of the Obeahmen fascinates me."

"But Obeah is not the same," said Bita, "it is an awful crime."

"Oh, it's just our civilization that makes it a crime. Obeah is only a form of primitive superstition. As Christianity is a form of civilized superstition . . .

You're intolerant because of your education. Obeah is a part of your folklore, like your Anancy tales and your digging jammas. And your folklore is the spiritual link between you and your ancestral origin. You ought to learn to appreciate it as I do mine."[33]

As the narrative progresses Bita learns, through Gensir's guidance, to appreciate the manifestations of her "ancestral origin," and eventually joins in the rituals of black peasant life. After Bita has broken her class restraints, gone to tea meetings, married Jubban (who, the essence of folk life himself, is almost entirely silent throughout the narrative), and exhibited other manifestations of heightened black consciousness, it might appear strange at first glance that she finds renewed appeal in the classic texts of her English education, the education which has alienated her from her people in the first place.

In a passage where Bita is poring over the English poet William Blake's poem, "The Little Black Boy," McKay explicitly deals with the question of what the "enlightened" West Indian must now do with all those great treasures of European thought with which the colonized subject has been indoctrinated into a sense of her own cultural and racial inferiority:

A splendid poem, she thought . . . yet not one to be recommended to an impressionable black child. For it was murder of the spirit, she reasoned, to cultivate a black child to hanker after the physical characteristics of the white. . . . But away from petty picking into little pieces a poem magnificent as a whole, to speculate about its great creator. What a marvellous *universal mind* was this William Blake's. A precursor of and King among the futurists, Shakespearean in comprehension. How perfect of music and phrasing, and far-reaching the implication of that thought: "When he from white and I from black cloud free." (268, emphasis added)

The novel concludes with a scene where Bita peruses her college copy of the *Pensées* and notes the line ". . . la vraie morale se moque de la morale; la morale du jugement se moque de la morale de l'esprit": "That was one thought from Pascal that her philosophy teacher had never chosen to expatiate upon as a Christian gem. She had come by it all by herself. . . . *Unbounded by little national and racial lines, but a cosmic thing of all time for all minds.*" (emphasis added)

Gauri Viswanathan asserts that "[m]aking the Englishman known to the native through the products of his mental labour removed him from the plane of ongoing colonialist activity. . . . The English literary text functioned as a surrogate Englishman in his highest and most perfect state."[34] The English literary text, then, arguably functions as the most reified form of English colonialism. Yet McKay is clearly not interested in dispensing with the qualities of Englishness, as represented by the English canon, that Bita has imbibed. Rather, the canon is an integral part of Bita's re-entry into the Jamaican landscape in its new incarnation as a *universal* philosophy, rather than as a colonial ideology. It allows Bita to participate simultaneously in Englishness as a universal, humanizing principle and West Indianness, which through its folk rituals is linked to all that is best in the European tradition. The English canon allows her to appreciate what the text posits as the universal truths of her own folk stories, just as Squire Gensir's intellectual authority gives Bita the insight—and approval—necessary to re-integrate herself into black peasant culture.

McKay's choice of a black female protagonist in the role of the alienated black middle-class person would appear to contradict my claim that the recovery of the folk and thus, the land, is constructed by male canonical writers as a masculine enterprise. And certainly, Bita's reintegration into the folk and the landscape suggests a feminization of blackness and the black national space, an idea that is reinforced by supportive critical interpretations. For example, Carolyn Cooper argues that McKay's novel anticipates revisionist readings of race, class, and gender in contemporary feminisms, and indeed asserts that the cerebral nature of Bita's rereading of Blake's poem — done while standing naked in front of the mirror — is "one of the great moments of black feminist literary criticism."[35] However, Bita's decision to "plant" herself back into the soil cannot be dissociated from her enlightenment on these revolutionary folk concepts by Squire Gensir, who is, symbolically, her intellectual half. It is *his* authority, *his* status, *his* linkage of West Indian peasant traditions to the European folk traditions, that allow her to "couple" herself with the land again.[36] Squire Gensir in effect "translates" Bita for the reader (and indeed for Bita herself), defines her role and her space — marks her. As such, Squire Gensir is the necessary masculine authorial figure, the English gentleman scholar, who illuminates the text or body of the West Indian space in Bita. Bita, for her part, would appear to stand in simultaneously for both the feminized body of the land *and* the black British-educated middle-class man, since Western knowledge here is implicitly masculinized through Gensir. However, if we consider that it is only *through Jubban* that Bita becomes reintegrated with the land, then, as Rhonda Cobham argues, Bita's body actually serves to unite two *masculine* entities — the earthbound Jubban to the cerebral Gensir — and is herself erased in the process.[37]

The question of whether or not McKay maintains a black masculine intellectual presence in this narrative in the face of the text's reverence for English masculine intellectual authority is rendered even more complex if we compare the Bita/Squire Gensir pairing to that of Ray and Jake, the two main black male characters in McKay's American novels, *Home to Harlem* and *Banjo*. Ray is an educated Haitian immigrant to Harlem who wants to be a writer and is embittered by the uselessness of his education to prepare him for life in the United States. Jake, on the other hand, is an African American vagabond, and his earthy pronouncements are presented in stark contrast to Ray's intellectual ruminations. Ray discovers that he has an affinity with Jake in their mutual history of oppression, and the reader is clearly meant to see the two as complementary versions of black reality, one marked as West Indian, the other as African American.

It is Ray, however, who translates the episodic nature of Jake's life into a novel, so in this sense Ray replays the Squire Gensir figure of *Banana Bottom*. Unlike the latter, however, the intellectual figure who translates the folk is a black West Indian man, implicitly playing the masculine role to Jake's implicitly feminized one — feminized in the sense that the characteristics associated with the folk such as emotion versus intellect, the needs of the body versus the needs of the mind, are signaled as feminine in this dichotomous arrangement. Despite the romance of the folk, there is a clear authorial distancing from the feminine land/body in all three of McKay's novels, since the author-figure always, ultimately, remains an intellectual. As McKay himself puts it, "I couldn't indulge in such self-flattery as to claim Jake in *Home to Harlem* as a portrait of myself. My damned white education has robbed me of much of the primitive vitality, the pure stamina, the simple unswaggering strength of the Jakes of the Negro race."[38]

McKay's need to conflate the "universalisms" of the English literary tradition with an incipient black nationalist aesthetic are essentially replayed in later West Indian literary discourse. It is the same characteristic found in Lamming's desire for the black West Indian "peasant feel" to be annexed to the eternal verities of Shakespearean prose or in Brathwaite's desire to create a revolutionary black writing tradition that could replicate the world of Jane Austen. Wayne Cooper notes that as McKay moved further to the political left, curiously his poetry became more like the conservative British poetic style of his Jamaican upbringing.[39] Indeed, McKay's black nationalist credentials were never an issue, since as a Marxist pan-Africanist who sought to influence Garvey's back-to-Africa movement, and as an anti-integrationist, his political views anticipated later generations of black West Indian and African American nationalists.[40] It appears that it is his political philosophy that accounts for his inclusion in both the West Indian and African American canon, despite African American puzzlement at his "English attitudes."[41]

Another writer of this period whose works strike similar chords in the way the protagonists vacillate between the need to return to folk culture and yet retain their elite English traditions is Jamaican poet and playwright Una Marson. A feminist who attended the congress of the International Alliance of Women in the 1930s, Marson experimented with the use of creole and blues forms borrowed from the southern United States in her poetry.[42] Some of her fellow female poets rejected her use of creole, even as they complained that she was not really an authentic Jamaican writer.[43] This, despite the fact that Marson's unpublished plays are treatments of nationalist Jamaican themes and parallel McKay's *Banana Bottom* in that they view the emergent black West Indian nation through black, middle-class female protagonists, like herself.

London Calling (1935) and *Pocomania* (1938), two of Marson's best-known plays, deal very explicitly with the question of how educated black West Indians negotiate their middle-class status while preserving their uneducated, peasant origins.[44] In the former, a group of educated black expatriates from the colonized island of "Novoka" are invited to dinner by an aristocratic English family. As if to burlesque British stereotypes of black West Indians, they speak in "broken" English and wear outlandish native costumes. All is discovered, and one of the broad-minded aristocrats asks the black heroine, Rita, to marry him, but she decides to marry a fellow Novokan instead, to the shock of all. Apparently this gesture, like Bita's marriage to Jubban, is meant to represent the heroine's emerging nationalist outlook. Yet the Novokans are merely black versions of the British and represent folk culture only in terms of how it is perceived by the British themselves.

In contrast to *London Calling*, Marson's play *Pocomania* explores the meaning of folk rural culture for the urban black middle class at more length. ("Pocomania" refers to the African-derived religion of Jamaica that involves ancestral spirit possession. The name itself is a false hispanization of a West African word, regionally known as "Kumina".) In a telling replay of Bita Plant, Stella, the black middle-class heroine, falls under the spell of the Pocomania revivalists, whose drums have mesmerized her since she was a child. (In *Banana Bottom*, Bita is momentarily held spellbound by revivalist drumming until Jubban removes her from the scene.) She is inducted into the religion via Sister Kate, who represents a kind of mother-figure for the motherless Stella. However, Sister Kate does not approve of middle-class people leaving their social place, and so represents one side of the black spectrum, a maternalized figure of the folk. On the other is Stella's admirer David, who "saves" Stella from the Pocomania revivalists after Sister Kate has died and her wake has turned into a drunken free-for-all fight. As the black middle-class gentleman figure, David must "translate" the folk, as he does at length at the play's conclusion: ". . . *these people* are not like the nordics with hundreds of years of discipline, restraint and orthodox religion behind them. *Our people* are made of sun and fire. Take from them the joy of life and you take everything." (22, emphasis added)

The movement from the distanced, patronizing "these people" to the familial "our people" reveals the ambivalence of the black middle class toward the folk themselves. David encourages Stella to have "balance" in her emotions, which is easily read as a need to "balance" the requirements of her social class with that longing to be a part of the peasantry. Despite the play's then-radical integration of Jamaican peasant songs and dances into the narrative, Marson clearly opts for middle-class ideology by critiquing the moral character of the revivalists through their fighting and drunkenness at the play's conclusion. If Sister Kate represents the lost black mother, the feminized landscape, and David the anglicized father, the authority of English tradition, then Stella as a black middle-class woman ultimately chooses the latter.

Honor Ford-Smith argues that "[i]n making a rupture with a previous [English] tradition, Marson steps into a kind of void; a place where there existed no precedent in form or content for women writers."[45] For this to be true, one would have to assume that Marson was neither influenced by the tradition of *male* West Indian writers already present in the region nor by English tradition, which is clearly not the case. In her nonfiction prose Marson writes of reading Claude McKay and having curiosity about America through her reading of other Harlem Renaissance writers, though "more familiar was England and I had a passionate longing for the land of Shakespeare, Milton, Tennyson, Keats, Shelley, Byron, Wordsworth."[46]

Marson's narratives reveal the same constructions of Englishness and West Indianness, masculine authority and feminized blackness, that we see in McKay, and to a different extent in Lamming, James, and Brathwaite. However, Ford-Smith's implied point that a literary tradition is needed for a West Indian female subjectivity to be fully articulated does hold true for both Marson and later generations. Marson's desire to represent the folk in a nationalist, anticolonialist frame is undermined by her invocation of masculine authority to "translate" them, which, even as the male writers do precisely the same thing, is particularly problematic in the articulation of a specifically black West Indian female marking of the national space. If the men invoke the subjectivity of the Victorian gentleman of letters, it is part of a subjectivity that has been "blackened," so to speak, since the nineteenth century. For Marson and later generations of black West Indian women writers, the challenge of writing is in how to invoke a literary authority that is itself both black, female, and yet part of this now West Indian tradition.

PART II

Writing Women:

Making the Nation

4

THEORIZING CARIBBEAN
FEMINIST AESTHETICS

At the top of the page I wrote my full name: Lucy Josephine Potter. At the sight of it, many thoughts rushed through me, but I could write down only this: "I wish I could love someone so much that I would die from it." And then as I looked at this sentence a great wave of shame came over me and I wept and wept so much that the tears fell on the page and caused all the words to become one great big blur. — Jamaica Kincaid, *Lucy*

I never wanted to be a writer because I didn't know that any such thing existed.
— Jamaica Kincaid

Books there were, but others wrote them. I read them.
— Marlene Nourbese Philip

Canadian-Caribbean author Marlene Nourbese Philip asserts that she never thought of writing as a profession growing up in post-independence Trinidad. Nevertheless, she is stymied by her own recognition that there *was*, in fact, a tradition of Caribbean writing in circulation at the time. Unlike the previous generation of writers, who had no tradition of Caribbean literature to write within, the post-independence generation of Nourbese Philip could look to the works of George Lamming, C. L. R. James, and V. S. Naipaul—though, as she notes of the latter, "*He* was a writer, but it meant nothing to me; furthermore, he was Indian. . . ."

As a *black* West Indian, Nourbese Philip cannot see a writer role model in Naipaul because of his Indianness, but the "furthermore" underscores that this criterion was an *additional* factor, not the primary one. What she cannot "see" in Naipaul is not just a *racial* reflection but, more particularly, a *gendered* reflection of herself. The result is that Nourbese Philip was an inveterate *reader* of texts in the Caribbean but becomes a *writer* of texts abroad.

Unlike Nourbese Philip, Jamaica Kincaid was not even aware of a prior generation of West Indian writers, having grown up entirely under colonial rule.[1] For her, writing was an even less accessible enterprise given her perception that all "serious" literature had ended after the nineteenth century:

[M]y education, which was very 'Empire,' only involved civilization up to the British Empire—which would include writing—so I never read anything past Kipling... I didn't know that people were still writing. I somehow thought that writing had been this great "thing" and that it had stopped. I thought that all the great writing had been done before 1900. Contemporary writers just didn't exist.[2]

Like Nourbese Philip, Kincaid was an avid reader, but, unlike Naipaul and James, the process of reading the English canon did not engender a desire in Kincaid to *write* novels of her own, nor to see herself as a writer. If anything, it seemed that reading the canon *prevented* such activity. Kincaid's desire to write — or, more precisely, her *perception* of herself as a *writer*—came only after she had begun working in the United States, as a domestic laborer.[3]

If the perception of the self as a writer is a critical component to the project of writing itself, then the tension between the reading self and the writing self for these women must be resolved in order to designate themselves as writers at all. Further, if the only "serious" anglophone Caribbean writers have been men recast in the image of Victorian gentlemen, what imaginative possibilities are available to the Caribbean woman in order to (re)cast herself as a writing subject?

Jamaica Kincaid's *Lucy* interrogates the meaning of writing for the Caribbean female, both "abroad" and "at home," in a fictive mode.[4] However, the novel's conclusion, which I have quoted above, presents a problem of interpretation for the feminist critic — such as myself — who is invested in reading the text as an example of feminist reclamation of colonialist, patriarchal literary authority. Helen Tiffin argues that the first sentence which is to begin Lucy's own narrative ("I wish I could love someone so much that I would die from it") "indicates a persisting enthrallment to written cliché." It is Lucy's *body*, in contradistinction to her *writing*, which rescues her from "the reproduction of the already-written."[5] Tiffin's assessment that Lucy's *body* has "erased a final act of scriptorial obedience" links this final writing act to Lucy's earlier imprisonment within the master narratives of colonialist discourse, represented first by her schoolgirl recitations of Wordsworth[6] and later by "new" Euro-American feminist theory introduced by her white, liberal female employer to "explain" Lucy as an entity.[7]

If Lucy's *body* is the locus of black, Caribbean female resistance to colonialist/white feminist cooptation, then what does this mean for her *writing* as an oppositional strategy? Is writing for the Caribbean woman writer then always a form of "scriptorial obedience," a rewriting of already-written narratives—a *treason* to the body's reality? Is the ultimate authentic narrative for the Caribbean woman writer no narrative at all?

Kincaid's anxieties over the act of writing as a Caribbean woman mirror Philip's seeming inability to find writing models for herself. Central to both stories is the issue of what constitutes a Caribbean female subjectivity. Philip must transform herself from reader to author, from passive receptacle or object of narrative to the subject/agent of narrative. For Kincaid, the narrative she writes must articulate a Caribbean female subjectivity that has no literary antecedents: hence, the body, as the carrier of female experience, is more authentic than the word.

Still, these women authors *are* writing narratives, and in so doing they give us and themselves a way of apprehending the essence of the Caribbean female subject. The formal properties of the writing are apparently as important as the subject matter itself, as Kincaid's conclusion suggests. How can we construct a theory of Caribbean female writing that identifies an "essential" Caribbean female subject? By way of an answer, I will lay a theoretical groundwork for Caribbean women's writing that finds its authority in the experience of being black and female in North America.

The traditional writing structure in anglophone Caribbean narrative, predicated as it is on the authorial construction of the gentleman scholar, presents special problems for female-authored Caribbean narratives. Female subjectivity lies outside of the paradigm. Moreover, that so many of the current spate of Caribbean women writers reside in North America and indeed write from within an African American tradition, makes the general project of self-definition through national definition particularly complicated. Paul Gilroy decries the trend in the current black discourse to construct canons on an exclusively national basis — African American, anglophone Caribbean, African, and so on.[8] Yet if canons of black critical discourse are not based on national categories, then the only other category is race, which returns us to the problem of essentializing blackness as a formal property of critical knowledge. What are the formal properties of black literary authority? Can, in fact, the construction of black identity in the African American tradition be used to articulate West Indian identity? Does the articulation of female subjectivity remain constant despite national differences and agendas? Can Caribbean women's writing be grouped as part of three different aesthetic traditions?

The theoretical framework provided in this chapter provides the foundation for my subsequent discussions of female-authored Caribbean narratives. I attempt to define the notion of cultural/gender essence to see whether we can speak of a uniquely Caribbean female authorial voice. Accordingly, I will look at the discourse on black aesthetics and feminist aesthetics. Together these methodologies have combined to dominate the discussions on essentialism within literary theory. However, none of these, taken separately, is useful for discussing black Caribbean women's writing. Thus I will construct an alternative model of analysis for the discussion of black women's writing generally and black Caribbean women's writing particularly. Obviously the use of black feminist aesthetics to establish Caribbean feminist aesthetics is still problematic for nonblack Caribbean women authors, but inasmuch as the defining characteristic of the nonblack women's texts we discuss here is the deliberate conflation of the black experience with the Caribbean woman's experience, the model will hopefully prove to be a useful one.

Black Aesthetics, Oppositional Aesthetics

In recent years American and more particularly European feminists have sought to identify a feminist aesthetics, or a purely feminine writing in order to distinguish the "true" female experience from its representation within canonical, patriarchal discourse. In the haste to identify and develop a discourse empowering to women, no particular distinction is made between "feminine" and "feminist," since the former is understood to embody the latter. The formulations of a feminist aesthetics vary greatly among its advocates: the American school presupposes a specifically female consciousness in its reading of canonical and noncanonical female-authored works while the French school privileges formal and linguistic experimentation. Nevertheless, the premises on which the formulations are based are the same: namely, that an essentially female/feminist discourse exists or can be created.

The polemics and political thrust of this line of feminist criticism bear a great deal of resemblance to the arguments of the Negritudinists of the 1930s for a pan-African aesthetic and more particularly, to the male African American literary theorists of the 1960s and 1970s, who similarly sought to define the "black" novel through the concept of an all-inclusive black aesthetics. However, while many American feminists have linked the political agendas of blacks and (white Western) women, and feminist scientist Sandra Harding has gone so far as to suggest that, in the way that these have been constructed, blacks and (white Western) women share a common world view,[9] no one would suggest that a feminist aesthetics and a black aesthetics are the same thing. (Indeed, a culture-based aesthetics stands on surer ground, I would think, than a gender-based aesthetics, though even to claim that black aesthetics is grounded in culture and not politics is to stand on shaky ground.) Yet the traits that are commonly identified as belonging to an intrinsically "feminine" discourse — that is, the fragmented, circular, or otherwise antilinear (some would call it "antiphallocentric") narrative — are also the bywords for the black novel. The mutability of this narrative category suggests that it might owe more to an oppositional tradition in literature than to a specifically culture-based or gender-based aesthetic. (Certainly some of the most revered canonical works in the Western tradition arose out of a tradition of "negative aesthetics.")

The disconcerting similarity between these two "camps" is further complicated by the recent advocacy by black feminist authors and scholars of a black feminist aesthetics, epitomized by Barbara Smith's germinal essay, "Toward a Black Feminist Criticism."[10] My intent is, first, to define and disentangle these overlapping definitions of aesthetics criteria; second, to identify any critical differences in black and feminist formulations; and lastly, to contextualize these issues in regard to the formulation of a black feminist aesthetics that might encompass female-authored Caribbean narratives. To this end I will discuss the various versions of the black aesthetics movement which have circulated within the diaspora and their correlative debates in recent feminist criticism. This will be followed by a consideration of theoretical attempts by Rita Felski and Henry Louis Gates to remedy the problems of what Anthony Appiah calls "the classic dialectic" of marginalized discourses.[11]

Locating Blackness: Negritude, Pan-Africanism, and the Black Aesthetics Movement

Before proceeding to compare black and feminist aesthetics, I will clarify precisely what I mean by black aesthetics, which connotes different things in different contexts. Indeed, where *does* blackness inhere? Is it in structure, theme, use of language, or depiction of black characters or communities? The debate over what constitutes the black aesthetic has dominated discussions of African American, African, and Caribbean literature. The problem of the term is self-evident: it suggests a cohesiveness of culture and context that simply does not exist to the extent that an orthodox application of the term would demand. Yet despite this the term persists and the debate continues because of the relative sameness of position that *all* black peoples find themselves in with regard to white culture in the Western world, an ironic but pivotal factor in the formulation of the black aesthetic. As such, oppositional racial politics are an intrinsic part of black discourse.

Like the French feminists, the Negritudinists — interestingly enough, all French colonials of Africa and the Caribbean — emphasized an essential blackness grounded in biology, which, they argued, was reflected in black art and literature. Ironically, Léopold Senghor, Senegalese poet, president, and a key figure in the Negritude movement, cites the racial theories of the racist French intellectual Gobineau and others in his insistence that emotion is the domain of black people.[12] And the poet Aimé Césaire, one of the founders of Negritude, writes, ". . . there flows in our veins a blood which demands of us an original attitude toward life . . . we must respond, the poet more than any other, to the special dynamic of our complex biological reality."[13] As such, while the black aestheticians of the later period stressed a shared history of suffering and resistance to white hegemony over any shared biological heritage, the result was the same: the claim to a literature which possessed essentially black discursive properties.

The cognizance of the political dimensions of African American art is commonly held to have begun with the Black Arts Movement heralded by Amiri Baraka, Addison Gayle, and Larry Neal in the 1960s, but recently some African American scholars have been arguing very persuasively that the very *genesis* of African American arts was itself political. According to bell hooks, whatever African Americans created in music, dance, poetry, or painting, it was regarded as testimony, challenging racist beliefs that blacks were uncivilized and that the measure of their savagery was their collective failure to create "great" art. Furthermore, she states, African slaves brought with them an aesthetic that art should emphasize kinship ties and help to ensure the survival of the community. These ideas formed the basis of African American aesthetics, since cultural production and artistic expressiveness were also ways for displaced African people to maintain connections with the past.[14]

However, as Kenneth Warren has argued, the earlier efforts of W. E. B. DuBois and the later Harlem Renaissance writers to formulate an African American aesthetic was in effect a move *not only* to counter white claims that blacks had no art and therefore no culture but also to erect an African American aesthetic as *the* American aesthetic, inasmuch as white America itself labored under a sense of its own lack of culture compared to Europe and searched for a peculiarly *American* aesthetic.[15] One might infer that though at one level the aim of these African American progenitors of the black aesthetics movement was to seek an African connection, at another their aim was to become an established influence in American society as a whole. There are echoes of this idea in J. Saunders Redding's observation in the mid 1970s that "even while [African American students] sloganize 'Back to Africa' and form study groups and forums as the means by which they will reclaim their African heritage, they are saying in the words of . . . Langston Hughes, 'I, too, am America.' "[16]

As I have already discussed, in the anglophone Caribbean, scholars such as Edward Brathwaite and George Lamming have attempted to remedy the problem of a black Caribbean narrative form by prescribing particular characteristics of peasant society for the West Indian novel. Despite the national concerns, however, arguments for both Caribbean and African American aesthetics presume a conception of a black aesthetic based on an implicit African aesthetic, to be uncovered whole under the layers of hegemonic European culture. Yet, African scholars and writers have been wrangling for decades over precisely this notion, inasmuch as an African aesthetic may be no more than a Yoruban aesthetic — something which Wole Soyinka advocates even as he does not particularly "buy into" the notion of an African or a black aesthetic[17] — or a Gikuyu aesthetic or a Wolof aesthetic, and so on.

A number of texts on the subject attempt a sort of codification to pin down what a "black" text really is, and the most common traits cited are, as I noted above, the so-called circular narrative which makes use of a myth-based, non-Western time found in agrarian societies of Africa;[18] orality (the discursive representation of oral narrative forms); realist writing that is accessible to the uneducated reader and which does not utilize any of the "elitist" stylistic innovations of the modernist and postmodernist schools; and, finally, use of an apparently authentic language of black people, whether that be African American dialect, Caribbean creole, or indigenous African languages.

Yet while these narrative traits are more or less observable in several African texts, the same cannot be said for "black" novels from North America or the Caribbean, where the debates over the black aesthetic were markedly different from their African counterparts in that the debates tried to establish what a "black" novel *should* do rather than for what the extant novels actually *did* do. The Black Arts Movement in the United States during the 1960s and the early part of the 1970s attempted to lay down criteria for black literature, with the end result that out of this emerged a body of literature and drama of a didactic and historically specific nature, which is not much referred to in present debates on black discourse. And yet art products *are* historical items, and any discussion of an all-encompassing black aesthetic must take into account the historicity of the black text rather than ground it in an essence of blackness. Interestingly, the best examples of a black aesthetic as it has been defined in these debates are to be found in the more recent fiction of African American women, such as Toni Morrison's *Song of Solomon*. Much of this literature, ironically, is often perceived as politically moderate or even conservative because of its indifference to analyzing or depicting white racism, instead focusing on the day-to-day lives of its black characters.

Feminist Aesthetics and the Question of Essence

One finds a similarly complex and factionalized debate over the constitution of a feminist aesthetic. These advocates of feminist aesthetics believe that current aesthetic criteria are chosen solely because they endorse dominant ideology; as Gayle Greene and Coppelia Kahn put it, "The criteria that have created the literary canon have, like the traditional conception of history, excluded the accomplishments not only of women but of people of races, ethnic backgrounds and classes different from the politically dominant one, which is Western and white. Feminist criticism questions the values implicit in the Great Works, investigating the tradition that canonized them and the interests it serves. . . ."[19] As such, recognizing that art is produced and given meaning through various ideological and social formations, one might infer that the primary thrust of feminist aesthetics is to replace one set of political underpinnings with another.

Yet much of this scholarship argues, paradoxically, for an ahistorical female essence, grounded in a biological imperative. This biological disposition presumably gives rise to an essentially female way of thinking, which in turn dictates a specifically female language, which consequently manifests itself in a female way of writing: Luce Irigaray's *parler femme* and Hélène Cixous's *l'écriture feminine*.[20] To confuse matters, *feminine* and *feminist* writing/language is conflated under this prescription, and because every woman must write as a female, and female language is intrinsically oppositional, it would follow that every female-authored document is inherently feminist.

Indeed, West Indian feminist scholar Evelyn O'Callaghan says as much when she writes, "For feminists, then, and by implication for the woman writer, the necessity of locating a coherent female subject is paramount. . . ."[21] Similarly, Caribbean feminists have identified Sylvia Wynter's narrative, *The Hills of Hebron*, as part of an embryonic feminist tradition in the region, regardless of the fact that the text evinces no particular engagement with the female experience.[22] Furthermore, as more than one outraged critic has pointed out, these theories depend on an essentialist construction of woman to make sense, and as everyone knows, essentialism is bad, bad, bad.[23] Lost in the acrimony is the most enduring point: any articulation of a female consciousness *necessarily* involves an essentialist construction of the subject.

Black Aesthetics, Feminist Aesthetics: Are They the Same Thing?

So: are the persistent epistemological similarities in feminist and black aesthetics the result of similar world views or similar desires for difference and sameness? By way of answering, let me point out a precursor of this connection between the interests of white women and blacks in the transient yet significant coalition in the United States of the Women's Movement and the Anti-Slavery Movement during the nineteenth century. As Angela Davis points out, white women invoked the analogy of slavery to express the oppressive nature of marriage.[24] One might argue that the invocation of black people was strictly a political tactic to highlight their own condition, but certainly it highlighted a mutual source of oppression. Of the current debates, it is conspicuously apparent that whereas white feminists continuously link feminist oppositional practices to black oppositional practices, the reverse is definitely not the case. Indeed, black scholars have traditionally remained ominously silent on this score. The connecting factor is, of course, the recent criticism by black feminists, but as we shall see this does not necessarily explain the situation.

The progenitors of black aesthetics have left their mark on today's black theorists who, while negotiating issues of gender and class, nevertheless adhere to a similar principle of blackness. Yet each criterion they raise as formulating part of an intrinsically black discourse is paralleled by similar moves in the feminist sphere. Just as black scholars have emphasized the personal narrative and the autobiography as particularly suited to black authors, so have feminist scholars claimed the same for (white) women. For instance, Selwyn Cudjoe claims that "the Afro-American autobiographical statement is the most Afro-American of all Afro-American literary pursuits": this is because it is "bereft of any *excessive subjectivism* and *mindless* egotism," and represents the autobiographical subject emerging as an almost random member of the group, selected to tell his/her tale.[25] As such, black autobiographical literature emphasizes the commonality of black experience in its position as an alternative history. Similarly, feminist scholar Rita Felski observes that, in its effort to document a distinct women's history, "feminist confession . . . is less concerned with unique individuality or notions of essential humanity than with delineating the specific problems and experiences which bind women together. It thus tends to emphasize the ordinary events of a protagonist's life, their typicality in relation to a notion of communal identity."[26]

Furthermore, just as black scholars, echoing W. E. B. DuBois's famous declaration that the black American possesses a "double consciousness," argue for the innate double-voicedness of black speech, so do (white) feminists argue the same for female language. Henry Louis Gates Jr. formulates this hypothesis in *The Signifying Monkey* and used it a few years ago to defend the rap group Two Live Crew on charges of obscenity by arguing that black speech is inherently double-voiced, such that what sound like obscenities to the nonblack ear are in reality an ironic commentary.[27] (Gates's intellectual virtuosity notwithstanding, this black listener could discern no finely veiled irony in "make the pussy splat.")

Similarly, Elaine Showalter states that "in the reality to which we must address ourselves as critics, women's writing is a 'double-voiced discourse' that always embodies the social, literary, and cultural heritages of both the muted and the dominant."[28] Rachel Blau DuPlessis claims even more unequivocally this double-voicedness as inherently female:

Insider-outsider social status will also help to dissolve an either-or dualism. For the woman finds she is irreconcilable things: an outsider by her gender position, by her relation to power; may be an insider by her social position, her class. She can be both. Her ontological, her psychic, her class position all cause doubleness. Doubled consciousness. Doubled understandings. How then could she neglect to invent a form which produces this incessant, critical, splitting motion. To invent this form. To invent the theory for this form.

Following, the "female aesthetic" will produce artworks that incorporate contradiction and nonlinear movement into the heart of the text.[29]

However, DuPlessis does acknowledge that other writing — nineteenth-century Russian fiction, "high" modernism, and most particularly the *Negritude* literature — exhibits the "nonhegemonic" tenets ("pointless" or "plotless" narratives, and so forth) that she has assigned to the feminine aesthetic. She does not perceive this to derail her argument because she separates what she perceives as oppositional convergences from aesthetic practices. This is most difficult to do in comparing the case of black writers; nevertheless, she asserts, though blacks will also "affirm a connection to rhythms of earth, sensuality, intuition, subjectivity," yet they will only "*sound* precisely as some women writers do."[30] The similarity, in other words, is a surface one.

Replacing Female Essence: The Feminist Public Sphere

In *Beyond Feminist Aesthetics* Rita Felski critiques the entire notion of feminist aesthetics and instead advocates what she terms a feminist public sphere as a better model from which to develop a counter-discursive space for feminism. Felski argues that it is impossible to define a feminist aesthetic, correctly pointing out that "women-centered" writings are not necessarily, ideologically speaking, feminist, and that even texts with an explicitly feminist agenda usually owe more to various oppositional literary genres (for example, postmodernist, avant-garde writing) than to a specifically feminist way of writing.

Indeed, as Felski notes, the common equation of the feminine with the oppositional collapses crucial distinctions in ideology, culture, and class through an appeal to a common negativity — describing oneself through what one is not — which in turn is equated with the feminine. This is hardly the way, it would seem, to articulate a useful theory of feminist aesthetics. Because the Western ontological concept of Man has traditionally depended on such attributes as rationality and linearity, the attempt to empower the category of Woman by merely revaluing the antithesis of these traits would not only preserve but ironically reinforce this formulation of Man. Furthermore, this binary relation would then subsume everything that is not Man under the category of Woman.

In concluding her critique of aesthetics, Felski notes that stylistic innovations, or any particular literary technique, for that matter, can be used to generate conservative or radical meanings depending on the agenda at hand. She concludes that "[i]t is thus increasingly implausible to claim that aesthetic radicalism equals political radicalism and to ground a feminist politics of the text in an assumption of the inherently subversive effects of stylistic innovation."[31] However, I am not sure that this is what feminist aesthetics — as a broad category — tries to do (the French school being an obvious exception). As is the case with black aesthetics, it seems that the focus is rather to *retrieve* radical meanings from extant texts and construct an aesthetics out of a literary tradition spanning different eras and stylistic genres.

Furthermore, having dispatched of the premise for a feminist aesthetics, Felski then argues *against* the dissolution of aesthetic categories, stating that "this repoliticization of the aesthetic sphere does not imply, in my view, that aesthetic categories are to be interpreted as a direct reflection of the interests of a political ideology, or that literary meaning is limited to its current political use-value for the women's movement." She goes on to assert that the correct relationship between aesthetics and ideology is "a continuum in which the aesthetic function may be more or less dominant but always intermeshes with the ideological conditions governing the text's own historical location."[32]

I should point out, however, that it would be an injustice to Felski and a misreading of her very thorough argument to lump her in with the orthodox poststructuralists who believe that any conception of the subject is founded on an inevitable phallocentrism because it necessarily involves the repression of other groups or ideas. And unlike those poststructuralists who critique the very premise of race and gender-based discourses, Felski sees the need for a conception of subjectivity in feminist discourse even as she warns against its becoming dissociated from its origins as a political construct erected to address particular strategic concerns:

> to expose critically the inadequacies of the rationalistic and self-sufficient individualism of liberal political theory is not thereby to argue that subjectivity should be abandoned as a category of oppositional political thought, nor does the decentering of the subject in contemporary theory mean that discourses which appeal to an experience of self are therefore anachronistic. Subjectivity remains an ineradicable element of modern social experience. . . .[33]

And furthermore:

> *even the most subjective feminist writing . . . appeals to a notion of communal identity which differs significantly from the literature of bourgeois individualism.*[34] (emphasis added)

Yet elsewhere she emphasizes that there is no archetypal female subject and warns that "[t]he ambiguous status of subjectivity in contemporary women's writing will become apparent . . . [in] the possibility that the very pursuit of authenticity can become a self-defeating process."[35] This last clause is crucial to understanding Felski's notion of subjectivity and forms the basis of what I see as a fundamental contradiction in her position — a contradiction which is symptomatic of a larger tension in feminist and black discourse in general and a problem addressed later.

Felski does, however, put forward some useful ideas for the rehabilitation of the notion of subjectivity in her analysis of the so-called death of the subject in postmodern society. She argues that reconstitution of the subject does not have to entail the mere replacement of the white heterosexual Western bourgeois male subject with the black/non-Western/lesbian/female subject — the problem here is in our very *notion* of what constitutes subjectivity. As a solution, she advocates the creation of a feminist counterpublic sphere, modeled on the Habermasian definition of the public sphere of bourgeois white Western men of the eighteenth century, where all men were equalized by their participation in rationalism and enlightenment.[36] In this countersphere, the various factions of the feminist movement would be united by their common gender and oppressed status to men:

Like the original bourgeois public sphere, the feminist public sphere constitutes a discursive space which defines itself in terms of a common identity; *here it is the shared experience of gender-based oppression which provides the mediating factor intended to unite all participants beyond their specific differences.... the 'we' of feminist discourse is intended to represent all women as collective cosubjects.* As a consequence, the women's movement can accommodate disparate and often conflicting ideological positions, because membership is conditional . . . on a more general sense of commonality in the experience of oppression.[37] (emphasis added)

While I find Felski's notion of the feminist public sphere useful in theory, and certainly desirable in practice, it has universalizing overtones which gloss over difference: that is, is common female status enough to generate a conversation? Especially when the very conception of womanhood is at issue? I am thinking particularly of black women's relationship to feminism and the history of womanhood in the Western world, where black women — and men, for that matter — were in a sense degendered altogether. As Hazel Carby notes, the cult of true womanhood in nineteenth-century America, which drew ideological boundaries to exclude black women from "woman" (woman being that which is virtuous, chaste, and so forth), has its reflection in twentieth-century notions on the subject.[38] We might infer the same of manhood, which could never be achieved by black men because as slaves they could not protect and make inviolable the body of the black woman, a necessary prerequisite of manhood.[39] Correspondingly, there was very little gendered division of labor on the slave plantation, and certainly throughout most of the twentieth century Western black men and women have been in the workforce in comparatively equal numbers.[40] As such, current calls for the dissolution of gender roles will not have the same effect in communities where they still have the aura of luxury. There is also a certain irony in her choice of model, in that membership to the public sphere of the eighteenth century required rational thought, of which women, and more particularly nonwhites, were deemed to be incapable.

Moreover, debate within a public sphere is not so much contingent upon possessing common social status as on speaking the same language, and I am not altogether convinced that this should be taken as a given in feminist discourse. One might argue that the very language of feminism is fiercely contested. For instance, although Felski acknowledges that the "ideal of a communal gendered identity generated by the feminist public sphere . . . can be viewed negatively as ideology insofar as it fails to come to grips with the material reality of class — and race — divided society," she then argues that radical critiques of white feminists such as bell hooks's presupposes and is only made possible through a preexisting ideal of a feminist public sphere which claims to represent all women.[41] And while I agree with this argument to a certain extent, it does not take into account the discourses generated *within* particular groups which do not engage "mainstream" feminism. Consider, for instance, Toni Morrison, an African American author much cited in feminist and black literary criticism, who has rejected not only feminism as the prerogative of white women but also the notion of an all-inclusive black aesthetic. Morrison argues that "Black men don't write very differently from white men" but that there is an "enormous difference" in the narratives of black and white women.[42] Morrison is in the curious position of disavowing a feminist aesthetic and a black aesthetic yet affirming a black feminist — or rather, *female* — aesthetic. At what point does — or can — a position such as hers enter the feminist public sphere? Can Morrison inhabit a position with the feminist public sphere when for all practical purposes she does not believe it to exist? Significantly, Morrison's position is echoed by that of Jamaica Kincaid's, who disavows feminist interpretations of her work: "I think I owe a lot of my success, or whatever, to this idea of feminism, but I don't really want to be placed in that category."[43] Therefore it would seem to be a not-uncommon — if ideologically awkward — position for black women writers whose works are read as feminist to take. This dilemma would also seem to highlight the problem of reading as a critical component of the feminist aesthetic but one which I will not be addressing here.

As a parallel issue in black aesthetics, we must also ask ourselves how, in fact, can black women's writing be "blacker" than that of the men? Since, according to Morrison, black men's writing is structurally indistinguishable from white men's, does this mean that black women's writing embodies the "authentic" black experience? Morrison's logic seems grounded in the sort of essentialism that advocates that women are "natural" bearers of culture, and therefore black women write with a sort of cultural intuitiveness that "transcends" the adversarial (as I think she would see it) phallocentric writings of black men, engaged as they are with racial politics.

Nor does Felski's formulation address the fact that it is the parameters of the debate within feminist discourse that are themselves defined by power relations among its participants. Consequently, much black feminist criticism, for example, is marginalized within the discourse by being categorized as merely "celebratory" because of its emphasis on personal experiences of black women, or as solely "political," a symbol or signifier for white feminist theory, but not theoretical in itself.

These reservations notwithstanding, I find Felski's theory of a feminist public sphere convincing enough to apply its logic to the black aesthetics debate. If Felski's arguments against the essential properties of art or discursive formations hold true for feminism and its constituents, should this not also hold true for black aesthetics and *its* constituents? This is an issue which logically leads to a larger concern of whether *all* oppositional social movements are not in some key sense endangered by the move to dismantle a discourse which is vitally bound together by an essential — and yes, essentializing — concept of their own subjectivity, on which aesthetic theories are inevitably based.

Back to the Body: Black Feminism and the Caribbean Woman Writer

Irigaray's notion of a *parler femme*, a feminine syntax, blurs the divisions between the social and the biological, and this accounts for much

of the vehement reception accorded it—and French feminism generally—among American feminists. Yet Diana Fuss finds it useful to re-
read Irigaray's (in)famous description of an autonomous female pleasure mechanism ("two lips rubbing together," etc.) as essentially a
political metaphor.[44] In another context, Gayatri Chakravorty Spivak
finds in French feminism a potential benefit for Third World women
not for its advocacy of an intrinsic female language but because it
provides a framework in which to deconstruct the ideological-material
opposition endemic to Western theoretical discourses, an opposition
which has served to exclude Third World reality from, or subjugate it
within, theoretical debates. Its conflation of the feminine and the feminist can be transposed to a similar principle at work in black (principally African American) feminist discourse, inasmuch as the essence
of the body implied by "feminine" and the politicization of the author
inherent in "feminist" embody the contradictory impulses of a theory
that seeks to be both. In much the same way, black feminist discourse
seeks to articulate black femaleness as a transhistorical entity and an
immediate political category. However, what separates black feminist
discourse from black discourse or feminist discourse is how it arranges
blackness and femaleness in terms of essences and political strategy.
Thus, unlike the conceptions of "feminine" and "feminist" used in
white feminist discourse that I critique earlier in the chapter, it becomes
necessary to speak both of "feminine" and "feminist" together with
regard to black feminism, in that what we understand to be the feminine has different political connotations for black women. I will illustrate this arrangement in the following examples.

   One anthology of criticism on black women's writing that has come
over the past decade[45] contains several assumptions that are important
to our discussion. In her introduction, the editor asserts a "black *feminine* consciousness," and at every point in her essay "feminine" is used
before "feminist," presumably to bespeak a cultural essence extending
across geopolitical lines. However, in her description of a global Renaissance of black women writers the author describes a "distinct generation of *culturally Polynesian*, yet *politically Black*, Maori women
writers." Elsewhere she speaks of blackness as a "political-class consciousness" and "a popular means through which [global 'black'
women] empower themselves." One would infer from these applica-
tions that whereas *woman* is an ahistorical, essential category, *black* is

a political construct. Yet, "[black female] contemporaneous political-class identities suggest qualitative change is brought about by the community who opposes domination and not by a 'nationality', a 'race', a 'gender', or an ethnic group per se."[46] What, then, one asks, is the *point* of race and gender distinctions in the first place, if they are simply signifiers for an indeterminate and interchangeable community of color? In her effort to politicize what started out as essential categories, the author has *re*-essentialized them to the point where we can only make sense of her argument if we understand that the essence of race and gender lies *outside* of the discursive realm. Paradoxically, the construction of racial and gendered essence is thus effected by its deconstruction.

Hortense Spillers articulates the idea that the radically altered consciousness of motherhood caused by slavery in the black American community has engendered a radically different black, *Western* conception of the female within that community.[47] Discussing black motherhood in its received context as a pathology, a castrating mechanism resulting from slavery and the lack of the Father, Spillers notes that the distinction between the illegitimacy of "mother" and "enslavement" is elided "inasmuch as each of these synonymous elements defines a cultural situation that is *father-lacking*." The slave mother, whose status "marks" that of her descendants, becomes responsible for the "fundamental degradation" of an identity inheritance that comes through the female line instead of the male, despite the fact that matriarchist value has been assigned where it does not belong, since the slave mother could not actually claim her child. In this context, she concludes,

This different cultural text actually reconfigures, in historically ordained discourse, certain *representational* potentialities for African-Americans: 1) motherhood as female bloodrite is outraged, is denied, at the *very same time* that it becomes the founding term of a human and social enactment; 2) a dual fatherhood is set in motion, comprised of the African father's *banished* name and body and the captor father's mocking presence. In this play of paradox, only the female stands *in the flesh*, both mother and mother-dispossessed. This problematizing of gender places her, in my view, *out* of the traditional symbolics of female gender, and it is our task to make a place for this different social subject. In doing so, we are less interested in joining the ranks of gendered femaleness than gaining the *insurgent* ground as female social subject. Actually *claiming* the monstrosity (of a female with the potential to "name"), which her culture imposes in blindness, "Sapphire" might rewrite after all a radically different text for a female empowerment.[48]

From this we may conclude that a black (Western) woman as an ontological entity lies outside the category of Woman, the result of a fundamental paradox in gender schemas. Yet if the black mother is a "monstrosity" and the inheritance of the law of the Mother a distortion of natural law, then the reclamation of black identity becomes an effort to reclaim — or claim — the law of the Father: a quest for patriarchal authority.

Madhu Dubey argues that, in black nationalist literature, the black woman is a symbol of the undesirable slave past which has to be destroyed before the new black writer can articulate a new black revolutionary sensibility.[49] The result of this is the consistent erasure of the figure of the black woman in both African American and Caribbean male-authored texts, as I discuss at length in chapter 5. Accordingly, the putative complicity of femaleness with enslavement would help to explain the traditional view in the black community that feminism is incompatible with the project of black liberation and the caution displayed even by black feminists not to alienate black men from the discussion.

Though this desire for gender inclusiveness is important and desirable, it can lead to a re-inscribing of some of the categories under critique; in one example, an Afro-Caribbean feminist literary critic articulates "the need for drawing men and the condition of men into the discussion of Caribbean women's experience." This is necessary because "[m]en in the Caribbean certainly need to feel that women's issues, and development, need not mean *the further erosion of their manhood.*"[50]

The statement is particularly interesting for its implication that Caribbean men have been "emasculated" by colonialism and therefore any liberation project, such as that which feminism seeks for women, must by implication acknowledge the necessity of "re-masculinizing" Caribbean manhood. Yet, according to the definitions of masculine subjectivity as they have been traditionally defined, this proposition would mean investing Caribbean men with the authority of male power associated with the male colonizer. The traditional assumptions underpinning the category of Man here are wedded to the corollary assumptions underpinning the categories of Woman and Black within both white and black Western communities: in other words, you cannot take one and leave the others. To "buy into" any one of these categories as they are thus defined is to effectively exclude black women from occupying any.

Turning to black women's literature, then, we must look for evidence not so much of its link with a feminine literary tradition or with a black discourse in order to identify its essential properties, as for its dual, seemingly contradictory focus. A reading of black women's literature should not focus, as so many critical readings of it do, solely on its "doubly oppressed" status; black women's fiction is not necessarily doubly enlightening on the subject of oppression and this is not where its particularity lies. I submit that the project of a black feminist aesthetics inheres in its apparent paradox: to re-engender black women as women, not as monstrous matriarchs but as "natural" women, within the black community; and to racialize black women within the feminist community and therefore to establish difference and a separate category of essence.

Let us return once more to the examples of Jamaica Kincaid and Toni Morrison. As I have already observed, Kincaid resists being categorized as a feminist writer. (Nevertheless, it is almost impossible to read her work without encountering the recurrent motif of the Afro-Caribbean mother/black daughter conflict that engenders such responses.)[51] At the same time, she believes that her writing is placed outside of a Euro-American aesthetic: "I can't write like a white American. I'm not a white American, and I don't have the same experience. . . ." This, despite her admission that she knew of no body of West Indian writers until recently and despite her horror of being "in a group of any kind, or in the school of anything."[52]

By contrast, as we have seen, Morrison believes that black men and white men do not write differently from each other, though she *does* concede the concept of an intrinsically "black" novel ("I try to incorporate, into that traditional genre the novel, unorthodox novelistic characteristics — so that it is, in my view, Black, because it uses the characteristics of Black art"). She states that she thinks that "women probably do write out of a different place. There's some difference in the ways they approach conflict, dominion, and power." However, she emphasizes that "it's not so much that women write differently from men, but that black women write differently from white women." Elsewhere she describes the household of women headed by Pilate in *Song of Solomon* — often approvingly cited in critical readings for its black female communality — as degenerative because of its lack of connection with men and warns that this "is the disability we must be on guard against for the future — the female who reproduces the female who reproduces the female."[53]

Therefore on one hand we have a distinction made between black and white discursive practices but one which is made visible only through the prism of gender; on the other is a negation of a discursive female community across racial lines. Blackness as a discursive feature thus is reliant upon an essential black female matrix which bears no relation to the feminine/feminist tradition outside its parameters. It is this seeming paradox which I believe accounts for Kincaid's and Morrison's curious insider/outsider positions within feminist criticism and is a feature which, as I have shown, has significant parallels in much black feminist scholarship.

The conflicting intersection of feminist theory and black liberation projects is an appropriate place to begin an inquiry into African American feminist theory to apprehend the Caribbean female-authored text. The black community of the diaspora has traditionally held a dismissive attitude toward feminism as a white woman's problem or as a divisive imperialist foreign import. In the words of one West Indian male scholar: "[W]hile the need to address Caribbean literature and society through feminist or pro-feminist perspectives has been embarrassingly neglected [nevertheless] there is the possibility that the exercise can be little more than the smuggling in of so much foreign . . . baggage rather than a demonstrated reality of West Indian life."[54]

In recent years, however, with the advent of a powerfully influential group of African American feminist writers (Alice Walker, Toni Cade Bambara, and Terri MacMillan, to name the most prominent) there has come a reassessment of the value of feminist theory. Alice Walker's redefinition of feminism for black women as "womanist" exemplifies this change perhaps most succinctly:

Womanist 1. From *womanish*. (Opp. of "girlish," i.e., frivolous, irresponsible, not serious.) A black feminist or feminist of color. From the black folk expression of mothers to female children, "You acting womanish," i.e., like a woman. . . . Interchangeable with another black folk expression: "You trying to be grown." . . .

2. *Also:* A woman who loves other women, sexually and/or nonsexually. Appreciates and prefers women's culture, women's emotional flexibility (values tears as natural counter-balance of laughter), and women's strength. Sometimes loves individual men, sexually and/or nonsexually. Committed to survival and wholeness of entire people, male *and* female. Not a separatist, except periodically, for health. . . .

4. Womanist is to feminist as purple to lavender.[55]

The significance of this definition lies principally in its effort to include black culture as an *ideology* of feminism; hence its critical clause, "Committed to survival . . . of entire people, male *and* female. Not a separatist . . ." is intended to allay the suspicion that feminism will divide the black community by aligning black women's interests with those of white women. Not surprisingly, the definition has been seized upon by black Third World feminist scholars in their quest for a theory that will allow them to speak simultaneously of gender and national liberation issues. African feminist Chikwenye Ogunyemi uses the term to describe any work by a black female author which is closely linked to an afrocentric cultural identity,[56] and the editors of a significant anthology on Caribbean feminist literature and criticism confer their approval of womanism as a way of theorizing Caribbean women's literature, arguing that the term has "strong Caribbean roots."[57] Further, they discuss the ongoing project of Caribbean women writers to create an "aesthetically female" novel form, and describe its narrative technique as bridging the gap between the "phallocentric" linear text and the "quilted/fragmented" text.[58] Even if one does not agree — as I do not — that this particular narrative device is more inherently "feminine" than more traditional devices, its deployment further underlines the political nature of the choice of form in Caribbean women's writing.

Accordingly, many Caribbean female-authored texts and readings of those texts are inevitably refracted through the prism of African American feminist theory and narrative, which jointly have provided the only theoretical framework for the engenderment of the black and female subject. (Indeed, Michelle Cliff explicitly outlines their influence when she tells an interviewer that she has been influenced "enormously" by Toni Morrison, particularly by the formal properties of her narratives.[59]) Caribbean feminist literary critic Carol Boyce Davies reflects that, as a student of literature in the Caribbean, "I could never feel the same excitement and involvement [for Caribbean literature] that I felt for African and African-American Literature without exorcising the meaning of Naipaul and some other troubling concerns."[60] In this statement coalesces the distinct conflict between black diasporic identity and the Caribbean canon, which Davies was compelled to read and of which Naipaul is an entrenched component. It also returns us to the disjuncture between Caribbean female reading and the "problem" of writing to which Marlene Nourbese Philip and Jamaica Kincaid explicitly and implicitly refer at the beginning of this discussion.

Naipaul, despite what some might call his neocolonialist — even racist — views, represents one extreme pole of the continuum of West Indian narrative. The African American canon, by contrast, with its small but consistent tradition of women writers, must have appeared to be much more accessible to the black West Indian female reader. Inasmuch as African American feminists have been the first in the diaspora to theorize the issue of a black female subjectivity, it is not surprising that many anglophone Caribbean women writers have been heavily influenced by their reconceptualization of female subjectivity for black women. As in the United States, historical and contemporary discussions of black identities and female identities in British discourse have situated them so as to be outside the purview of black womanhood. (For instance, if Victorian debates on race and imperialism provided a way for black West Indian men to assert themselves as West Indian subjects, they also provided a way for white Victorian feminists to assert themselves as British subjects, since British feminists of the nineteenth century invoked Englishness as a way of arguing for female equality.[61] Between the two, there was no place for West Indian women, black or otherwise.) The African American feminist paradigm of black female subjectivity outlined here thus provides a critical frame for Caribbean women writers to begin reconceptualizing an authoritative literary space for themselves that simulates neither black masculinist nor white feminist constructions of the oppositional subject.

By way of conclusion, let me return once more to the problem of narration in *Lucy*. If the tears on the page reflect the Caribbean female subject's rejection of narrative as a strategy for self-definition, they also reflect the *fusion* of the body *with* the page: "all the words become one great big blur." Using Spillers's argument for the reinscription of the "monstrous" black female, Lucy, the "monstrous" black female who has become the "slut" that her mother has warned her against, has not so much *rejected* narrative as *disrupted* it: the *feminine* and the *feminist* have found a point of contact. The blur of words suggests a raw material of body and language that will engender the new discursive features of a Caribbean black female subject.

5

ᴧᴧᴧᴧᴧᴧᴧᴧᴧᴧ

The Novel of Revolution

and the Unrepresentable

Black Woman

Caribbean discourse has long had a central engagement with revolutionary discourse, a concern with narrativizing and deconstructing historical revolutionary events or movements in the Caribbean. From classic West Indian novels such as V. S. Naipaul's *Guerrillas* and Earl Lovelace's *The Dragon Can't Dance*; to critical discourse such as C. L. R. James's *The Black Jacobins*, Lamming's *The Pleasures of Exile*, and Selwyn Cudjoe's *Resistance and Caribbean Literature*, Caribbean discourse has consistently blurred the distinction between the historical and the fictional revolutionary moment.[1]

In a sense, the melding of real revolutionary events and the fictional project is inevitable, indeed necessary, given that much of the revolutionary history of the Caribbean was absent from traditional histories of the region in the pre-independence years — even of successful revolutions in the region such as the Haitian revolution, the events of which are documented as part of Caribbean history for the first time[2] by a Caribbean scholar in James's *The Black Jacobins*, published in 1938. The history of all the failed revolts, the attempts at resistance or rebellions, became part of what Derek Walcott calls the "amnesia" that is the "true history of the New World."[3] These silences of history lingered in half-remembered oral histories, myths, and legends that abound in the Caribbean; thus fiction takes over where history leaves off: fiction and fact become part of the same project of reclamation — the recovery of the almost-revolutions of Caribbean history.[4]

The emphasis on the discursive status of revolution as a means to literary *equality* with the metropole is perhaps an even more important component within Caribbean narrative. For example, in James's account of the Haitian revolution, literacy and revolutionary action are explicitly linked; James's account of the Haitian revolution emphasizes the writing and reading abilities of the Haitian leader Toussaint L'Ouverture, whose status as a "well-read" revolutionary, he argues, is crucial to the success of the revolution:

> We have clearly stated the vast impersonal forces at work in the crisis of San Domingo. But men make history, and Toussaint made the history that he made because he was the man he was.
>
> He had had exceptional opportunities, and both in mind and body was far beyond the average slave. . . .
>
> He had read Caesar's Commentaries, which had given him some idea of politics and the military art and the connection between them. Having read and re-read the long volume by the Abbé Raynal on the East and West Indies, he had a thorough grounding in the economics and politics, not only of San Domingo, but of all the great empires of Europe which were engaged in colonial expansion and trade. . . . The masses of the people learn much during a revolution, far more a man like Toussaint. . . .[5]

Elsewhere, James admiringly recounts the elegance and diplomacy of the various missives that L'Ouverture pens to the different factions, and remarks that he is "not only the born soldier but the born writer."[6]

This emphasis on L'Ouverture's exceptionality from his peers, the descriptions of the ex-slave's extraordinary intelligence, the constant references throughout the text to L'Ouverture's "natural" aristocratic habits and manners, all might seem odd in an apparently Trotskyist version of history. However, for James revolutionary thought and the figure of the literary man have been linked since his childhood readings of *Vanity Fair*. Consequently, his emphasis on one central, masterful personality in an otherwise Marxist account of revolution makes sense only if we understand it to be a particularly West Indian, particularly middle-class and male version of revolutionary discourse.

Toussaint's recasting as a Jamesian author-figure of the revolution is useful to us as a metaphor for the privileged relationship of the author to revolutionary engagement in Caribbean narrative: that is, [male] authors "author" revolution through fiction. From another angle, however, this desire to fictionalize Caribbean history is arguably a desire to *rewrite* the ending of the Caribbean historical script. The failures of slave revolutions and other revolts in a larger framework of colonization and systemic subjugation become a narrative problem of creation, according to V. S. Naipaul: "The history of the islands can never be satisfactorily told. Brutality is not the only difficulty. History is built around achievement and creation; and nothing was created in the West Indies."[7] The association of violence with the *impossibility* of narration corresponds to a discursive desire to mark history with conquest (which, in Naipaul's terms, constitutes achievement, since "real" history is the story of battles and wars fought and won) and thereby write the Caribbean into reality. Since violent conquest is in its turn associated with the rites of manhood, the reclamation of history has come to signify the "reclamation" — or the constitution, to be more precise — of Caribbean masculinity in much of Caribbean discourse. It is under these circumstances that Cudjoe can title one of his chapters in *Resistance*, "Back Into Manhood and Resistance," since acts of resistance themselves are associated with the masculinized characteristics of violent agency.

The desire of the novel of revolution to liberate the Caribbean space by remaking it, literally and figuratively, in the image of Caribbean man is tied to its corresponding impulse to "erase" the symbolic body of the black woman. As a symbol of the slave past, the black woman represents a double threat. For Caribbean men, on one hand, she carries within her the ability to "name" her descendants, which is, as Spillers suggests,[8] the ever-present discursive reminder of the subjugated status of [black] Caribbean men to white European men. For European men, on the other hand, the black woman's ability to "race" the mulatto child in her own image was a direct assault on the cherished European idea that male sperm was stronger than female, an idea that was the basis for European laws of inheritance. Lynda Boose suggests that this need to reestablish masculine genetic primacy is the reason for the many representations of romantic alliances between black men and white women in English Renaissance texts and the singular absence of representations of black women and white men:

by restricting themselves to narratives about offspring born to black fathers and 'faire mothers', [these writers] protect themselves and their readers from the ideological disruption implicit in the story they do not tell. . . . [T]he orthodox discourse about gender still works to contain the problem of colour dominance within the black man–white woman paradigm: that a white woman married to a black man should bear a son who replicates the father actually fulfills the deepest patriarchal fantasy of male parthenogenesis . . . in which women were imagined primarily as receptacles for male seed.[9]

For both black men and white, therefore, the body of the black woman becomes a threat to entrenched ideas of masculine patriarchal authority and dominance. Consequently, she must be "buried" in the new mediation between colonizer and newly decolonized subject.[10] The best-known discursive metaphor for the mediation of white colonizer and black subject in Caribbean revolutionary discourse is Shakespeare's *The Tempest*, an appropriately iconic representative of the English canon. The scenes in which Prospero and Caliban battle for ownership of the island—and for Miranda—is replayed in various Caribbean "takes" on the play. Miranda effectively displaces the body of the black woman in the revolutionary script by becoming, in Jonathan Goldberg's words, the "trope of ideal femininity, [the] fantasmatic female that secures male-male arrangements and an all-male history."[11] Miranda's status as the medium of exchange between English and Caribbean men is particularly telling not only for its displacement of the black woman's body but also for its relation to [Prospero's] language—and by extension, the English literary canon—as the medium by which these men negotiate the conditions of dominance and liberty.[12] Unlike the possession of the black female body, the "ownership" of Miranda is imbricated in the mastery of English literary tradition.

The following chapter shows that the erasure and replacement of the black female body is a necessary component of the canonical Caribbean male-authored revolutionary narrative that has fused the meaning of revolution to masculine authority; furthermore I intend to illustrate that this erasure is "exhumed" by women writers, who must refigure the meaning of "revolution" and "revolutionary" in order to envision anticolonial narrative that does not preclude the meaning of black womanhood. First I address the Caliban/Prospero/Miranda trope that structures so much of the discourse on Caribbean narratives of revolution, using as a backdrop a feminist critique of the Caliban argument. From there I engage in a close reading of Lamming's *Water with Berries*, which narrativizes his theoretical arguments for the Caliban paradigm of Caribbean revolutionary agency. I conclude by contrasting the above arguments with close readings of both Paule Marshall's novella

"Brazil" and Michelle Cliff's *No Telephone to Heaven*, which I pose as "responses" of sorts to the revolutionary paradigms of Lamming and other male Caribbean writers.

Rapists and Comrades: Caliban, Miranda, and the Language of Resistance

Laura Donaldson notes that while the relationship between Prospero and Caliban has received overwhelming critical attention by Third World scholars, the relationship between Miranda and Caliban has been virtually ignored. She wonders why "these two victims of colonialist Prospero cannot 'see' each other" and links this invisibility to that of the "native" female in the interpretation of women's texts by white feminist critics. In particular, she notes Gayatri Spivak's critique of Sandra Gilbert and Susan Gubar's reading of Jane Eyre as feminist heroine. Spivak claims that feminist methodology requires a "self-immolating colonial subject for the glorification of the social mission of the colonizer." In other words, it requires, for Gilbert and Gubar, "the annihilation of the 'native' female Bertha [Mr. Rochester's Jamaican creole first wife] for the glory of Jane's individuation."[13]

Donaldson is troubled by Spivak's contention that Bertha "dies on the pyre of feminist individualism" because she thinks that it implies that oppressed female status is congruent with ritual self-sacrifice and annihilation.[14] More particularly, she perceives it to be a repetition of the dialectic of colonialism: whiteness is masculinized, "imperialized," and dominant in contrast to blackness/racial "otherness," which in turn is feminized, colonized, and obliterated. Donaldson concludes that this vision of the white creole serves to render her invisible as much as does Gilbert and Gubar's "hermeneutics of suspicion."[15]

White women also suffer the "ravages of colonialism," Donaldson asserts, something not evident in Spivak's argument, because "like Caliban, [Spivak] distorts feminine ontology."[16] She quotes bell hooks's description of white southern plantation women watching the beating of black female slaves ("Incidents of this nature exposed to white women the cruelty of their husbands, fathers, and brothers and served as a warning of what might be their fate should they not maintain a passive stance")[17] and emphasizes that Caliban's great failing in his quest for freedom is that he does not grasp "how similarly Prospero dominates both 'daughter' and 'native'." (I am particularly unpersuaded by hooks's speculation that the white women on the nineteenth-century plantation read a cautionary tale for themselves in witnessing black women's physical torture. These women, by and large, would not regard black female slaves as the same order of beings as themselves, hence they would hardly think that they could be subject to the same subjugation. And they would be correct.)

Donaldson implies that Miranda and Caliban, white women and blacks, are similar in their ontologies of oppression if only critics could transcend the politics of reading wherein one oppression must be privileged over another.[18] Consequently, she claims that a more useful view is to see Miranda as a "feminine trope of colonialism." Miranda thus symbolizes, for Donaldson, the absence of feminist discourse in postcolonial narration and the absence of racial discourse in feminist narration.

For our purposes, Donaldson's view possesses a twofold significance: first, for its claiming of the "Miranda complex" as a specifically feminist paradigm, and second, for its conjoining of Miranda and Bertha as representatives of these twin moments of unnarratability. The figure of Bertha, of course, has become emblematic of the colonized Caribbean's invisibility within the English literary canon (note Jean Rhys's recreation of Bertha in *Wide Sargasso Sea*), as well as a symbol of the "other" woman's experience/voice in the European-American canon which feminist literary scholarship seeks to uncover. As such, Donaldson's analysis attempts to provide an important bridge between two heretofore exclusive modes of discourse.

However, in her desire to point out the similarities in the epistemologies of oppression between white women and colonized races, Donaldson herself risks making a dangerous conflation between the two. While no one form of oppression should be "privileged" over another, it would be absurd, if not insulting, to argue that the types of subjugation experienced by a white female aristocrat and a black male slave are the same thing. How, then, to adequately theorize the congruences and divergences of the political meanings of white femaleness and blackness/nonwhiteness, symbolized in the Miranda/Caliban relationship?

While I would agree that until recently feminist and Caribbeanist discourse have had nothing to say to each other, Caliban and Miranda as gendered symbols of colonial empowerment have been both implicit and explicit in much Caribbeanist fiction, though not in the configuration that Donaldson would desire. What Donaldson does not mention is the obvious: Caliban is a symbol of *black* Caribbean manhood in francophone and anglophone discourse, Miranda a symbol of *white* European womanhood. Therefore, the following argument is predicated on the "raced" and gendered meaning of Caliban in Caribbean narrative.

George Lamming, more so than any anglophone Caribbean writer, is responsible for establishing *The Tempest* as the primary text for discourse on the West Indies' relation to Europe and for erecting Caliban as the revolutionary symbol of Caribbean manhood and independence. Accordingly, I will read Lamming's interpretations of the Caliban metaphor as paradigmatic of its specifically anglophone Caribbean construction.

Before I proceed to Lamming's analysis of Caliban, I should note that *The Tempest* is treated somewhat differently as a parable of colonization. In particular, the Cuban critic Roberto Fernández Retamar appropriates Caliban not as a symbol of the enslaved black man but rather as a symbol of *mestizaje*, the racially mixed figure who has come to represent what José Martí called "our *mestizo* America." Retamar acknowledges Lamming's status as the "first writer in our world to assume our identification with Caliban," but he criticizes Lamming's depiction of the Caribbean Caliban as one who suffers from the "Prospero complex."[19]

Retamar's image of the mestizoized Caliban thus updates Martí's dream of a colorblind New World. It also defuses the negative image of Caliban in the novel *Ariel*, by early Latin American nationalist José Enrique Rodo. In this novel Caliban, as the brute who terrorizes his compatriot Ariel, is meant to symbolize U.S. aggression. By contrast, Ariel is depicted by Rodo as a creole intellectual embodying the essence of nascent Latin American nationalism and culture. "Our symbol then is not Ariel . . . but rather Caliban," says Retamar, "[t]here is no Ariel-Caliban polarity: both are slaves in the hands of Prospero, the foreign magician. But Caliban is the rude and unconquerable master of the island, while Ariel . . . is the intellectual."[20]

Thus, while Retamar negates racial distinctions between Caliban and Ariel, he still retains the idea that Caliban is a symbol of the place itself, not an intellectual creator. It is in this assessment, and the question of blackness, that Lamming's reading of Caliban differs markedly from that of Retamar and the hispanophone critics generally. Aimé Césaire also uses Ariel as a figure of the mulatto intellectual in *A Tempest*, but as a counterrevolutionary one, implying a kind of natural treachery of the educated brown-skinned middle class that would be anathema, I think, to Lamming's purposes.

Rob Nixon argues that Retamar's analysis of the Caliban/Prospero struggle hinges on class rather than on race and explains that this is because Retamar's homeland, Cuba, is one where mulattoes predominate, as opposed to the reading of the mulatto as counterrevolutionary in Césaire's play, where Ariel is the favored mulatto and Caliban the oppressed black.[21] The class-versus-race reading tends to mystify Caribbean attitudes on race, in my view, since the emphasis on one does not preclude the other, even if we are meant to see it that way. After all, Retamar's vision of a Martí-inspired mestizoized America is based on the idea of a new relationship between culture and race, one that opposes what Retamar sees as the oppressive binary race logic of Latin America's northern neighbor, the United States. A romantic vision, perhaps, given that Latin America has a distinct racial hierarchy itself, albeit of a different character and makeup.

Why hispanophone and anglophone Caribbean nationalists should choose such markedly different interpretations deserves more analysis than I can give here. However, it seems obvious that the majority of African-descended peoples in the anglophone Caribbean, with the corresponding emphasis on African culture and identity in the independence struggles of those nations, coupled with the comparatively subordinate role that black culture has played in *political* (not social) terms in Latin America, in good measure explains this discrepancy. Furthermore, Retamar's insistence on the primacy of the intellectual in symbolizing political potential suggests that the ability to master the political discourse of the master — the intellectual's stock-in-trade — is the more critical criterion for political accession/national masculinization, particularly given the unmanly qualities associated with Calibanness/blackness.

Lamming's Caliban: Revolutionary Masculinization

In *The Pleasures of Exile*[22] Lamming interprets the Haitian revolution in terms of the Prospero/Caliban relationship and argues that Haiti provides a perfect example of how Caliban uses Prospero's weapons to claim his island and his identity. Napoleon of course is Prospero, Toussaint L'Ouverture is Caliban, and Josephine, the white creole from Martinique, is, significantly, Miranda (118). Lamming argues that C. L. R. James's definitive text, *The Black Jacobins*, is an example of how Prospero's most potent weapon — Language — can be transformed into Caliban's language, and by extension Caliban's weapon in seizing back the means to create history: hence the title, "Caliban Orders History." Therefore, it is Toussaint and James together who have made the reality of the Haitian revolution, actor and chronicler alike. What is significant for us here is the cast of characters assembled to play the leading roles: a white male European leader and a black male West Indian slave, mediated by that hybrid of Europe and the Caribbean, the white creole female. We will come back to this arrangement presently.

Lamming reads *The Tempest* as an allegory of the struggle for power, and the power of language, between the European man and the colonized African (descended) man. Though, as historical categories, blackness has been associated in the West Indies with primitivism and whiteness with modernity and "progress," the region's image as a geographical, historical, and cultural "blank slate" — halfway between Europe and Africa, representing neither — is the feature that has made it at once the object of fascination and revulsion in the European imagination. Caliban represents this limbo-state of existence, the Neither-Nor, this sense of simultaneous possibility and impossibility. The moment of becoming "white" through mastery of the English language is simultaneously the moment of Caliban's realization of his "otherness," since, as "real" white people, only the English can "own" the language.

It is worth noting here that if one attempts to find direct and precise parallels in Caribbean history then Caliban would be best represented as the figure of the original inhabitant, the Amerindian, and not the African slave. However, in the debates for independence of Caribbean nations from the nineteenth century through the twentieth Europeans were not concerned with the fitness of Amerindian peoples to rule — there was no possibility of such an event since they were all but extinct — but rather, they were concerned with the question of whether white creoles and black peoples of the region were sufficiently "civilized" to do so. Black peoples had already made a successful bid for independence in Haiti, and the newspapers in Europe were full of sensational reports of cannibalism and other horrors that were — to many — the inevitable result.[23] Thus, according to Lamming, "Caliban may become Man; but he is entirely outside the orbit of Human. . . . If Caliban turns cannibal, it is not because human flesh may appear a necessary substitute for food which is absent. It is rather because he is incapable of differentiating between one kind of reality and another. . . . Word and concept may be part of his vocabulary; but they are no part of his way of seeing . . . Caliban is a condition."[24]

This distinction between Man and Human parallels the distinction between the black gentleman, created from careful English cultivation, and "natural" black savagery, erected by the Victorians. If we apply Victorian ideas regarding the inhabitants of the Caribbean — and of black men in particular — as the historical measure, then Caliban is Not-Man and Not-Cannibal: he is the crossroads of possibility itself.[25] The factor which can decide either way is Prospero's "gift" of language, which Caliban finds useful only to curse his master. But, as Lamming points out, ". . . . Prospero lives in the absolute certainty that Language which is his gift to Caliban is the very prison in which Caliban's achievements will be realised and restricted. *Caliban can never reach perfection, not even the perfection implicit in Miranda's privileged ignorance*" (emphasis added).[26]

Therefore, while Language heralds future possibilities of revolt and accession to power, it simultaneously brings to Caliban the realization of the impossibility of achieving Humanity. The parallel that Lamming makes between Caliban's natural state, which Shakespeare paints as innately savage, and Miranda's, rendered as the epitome of innocence and grace, emblematizes the intrinsic difference between circumstance and racial/cultural essence. In other words, Miranda's essence, based on class and culture assumptions and rooted in racialist thinking, is such that it is genetically incapable of succumbing to the savageries of the island, which affects less noble natures than hers, such as the ship's crew. Yet Lamming finds the similarities between Caliban and Miranda to be significant: he points out that "like many an African slave child," Miranda has no recollection of her mother and that while Caliban's mother, Sycorax, is dead, he has the advantage in that he actually remembers her, and therefore knows her symbolic power and meaning.[27]

One may infer that Sycorax represents the past might of black Africa — the black Mother in contrast to the present European Father — further underscoring the fusion of gender and racial roles, in that Caliban has no father.[28] His savage Otherness is the result of a solely black and female progenitor. Caliban is not simply then a *racial* aberration but a *gender* monstrosity as well. This schematic placing of Caliban further underscores the "monstrosity" of black femaleness in the Western epistemological frame, the result of the slave mother's ability to mark her descendants with her status and thereby "erase" the mark of the slave Father. Caliban is therefore a peculiarly apt symbol for black colonization. Yet in this particular schema it is aberrant *manhood* that is the focus; in that Caliban represents Not-Man, his father-lacking, mother-descended genealogy illustrates the impossibility of his becoming Man even as it explains his able mimicry of manhood.

Lamming also surmises that Caliban must have played the role of nanny/servant to Miranda before his attempted rape and subsequent imprisonment. He goes even further, stating, "Miranda is the innocent half of Caliban; Caliban is the possible deformity which Miranda, at the age of experiment, might become" and "In some real, though extraordinary way, Caliban and Miranda are seen side by side: opposite and contiguous at the same time. They share an ignorance that is also the source of some vision. . . . In different circumstances, they could be together in a way that Miranda and her father could not."[29] The question, then, of where the Miranda/Caliban relationship fits into the schema of West Indian discourse, becomes implicit in any further use of Caliban as a symbol of the displaced West Indian subject.

Sylvia Wynter makes an important point when she asserts that the primary traditional/religious opposition of male/female in European epistemology underwent a radical revision during the Renaissance, when European civilization began its incursions into Africa and the nonwhite New Worlds; the discursive construction of the male/female binary was replaced by the distinction between "men" and "natives," such that "native" came to function as the primary antithetical relation to "Man" in the European lexicon and the male/female distinction came to play a secondary role.[30] In other words, the colonized subject replaced the white woman in the binary oppositional paradigm of white Western culture, and thus the European woman could accede to a form of subjectivity—albeit a subjectivity of a greatly inferior kind. Wynter illustrates this point through the use of the Prospero/Miranda/Caliban relationship, noting that Miranda escapes ultimate subordinate status by her juxtaposition with Caliban. Therefore, if we connect Wynter's point to Lamming's characterization of Caliban as Not-Man, Miranda's placement is in fact *crucial* to the fixing and maintenance of Caliban as the permanent Other, the essential Not-Man, a logical extension which Lamming's reading suggests but does not complete.

Inasmuch as Lamming's emphasis is on Caliban's and Miranda's *similarities*, his reading of their relationship is one of political expediency and missed political alliances. Particularly important is Lamming's interpretation of Caliban's attempted rape of Miranda. Lamming places special emphasis on Caliban's reply to Prospero's charge that he attempted to rape Miranda. ("O ho, O ho! would't had been done! / Thou didst prevent me; I had peopled else / This isle with Calibans.") Caliban does not wish to rape Miranda for "the mere experiment of mounting a piece of white pussy," he argues, but rather because Caliban is thinking in *political* terms; little Calibans mean future organized resistance to Prospero: ". . . it is most unlikely that Prospero and his daughter could endure a brown skin baby. . . . It would be Miranda's and Caliban's child. It would be *theirs*: the result and expression of some fusion of both physical and other than physical: a fusion which, within himself, Prospero needs and dreads!"[31]

Leaving aside Lamming's misogynistic representation of white women ("a piece of white pussy"), one might wonder: why does Prospero *need* such a fusion? Lamming's interpretation of the attempted rape suggests that the violation of Miranda's white body by a black man would not simply produce a monstrous hybrid for Prospero and an ally for Caliban, but it would irrevocably change Prospero's relationship to Miranda, who would now become bound to the island, to Nature, and to Caliban. Prospero would *need* such a fusion to continue the imperative of domination and subordination which gives him identity (that is, complete power over his "subjects"), but it must be done at the cost of his own child. Miranda thus represents a condition of threat and possibility, being Not-Yet-Man (as opposed to Caliban's Not-Man) and the means by which Caliban can reproduce, seize control of the island, and accede to the terms of power understood to be Manhood.

The absence of the body of the black woman, both in Shakespeare's play and in Lamming's re-creation of it in his allegorical novel, *Water with Berries*, affirms Boose's argument that, in these narratives of racial power negotiations, black manhood is representable more so than black womanhood. In that the black woman's body would seem to be the logical choice as the central symbol of the female body as political weapon, having suffered the historical victimage of institutionalized rape at the hands of white male slave owners, it is significant, if not deeply ironic, that the most potent representations of rape and/or violation of a female body as a political act in male-authored West Indian fiction — and for that matter, male-authored African American fiction — is often effected through the use of a white female character.[32]

In much male-authored anglophone and francophone narrative the black woman's body, unlike the white woman's, is often figured as maternal, like Sycorax, when it figures at all.[33] In these masculine narratives of Caribbean history, the silence of the raped white female body is not the same as the silence of the black maternal body, since rape is figured as one kind of displaced desire *for* something *through* violence, whereas the black female body represents both unrecoverable, nostalgic history associated with Africa (the land, the folk) and the tainted history of slavery that requires erasure. The white creole female body becomes a metonym operating in two spheres: it displaces the history of black female rape even as it registers black male desire for contemporary power, signified here as a political conflict with masculinized European imperialism.[34]

The body of the white woman, then, could be said to represent the site of possible future interactions between the Colonizer/Prospero and the Colonized/Caliban, a site where both must renegotiate the terms of dominance and subordination; a site where both can meet as *men* — a variation of Habermas's conception of the eighteenth-century public sphere,[35] except that the terms of equality rest on the ability to violate the female body. In this particular logic of gender domination, the rape of the black woman does not count in that she is not a Woman, nor is she human. I will elaborate on this symbolic use of the white woman in my reading of Lamming's *Water with Berries*.

In the novel Lamming allegorizes *The Tempest*, to which the title makes explicit reference, the "water with berries" being Prospero's gift to Caliban when he first landed on the island, representing the gift and prisonhouse of Prospero's language.[36] However, the circumstances of the encounter between colonizer and colonized are reversed in some important ways. This encounter takes place almost entirely in the homeland of the colonizer; the movement of the novel reverses the movement of contemporary immigration so that the figure of Caliban travels from England to the Caribbean. Even more interesting is that Lamming re-creates the allegorical figure of the English colonizer as an old white Englishwoman.

Teeton, the protagonist of the narrative, is a West Indian painter exiled to Britain from his homeland of San Cristobal for fomenting revolution. He is the central character in a trio of three fellow revolutionary West Indian artists in exile, the other two being Derek and Roger. Lamming's conflation of artist and revolutionary in these characters is a clear indication that he is making an argument that art and revolution are, ultimately, the same. The name of the fictional Caribbean island, San Cristobal, is a play on the Spanish version of Columbus's first name, clearly suggesting that the West Indian's revolutionary struggle begins with the originary point of Caribbean misnaming by the European conqueror.

Teeton rents a room in the home of Mrs. Gore-Brittain (the obvious metaphor of the name requires no explanation), whom he refers to as the Old Dowager. Their relationship is affectionate; she daily dusts the old black tree trunk (a metaphor of subjugated black masculinity) which he brought into his room over her objections and which he now cannot get rid of because she insists it must stay. In short, the once-powerful revolutionary is domesticated.

However, Mrs. Gore-Brittain is the widow of a San Cristobal plantation owner, a cruel authoritarian who abused his servants and whose servants in turn set fire to his estates and raped his daughter, Myra (Myra, of course, represents Miranda). When the body of Roger's white wife is found, inexplicably, by Mrs. Gore-Brittain in Teeton's room, both she and Teeton hide the body in the garden and flee to her husband's private island in the Orkney Islands. Here they are found by her lover and her husband's brother (and murderer), Fernando (who represents Antonio from *The Tempest*).[37] In a jealous rage Fernando attacks Teeton and is killed by Mrs. Gore-Brittain. Teeton, now finding himself bound to the Old Dowager more tightly than ever, kills her to escape permanent dependence on her. In the meantime, Derek is arrested for arson, and Roger, in a fit of fury, rapes a white actress onstage while he is performing as a dead body in, significantly, a play entitled "A Summer's Error in Albion." By the close of the narrative, the reader is presented with three dead white female bodies, killed directly or indirectly by three black male revolutionaries.

The narrative moves in parallel to the original slave ship journey; to escape the murder charges, Teeton travels from England to the islands. This movement suggests that the revolutionary's desire to substitute himself as the discoverer/conqueror of the Caribbean is bound to the artist's desire to transform the colonizer's gift/curse of language so that through it he can "speak" his own reality. But this geographical space, like this revolutionary and his oppressor, are specifically gendered entities. The narrative logic of the plot dictates that in order to transform the Somewhere Elseness of the Caribbean space to a discrete political reality, and the Caribbean would-be revolutionaries into "real" revolutionaries, three specific textual events must be enacted through the allegory of *The Tempest*.

First, the gendered terms of the binary interplay of dominating and dominated regions that structures the narrative must be maintained even as the terms are being renegotiated: the space of the "Fatherland," England, must be feminized in order for the Caribbean space to become masculinized. Second, the attempted rape of Miranda in *The Tempest* must be completed by Caliban's heirs in *Water with Berries*. Finally, Teeton must first rid himself of dependency on the Old Dowager — he must be transformed from child to Man.

In that Caliban is subordinate to Prospero because he is Not-Man, he can never effect a true revolution because a revolutionary is a Man. Teeton is a revolutionary without a revolution — he is displaced from the space that gave him the terms of his existence. Therefore, Teeton himself is a disembodied space that must be defined before he can in turn define the space that is his referent.

Clearly, the Old Dowager is an allegory. The most obvious problem of interpretation becomes precisely *who* or *what* does she represent if we are to read this narrative as an extension of *The Tempest*? In that her husband is the abusive plantation owner, and her daughter is Myra, one obvious answer is that she is the unknown (dead) wife of Prospero, mother of Miranda. However, she is also Britain, as her name suggests, and is the direct source of oppression from which Teeton must liberate himself. The fact that Teeton rents a room in her house alludes to the paradoxical relationship of the Caribbean to Europe — the intimacy suggested by the familial relationship, the home, and the fundamental inequities of power and antagonism suggested by the fact of renting. If Prospero represents power, being a conflation of England and Manhood, as Lamming's interpretation implies, then the replacement of a male figure with a female suggests, among other things, that England's status as a crumbling colonial power has effectively feminized it. Lamming himself says as much in an interview, where he is discussing the symbolic importance of the Old Dowager:

. . . She's sort of taken over the role of Prospero, with this difference: whereas Prospero in *The Tempest* is a *male force* because the world from which he is operating is aggressive, expansionist and conquering, by the time we get to *Water with Berries*, that world has now contracted in a way. It has now retreated; it has aged. And what we see in the Old Dowager is the age, the remoteness, in some ways the *impotence* of the earlier Prospero.[38] (emphasis added)

Yet the feminization of the English space also rearranges the terms of the relationship so that whereas Prospero and Caliban were engaged in an exclusively antagonistic relationship, Prospero's female successor has managed to bind Caliban even more intimately to England — the relationship is characterized by, in the words of one critic, Teeton's "castrating dependence" on the Old Dowager. Caliban must therefore assert his masculinity (in the form of independence) not merely over the historical (masculine) presence of England in the Caribbean, but against the seductions (I use the word deliberately) of the maternal bond between England and the Caribbean in England.

The Old Dowager thus must be read as both a masculine and a feminine entity. Her status as Myra's mother is accordingly ambiguous; she has no idea of the whereabouts of her daughter, who has become a prostitute in London. Myra, as the ultimately displaced white creole, at home neither in San Cristobal nor Great Britain, extends Miranda's position as motherless child in an alien country. A pivotal scene in the narrative occurs when Teeton and Myra meet, in symbolic and real darkness, on the heath. In this exchange Teeton learns about Myra's rape during the revolt in San Cristobal. The scene enacts Lamming's suggestion in *Pleasures* of similar circumstance and potential political alliance between Caliban and Miranda; both are displaced individuals disconnected from their place of origin, both the result of English colonizing practices in the Caribbean. Myra represents whiteness/Englishness in its most acquiescent state: feminized, subordinate, and West Indianized.

Teeton and Myra can only meet as equals *after* the rape has occurred, because the rape represents the necessary — and necessarily brutal — changeover in gender and power roles. As I have discussed elsewhere, Lamming's vision of historical change necessitates such violence.[39] His belief that violence is an inevitable part of the decolonizing process can be linked to his acceptance of Caliban's (attempted) rape of Miranda as a similarly inevitable process of reassertion of power by the native over the imperial presence. Richard Halpern argues that Cuban critic Fernández Retamar similarly accepts Caliban's attempted rape of Miranda as part of his vision that Caliban's counterutopia is a model for a revolutionary postcolonial Caribbean/Latin American national culture. Halpern suggests that the multiple desires of the characters in the play to produce utopias implies that

> . . . utopian solutions only multiply the violence — so the moral seems to go. Yet this symmetry — or rather, this double bind — is rather artfully contrived, for despite their own fantasies it was the colonizers themselves who held a virtual monopoly on rape and sexual violence. Readers who find themselves casuistically tallying Caliban's sexual assault against the prior wrongs done to him, then, or who try to 'revalue' this assault in light of the anti-colonial utopia it projects, are caught in a false historical premise, one which builds specious symmetries for anti-utopian ends. Retamar's choice of Caliban as anti-colonial hero falls into this same trap. To embrace Caliban's counter-utopia means having to embrace his rape of Miranda.[40]

This unhappy congruence of thought suggests that the criminal nature of rape is assigned different value depending on its context: rape as a gesture of colonization somehow differing from rape as a means of decolonization.

The scene in which Derek, while playing a corpse onstage, rapes the white actress in front of a horrified English audience, reaffirms the narrative logic of the rape of the white female body in Lamming's novel. As a parallel Caliban figure, Derek in his role as corpse suggests the passive quiescent position of the colonized mapped out by grand design in the European play of imperial conquest. That the play is titled *A Summer's Error in Albion* of course reminds us of Shakespeare and the relationship of the West Indian artist to the British literary tradition, wherein all these power relationships are encoded in the very language itself. Derek's fury at playing the "feminine" role — the body, literally — suggests his emasculation within the narrative as an entity without agency. His rape of the white actress, then, reverses the roles such that *he*, and not she, becomes the actor, and she becomes the body, the entity acted upon.

In this way, the narrative of *Water with Berries* establishes the gendered terms by which nationhood must be established. The dialectics of rapist and victim, landlady and tenant, owner and owned, are used to illustrate the necessity of masculine agency for the West Indian intellectual in his quest to define the disembodied region of the Caribbean on the European map. Like James, for Lamming revolutionary success ultimately lies with one central figure, the intellectual. The rape metaphor plays on the implication that the colonization of the Caribbean constituted a national rape which must be repeated but reversed so that racial and gender roles are reversed. It also, in identifying European colonization as rape, functions to embody, or make material, the indistinct character of the region in the European imagination. The residue left by this dialectic is of course the figure of the white female creole, who represents for Lamming simultaneously a future political possibility of fusion and reconciliation as well as the unassimilability of the features of whiteness, femaleness, and West Indianness within the new West Indian nation.[41]

Caliban and Miranda Redux: Rewriting Resistance

If Lamming's Caliban is representative of the masculinist structure of Caribbean literary symbolism, this does not necessarily mean that the Caliban/Miranda paradigm cannot be utilized in ways that subvert its masculinist presuppositions. Rob Nixon notes the play's declining pertinence to the contemporary Caribbean and Africa given the problem of "wresting from it any role for female defiance or leadership in a period when protest is coming increasingly from that quarter. Given that Caliban is without a female counterpart in his oppression and rebellion, and given the largely autobiographical cast of African and Caribbean appropriations of the play, it follows that all the writers who quarried from *The Tempest* an expression of their lot should have been men."[42]

While I generally agree with Nixon's assessment, this is not to say that women intellectuals and authors have ignored the symbolism of Caliban altogether in their assessment of the place of women in liberation struggles. To the contrary, I think it is particularly important to note and understand how West Indian women authors have addressed the "problem" of Caliban, if you will, in more indirect ways. Paule Marshall's 1961 novella "Brazil," and Michelle Cliff's 1987 novel *No Telephone to Heaven* illustrate a two-pronged assault on the gendered meaning of Caliban and revolutionary discourse in anglophone Caribbean narrative.

On one hand, Marshall's subversive reading of the Caliban/Miranda relationship refigures the dynamics of race, gender, and power at play in the white woman/black man motif in nationalist discourse. On the other, Cliff attempts to (re)write the Caribbean novel of revolution by re-inscribing both the authorial voice and body of the erased black woman through a "white" creole female subject. If revolutionary action has been marked as a contest of competing masculinities in Caribbean metanarrative, and the site of struggle is correspondingly marked as (white and) female and/or feminized, Cliff must activate and thereby render visible the black woman's literary and material place in historical/fictive discourse. Readers are forced to confront the question of whether white and black female voices can simultaneously occupy the same discursive spaces.

Brazil is set in Rio de Janeiro and features two main characters called Caliban and Miranda. Placing the story of Caliban and Miranda within a multiracial Latin American nation — a region with many cultural parallels to the Caribbean — gestures to a concern over the effects of colonialism and national independence beyond the borders of the Caribbean. This placement manages to reaffirm Retamar's vision of a unified Latin American/Caribbean political identity and the concerns of "Caliban" proponents of Caribbean nationalism generally, even as it sets the stage for a critique of the same.

Caliban, the stage name of the protagonist, is a famous but aging, dwarfish black night club performer in Rio de Janeiro. He performs a comedy/dance act with his sometime lover, the blonde, white-looking Miranda. The title of the pair's act is "The Great Caliban and the Tiny Miranda!" An ironic title, given their respective physiognomies — Caliban is old, greying, and short, while Miranda is comparatively young, tall, and strong:

Their act was mostly slapstick, with Caliban using the cowed Miranda as a butt for his bullying and abuse. And it was this incongruous and contradictory relationship — Caliban's strength, his bossiness despite his age and shriveled body and Miranda's weakness, which belied her imposing height and massive limbs — that was the heart of their act. It shaped everything they did. . . . They broke into a dance routine and Miranda took little mincing steps while Caliban spurred his body in a series of impressive leaps and spins, and forced his legs wide in a split.[43]

The pair enact — caricature — the gender stereotypes expected of them, which is the source of the routine's perceived hilarity. Yet Caliban has begun to feel the futility of his act and has decided to retire. He desires to return to his old life, before he became famous, when he was just Heitor Guimares from a small mining town. But Caliban's own memories of his past life are disappearing, and he cannot remember who he used to be before he became O Grande Caliban:

He avoided looking at his face now that he was old. Without the make-up it reminded him of a piece of old fruit so shriveled and spotted that there was no certainty as to what it had been originally. Above all, once he removed the make-up, his face was without expression, bland, as though only on stage made up as Caliban in the scarlet shirt and baggy trunks was he at all certain of who he was. Caliban might have become his reality.[44]

Recognizing the danger that he has in fact *become* the stage persona, Caliban seeks validation of his original identity but finds that no one else remembers his real name — not his young wife, nor the old man who encouraged him to go onstage, nor Miranda, who in fact was also responsible for creating his stage persona.

Since the usage of Caliban and Miranda points the reader to the obvious allegory that Caliban represents — that is, the Caribbean — the issue then becomes: What precisely is Marshall saying by establishing Caliban in these terms? Caliban's loss of his true name and his imprisonment within his stage name clearly allude to the misnomer of the West Indies and its symbolic importance as mis-history. That Caliban and Miranda are burlesque club dancers reminds us of the origins of the Caliban/Miranda trope within theater — *The Tempest* was, after all, created as *entertainment* for the English reader/audience. By the time "Brazil" was written the figure of Caliban as a symbol of the defiant colonized Caribbean had been established, so that Marshall's Caliban clearly parodies this antiheroic depiction. He is not indigenous to the Caribbean but a product of the English fictive imagination, a tainted creation whose identity is irrecoverably compromised by his location within English discourse as the burlesque grotesque. As a shriveled, dwarfish figure, Caliban is the antithesis of the young, muscular animal-savage we envision from the Shakespeare/Lamming image. By contrast, it is Miranda who is young and muscular.

That Miranda is responsible for the creation of the stage persona is also significant, as is her role as his mistress: she is ambitious and has become Caliban's mistress for personal gain. Caliban recognizes that "she would quickly choose another jester to her court once he was gone."[45] Again, the roles are reversed: Miranda has agency in this particular tableau and in fact draws her power from her role as Miranda. The allusion to the court jester reminds us again that, if history is a masquerade, and the Calibans/blacks are disempowered by the roles that they are assigned to play out, there are those who benefit by the masquerade. Miranda, as an allegory of the white creole female, desires "to remain the child herself — wilful, dependent, indulged — and [now] that she had used [Caliban] to this end," would "use someone else now that she had exhausted him."[46] In other words, the masquerade of Miranda's dependency obscures the fact that she derives very real power from the relationship and from her own position as a coveted white body.

The difference between Marshall's interpretation of the Caliban/Miranda trope and that of Lamming and others is significant for more than Marshall's upending of Lamming's paradoxical rapist/comrade thematics. If it is Miranda who pays the price for Caribbean national liberation in the Lamming narrative, for Marshall it is Caliban who pays the highest price; by allowing himself to be "Calibanized," by inhabiting the role itself, he has lost all hope of liberation because he can no longer separate the role from the reality. A Caliban can be nothing else but a Caliban; Lamming's revolutionary, by extension, cannot recover a "lost" masculinity when he has so thoroughly imbued himself with the attributes of his slave persona. By tying the confining gender stereotypes of the stage act to the political meaning of racial and sexual identity in Caribbean history, Marshall reminds us of the larger context for national liberation that cannot be encompassed by merely exchanging the roles of victim and victimizer from a European play of conquest.

It is significant, too, that Marshall's reading of Caliban and Miranda dismantles Donaldson's attempt to iconize Miranda as a "feminine trope of colonialism." While Donaldson argues that Miranda is as much a victim of colonialism as Caliban, Marshall's Miranda suggests in 1961 what many black and Third World feminists have been saying about the vexed relationship between white and black/Third World women for the past two decades: Miranda derives very material and specific benefits from the colonial arrangement, and therefore her path to agency and power tends to a very different one from that of Caliban. Though the Miranda character in "Brazil" is clearly a mixed creole, the politics of color in the shade hierarchies of Latin America and the Caribbean maintain the essential white/black dichotomous paradigm of power in those places.

Black Miranda: The White Creole Woman and the Black Revolutionary Tradition

A somewhat more sympathetic rendering of the white creole female is to be found in Cliff's No Telephone to Heaven. Cliff's novel is particularly important because it is perhaps the only female-authored West Indian narrative — with the possible exception of Merle Collins's Angel — that explicitly thematizes revolutionary political action through a female protagonist. Cliff's concern with integrating the violent history of the Caribbean with issues of sexuality, race, and gender make this novel at once in the tradition of male-authored revolution narrative as well as a radical departure from — and critique of — it.

A sequel to Cliff's first novel Abeng, in No Telephone the protagonist, Clare Savage, a white-looking creole, searches for the meaning of her conflicting inheritance: she is a Jamaican living in the First World and therefore a member of the despised Third World. Yet as the recipient of the white skin of her slave-owning great-grandfather she has the privileges of apparent whiteness and functions as politically white in Jamaica. Clare is the daughter of an unhappy couple, Boy and Kitty Savage. Boy Savage, also a white-looking creole, is the direct descendant of Judge Savage, a white slave owner who burned his slaves. Boy wishes to preserve this "illustrious," historically approved heritage by identifying himself and his family with its European ancestors and all things European. His desire for whiteness is part of a national desire to claim the "winning side" of history, a history which plays itself out in the country every day, as Clare notes: "But we *are* of the past here. So much of the past that we punish people by flogging them with cat-o'-nine tails. We expect people to live on cornmeal and dried fish, which was the diet of the slaves. We name hotels Plantation Inn and Sans Souci. . . . A peculiar past. For we have taken the master's past as our own. That is the danger."[47]

By contrast, Kitty Savage, who cannot pass for white, is from "the bush" and silently opposes Boy's desire for whiteness. Kitty clearly represents the rural black folk in the narrative. Her ambivalent relation to Boy, and indeed to herself, suggests that Cliff is revising earlier images of the folk — such as those that we find in McKay and Marson — as people unmarked by or blissfully unaware of the psychological complexities of race and power in the Caribbean. Here, the folk are shown to actively participate in the production of national meaning, though their relation to the discourse is obscured.

When the couple emigrate to the United States Kitty works in the aptly named "White's Sanitary Laundry," a place peopled by black women who do the actual work even as the finished laundry is accompanied by a signed note from an imaginary "Mrs. White" giving laundering advice. The laundry's white owner subscribes to a philosophy of wifehood, motherhood, and general womanhood that makes crisp laundry an intrinsic part of being a woman — here signified as white — even as the labor that produces the white laundry is invisible black female labor (73). Kitty, who must pen the imaginary notes, one day writes "Hello. Mrs. White is dead. My name is Mrs. Black. I killed her." Her subsequent firing is the wedge that ultimately separates her and Boy, who is trying to "pass" as white in the United States. There is deliberate irony in the fact that Kitty's act of resistance is contained within the context of white America and that she never "speaks" in Jamaica, since she dies in the United States and is returned, dead, for burial in Jamaica. Kitty's silent resistance symbolizes the silenced discourse of blackness in the region. In contrast to the overt and public signs of whiteness that mark womanhood in Mrs. White's laundry, womanhood has now become silent and black. Kitty's body manages to straddle two disparate discursive worlds: that of the "author"/subject—she "authors" the antiracist notes in the laundry and thereby writes herself into subject status—and that of the laborer/land/object. Her dead black body becomes a silent and yet unburied legacy, part of Walcott's amnesia that must be remembered. The subsequent two-page chapter titled "Magnanimous Warrior!" ties the historical figures of female warrior/maroons, the runaway slaves who fought and beat the British, to the powerful mythic female spirits and "obeah" women who can "shed [their] skin like a snake and travel[ ] into the darkness a fireball" (163), and finally to "real" black, poor women:

What has become of this warrior? . . . She has been burned up in an almshouse fire in Kingston. She has starved to death. She wanders the roads of the country with swollen feet. . . . Her children have left her. Her powers are known no longer. They are called by other names. She is not respected. . . . She cleans the yard of a woman younger than she. . . . They tell her she is senile. They have taken away her bag of magic. . . . We have forgotten her. . . . Can you remember how to love her? (164)

Some years later Clare, who has been traveling in the United States and London, returns to Jamaica. There she meets a black transvestite, Harry/Harriet, who introduces her to a revolutionary group with international links. The leader of the group, a black woman, questions her desire to come back to Jamaica and fight for social change, and Clare replies that she has returned to Jamaica "to mend . . . to bury . . . my mother" (192) and because "[m]y mother told me to help my people" (196). The black revolutionary in turn asks her to "think of Bishop. Rodney. Fanon. Lumumba. Malcolm. First. Luthuli. Garvey. Mxembe. Marley. Moloise" (196). The list is (with the exception of First)[48] that of radical black men: African, African American, and Afro-Caribbean political leaders, thinkers, and artists. In this way Cliff establishes a direct link between a pan-Africanist male tradition of revolutionary agency and the discursive as well as material recovery of the black female body, since Clare, through radical political action, hopes simultaneously to bury and make visible her black mother and the black, silenced maternal space of Jamaica, through revolutionary action. It is a central contradiction of the narrative that Clare, who operates as physiognomically and socially "white" in the Caribbean (and indeed in Europe, where she is assumed to be white) must find a way to recover the black female body so that she may be "made black," so to speak, in her mother's image. The narrative attempts a resolution to this conflict in terms of how it reenvisions the gendered and "raced" idea of revolutionary struggle in the Caribbean.

In *The Wretched of the Earth* Fanon declares that violence is an inevitable part of the decolonizing process, and much of West Indian writing acknowledges this potential for violent social upheaval, as has been discussed. However, much of West Indian fascination with revolution centers on the *failure* of revolutionary action. Lamming's revolutionaries are exiled to London in *Water with Berries*; in Lovelace's *The Dragon Can't Dance* and Naipaul's *Guerrillas*, the revolution fails because of the internal incoherence of the would-be revolutionaries. In the latter, the black nationalist protagonist Jimmy Ahmed seeks only to be a "real" hero, like the one he is writing about in his novel, whose "reality" is sustained by the fact that he is much admired — and feared — in England, the site of white male power.[49]

Ahmed's novel also contains a gang rape of a white woman by black men, who after the assault offer her water, which she accepts gratefully. The fictional story of the white woman's rape is completed at the end of the narrative in the actual rape and murder of the white English female character, who is "offered" by Ahmed as a sacrificial victim to a berserk black boy, the product himself of the "madness" of black revolutionary desire.[50] For Naipaul, the violation of the white female body is a necessary staple for the ascendance of black nationalism. This is not to suggest that Naipaul's distinctly hostile view of Black Power is in any ideological way connected to Lamming's or other writers' views on the subject; indeed, Lamming castigates Naipaul for his "inadequacy" (*Pleasures of Exile*, 30), and Naipaul has established an overt antipathy to Lamming indirectly in his critiques of the Caliban model for Caribbean empowerment. Despite the ideological chasm between Naipaul and the nationalists, however, the arrangement of bodies and their meanings are remarkably similar.[51]

Naipaul's novel is particularly important to our discussion of *No Telephone to Heaven* because of its reading of Black Power movements in the Caribbean as a contest between black and white men mediated through the exploitation of a willing white woman. It is this model of race and power relations which is the site of an intertextual engagement in Cliff's narrative. In *Guerrillas* Ahmed's rape and murder is constructed as the ultimate act of black violence run amok. It is violence that is the result of an existential crisis of identity, an identity which can only conceive itself on the other side of "reality": the revolution is revealed to be an empty contemporary cliché that masks this "truth." The depiction of revolution as symbol, as sign without connection to referent, echoes Naipaul's emphasis on the guerrilla's writing fantasy scenarios of revolt — the implication is that his rage, like his writing, is only given expression by romantic European liberal ideas, and consequently his violence, like his writing, can only be a caricature, an echo, or inversions of a European referent.

In a scene that parallels Naipaul's, the gardener Christopher in *No Telephone to Heaven* murders his wealthy brown employers and their black maid because they refused to give him land to bury his grandmother, who had died some thirteen years before. Christopher too is "mad" in one sense, but his "madness" becomes coherent in the historical context of the narrative, where the injustices of the past and present converge into a single act of "random" violence.

Like Christopher, Clare's mother had died some time before. And, like Christopher's mother, Clare's mother is black, a significant element in the chronology of West Indian narrative where, as has been noted, the bodies which represent the site of dialogue have been those of white females. That these *other*, black, maternal bodies have been dead but not buried reminds us of the invisibility of black women in the narration of West Indian revolutionary discourse, as embodied by Caliban's mother, the absent Sycorax, who represents Caliban's past heritage of might and agency. Therefore, the attempt to "bury" the grand/mother becomes a metaphor for reconciling the "unburied" — that is, unrepresented, ghostly, "magical" — history of the people with the possibilities contained in the land, a fusion which requires violent rupture with present reality.

When Clare joins the revolutionary group and engages in a physical attack on an American movie set, this act of violence replicates Christopher's act, not solely for its intent to "bury" the black mother but also for the seeming randomness of its target, a Hollywood movie about the Jamaican maroons. One of the actresses in the film is a black woman who is to play the role of Nanny, the legendary maroon leader who was reputed to catch the British bullets between her buttocks. This actress,

called in whenever someone was needed to play a Black heroine, any Black heroine, whether Sojourner Truth or Bessie Smith, . . . wore a pair of leather breeches and a silk shirt—designer's notion of the clothes that Nanny wore. Dear Nanny, the Coromantee warrior, leader of the Windward Maroons, whom one book described as an old woman naked except for a necklace made from the teeth of whitemen. . . . Facing the elegant actress was a strapping man, former heavyweight or running back, dressed as Cudjoe, tiny humpbacked soul. (206)

The grotesque sexualization of Nanny to conform to romantic heterosexual Western ideas about black womanhood is completed, significantly, by the fake Nanny's partnering with a similarly sexualized "Cudjoe," who represents the historical figure of the small, deformed maroon leader. The film's Cudjoe also conforms to Western heterosexual ideas about what desirable — and desiring — violent black masculinity should look like. This [hetero]sexualization of black revolutionary action is paradigmatic of the sexualized figures in the Caribbean history of conquest, subjugation, and rape, a tableau which it merely continues in a modern, postcolonial framework.

Cliff attempts to dismantle this paradigm by inserting radical sexualities into her narratives. In *Abeng* the historical figure of Nanny is represented in the fictional character of Mma Alli, a black maroon leader/obeah woman who is also lesbian, though the text makes a point of letting the reader know that she "was a true sister to the men — the Black men: her brothers" (35). In *No Telephone* Mma Alli's literary heir is the character of Harry/Harriet, whose androgynous status, combined with his role as guerrilla, is meant to confuse the distinctions between male and female roles in a society where gender overdetermines one's relation to the state and to the kinds of action — or inaction — in which one may or may not participate.

When a European tourist notices Harry/Harriet's eyeshadow, he explains that he is a Crown prince of Benin, and that his name is "Prince Badnigga": "I see you have noticed my eyelids . . . these are the colors of our national flag. . . . At the first sign of manhood each young warrior in our country must do the same . . . going back to the days when we devoured our enemies. . . . I mean, we needed the means to distinguish, didn't we?" (125). Harry/Harriet's performance satirizes both European fears about black male savagery as well as a brand of black nationalism which equates black liberation with a dominant heterosexual masculinity that wishes to divorce itself from the "taint" of the feminine, associated as it is with failure and rape. He therefore marks the African national flag with that most trivial of "feminine" pursuits, makeup, implying that the masculinist nationalist project is itself "in drag."

We later learn that Harry/Harriet is the child of a housekeeper and her employer. He has been taken into the household of the employer "on sufferance," and his first sexual experience is a rape that he has suffered at the hands of a white military officer who threatens him if he dares to speak of it (129). As a young black boy whose status is already contingent on silence — his mother, the maid, was fired so that his father could preserve the myth of his son's "legitimate" origins — this further silencing of sexual violence imbricates black masculinity in the national silence that is discursively as well as materially feminized and racialized.

Therefore, Harry/Harriet must learn to "speak" of this history — both his own as a raped black man and his mother's as raped black woman (I submit that sex under these conditions of power inequity constitutes a form of rape) — in ways that will allow for both voices and yet not repeat the historical pattern of sexual and racial violence. As Harry/Harriet tells Clare, "the time will come for us to choose . . . [we cannot] live split. Not in this world" (131). But their options are different, though related ones. Harry/Harriet must choose between gender roles and the political consequences of being a black man or woman in Jamaica; Clare must choose whether she is to be politically black or white, which are, for her, also gendered roles.

By having Clare read *Jane Eyre* Cliff shows Clare's direct relation to Antoinette Cosway (called Bertha by her husband), the madwoman in the attic of *Jane Eyre* who is also the subject of Rhys's *Wide Sargasso Sea*: "The fiction tricked her. Drawn her in so that she became Jane. . . . No, she could not be Jane. . . . No, my girl, try Bertha. . . . Yes, Bertha was closer the mark. Captive. Ragout. Mixture. Confused. Jamaican. Caliban. Carib. Cannibal. Cimarron. All Bertha. All Clare" (116).

This passage is particularly important for the link it provides between Caliban and Bertha, the two gendered and racialized symbols of Caribbean independence and invisibility. Both inhere within the identity of Clare, who has been characterized as an epistemological paradox in the narrative. That the misnomer of Bertha — this is the name that Rochester forces onto Antoinette — is the name designated as "closer the mark" reminds us of the misnomer of "West Indies," and the struggle between the imposition of hegemonic history and uncoded reality which it embodies. The name represents a locus of struggle over identity, and we are guided to read Clare's name in this way. As the inheritor of her father's cultural and racial whiteness, Clare is, unlike her darker-skinned sister, the "masculine" daughter. Boy has designated Clare to be the "white" child, to whom he imparts the "gift" of European history and knowledge, and this whiteness is in turn associated with the figure of the gentleman scholar.

Yet whiteness, as a masculinized epistemology, and femaleness, which is aligned with blackness and historylessness, cannot be assimilated to each other. Clare's name points to this fundamental schism: "Clare" represents, obviously, the "light" of European ancestry, and yet from *Abeng* we learn that Clare is named after a black mother, a maid, who saves her mother's life — the sign of good, therefore, is black. (Indeed, maids, nannies, and domestic laborers consistently appear in binary relation to the gentleman scholar in these stories, providing an alternate model of learning through what they *do* and not through what they have read.) "Savage" is an illustrious Jamaican name, and yet, as the name implies, it carries with it a barbaric history. Thus even *within* the paradox of the name are concealed paradoxes. The "Savage" reminds us of Caliban, and yet this is not to whom the name refers — Caliban/Black/Man and Bertha/White/Woman are reversed within Clare. The above passage also engenders within the reader a full realization that the site of dialogue is not simply with an ambivalent white creole tradition but also with the European literary canon itself, which freezes the colonized subject in an eternal relation of subject/object.

The English canon, so useful to Lamming, Naipaul, James, and McKay as a means of constructing literary authority for themselves as literary subjects, is useless to this female "heir apparent." When Boy Savage takes Clare to an American high school, they are told that, like all foreign students, she will have to begin a year behind her class. Boy suggests that his daughter be made an exception, as she is proficient in Latin, Greek, and French, and has read Dickens, Shakespeare, and Milton (97). The principal, pointing out that she is from an "underdeveloped" country and moreover has black blood, refuses. In ironic reference to the meaning of Miranda as complicit with the authorizing power of the English literary tradition, Clare's "purchase" of the instruments of Western patriarchal knowledge is shown not to be hers at all, but rather her *father's*, who deeply desires to be *himself* recognized as a (white) gentleman. Ironically, the confrontation with American-style whiteness and racism symbolically "unmasks" Clare's hidden, black identity, an identity that finally liberates her at the novel's conclusion. Cliff's invocation of an American experience of race relations illuminates the limitations of the English-style gentleman scholar model for black immigrant women, and indeed for revolutionary black women.

Mary Lou Emery points out that "feminist and Third World perspectives rarely combine in readings of Rhys's work. When they do, the resulting analysis usually depends upon a structural analogy between colonial hierarchies and sexual oppression that still positions the protagonist as a victim who lacks agency and offers little or no resistance."[52] I would extend this observation to most analyses of white creole women.[53] In many ways Cliff is Rhys's literary heir, therefore it is important to know the critical context of Cliff's narrative and how it seeks to rearrange the white creole female body so that it can act without acting *upon* the black female body, since in the Caribbean historical script the silent body becomes metonymy for quiescent land, ripe for exploitation.

In *The Politics and Poetics of Transgression*, Stallybrass and White emphasize that to properly understand discourse one cannot separate it from its social space. ("It is only when such related concepts as critical judgement, taste, authorship and writing are reconnected to their 'planes of emergence' as Foucault has called them, the social points at which such ideas surface, that they can be fully understood.")[54] In returning Bertha Mason back to the West Indies where her "real" name is revealed, Rhys acknowledges that geopolitical location is the crucial referent to "reading" Bertha and by extension to making sense of West Indian discourse. Similarly, in *No Telephone to Heaven* Clare Savage returns to Jamaica after moving first to the United States and then to London. Cliff's novel reveals Clare Savage at different stages in her life, and yet the point is not to embody Clare as a character separate from her "plane of emergence" but rather to read that location through the conflicting and multiple identities that are Clare Savage: she is, as such, not a "character" in the traditional sense at all. Clare's final destination is not England and a descent into madness, but Jamaica and conscious, *political*, public resistance, though she, like Bertha, dies in the act of resisting.

Whereas Antoinette Cosway dreams of a location that is "somewhere else" to remove her from the Manichean world in which there is no psychic or social space for someone such as herself, Cliff seeks to *actualize* that location of "elsewhere" for Clare by creating within her novels a geopolitical space of memory arising from Clare's slave owner, slave, and Arawak ancestry. In this way she deconstructs the traditional historical, chronological narrative, with its understanding that the "conclusion" allows us to elucidate the meaning of the history. In the history of the Caribbean, the "conclusion" of which was one of slavery, colonization, and consequent Third World status, the historical narrative has functioned to contain or erase other histories by reading the region solely in terms of how it served to construct the historical realities of Europe or America.

Barbara Harlowe notes that narratives of resistance must not only undo hegemonic recorded history, but they must also invent new forms of encoding resistance by inventing spaces of resistance.[55] West Indian authors similarly emphasize the spatial aspect of narrative for West Indian literature. Wilson Harris suggests that the "authentic" West Indian novel uses the historical memory of the land, with its unknown past and infinite possibilities, to deconstruct the colonizer/colonized opposition and thus destabilize the subject/object relation of European discourse to West Indian literature.[56] Others, notably Alejandro Carpentier, have advocated magical realism as a way of recovering the true history of the region. But as Selwyn Cudjoe observes, what they understand to be the "magical" properties of West Indian history — conquistadores, obeah, an extinct Amerindian culture — are in fact based on a *critical* understanding of reality, and that as such West Indian narrative should not be read as circular but rather as a spiral, not a repetition but an extension, what he terms a "critical realism."[57]

This is a useful concept for explicating Cliff's narrative in that Cliff explicitly seeks to *rewrite* and yet not to *repeat* history. In the following

passage we hear the "official" history of Jamaica, one which resurrects
Naipaul's vision of West Indian history ("We pretended to be real . . .
we mimic men of the New World" who are irretrievably "sunk in the
taint of fantasy"),[58] but infuses it with different meaning:

> These are the facts as I believe them. But as you no doubt are well aware, there
> are no facts in Jamaica. Not one single fact. Nothing to join us to the real. Facts
> move around you. Magic moves through you. This we have been taught. This
> fact that there are no facts. Wait. I can call up one fact. "The adamantine refusal
> of the slave-women to reproduce" — a historian report that. What of Game-
> some, Lusty Ann, Counsellor's Cuba, Strumpet called Skulker — not race-
> horses, mi dear, women: barren. Four furious cool-dark sistren. Is nuh fact dat?
> Fact yes, but magic mek it so. (92)

By blending the voice of the "official" history, which denies that there is
a history, with the oral transmission of historical resistance encoded in
the "magical" narrative of myth, the passage reveals historical representation in *discourse* to be the site of conflict. This political fusion of
fact and fiction ("magic") becomes a female project: black slave women
as magic-makers, producers of the "fictions" of Jamaica, re-create the
"facts" of Jamaica history. The "fact" is shown to be fictional (the
distorted interpretation of black women's "refusal to reproduce"); and
the "fiction" is shown to be fact (the women's "refusal" is the result of
obeah, part of a specifically female tradition of resistance to slavery).

The conclusion of No Telephone, in which the international, multiracial, socially, and sexually diverse band of guerrillas attack the film
set and are in turn attacked by the military, is an ironic replication of
the failed revolutionary actions of the male-authored narratives. Unlike
its predecessors, however, No Telephone highlights its engagement not
with material revolution and the whys and wherefores of its failure, but
rather with the discursive formulations of revolution. Clare's last memory is of sounds: patois, English, bird noises. The reduction of revolutionary action to basic components of language suggests that before the
material revolution can be actualized, there must be a revolution of
words, of the values and determinants of language, symbols, names.

Earlier in the story Harry/Harriet signals to us that the real enemy is
the narrative construction of history and violence, which has impris-
oned all of the historical players in fixed racial, political, and sexual

roles. Entering an expensive restaurant with a swashbuckling pirate colonial theme, s/he says:

"Of course, if they were really imaginative . . . they would hang some whips and chains on the walls, dress the waiters in loincloths, have the barmaid bare her breasts, and call the whole sorry mess the Middle Passage . . . these places bring out the worst in me . . . especially since I know I am more welcome here than I would be in a rumshop at Matilda's Corner. . . . Our homeland is turned to stage set too much." (121)

With Harry/Harriet's observation that his relative acceptance by the island's elite is due not to tolerance but class mores comes the realization that Caribbean historical identities — racial and sexual — have become so shaped by the stereotyped distortions of hegemonic discourse that, like Marshall's Caliban, the distortions threaten to become that identity: the Caribbean has become the "stage set," the performance of itself.

Among elite Jamaican society, the radical sexual identity of Harry/ Harriet is rendered harmless because he is perceived as only one more performance among many performances, one that cannot change the material conditions of power and powerlessness. The privileged site of performance, consequently, is also the place wherein is produced the language and the categories which will inflict "real," material consequences on those who are forced to identify themselves through those performances.

In one sense, Cliff's emphasis on the centrality of language and canonical fictions in the colonizing project brings her into line with McKay, Lamming, and James. In another, her critique of the limitations of literary mastery as a resistance tool marks her departure from the male West Indian tradition of revolutionary discourse because, for Cliff, revolutionary engagement can only begin by the de(con)struction of the narrative itself. The deconstructive narrative by its very nature is decentralized, such that Clare, who starts out as the heir apparent to the gentleman scholar legacy, concludes by vanishing altogether in a whirlpool of the sounds of life. Like *Banana Bottom, No Telephone to Heaven* poses the problem of how to re-integrate the educated female, the gentleman heir apparent, back into Caribbean society. Unlike McKay, however, Cliff does not — and cannot — conceive of the Caribbean as an idyllic space, untouched by colonialism, to do so. Clare's status as a descendant of slave owners makes such mythification impossible, even dangerous. Consequently, the character's final dissolution into the landscape symbolizes the only way in which Cliff's white creole female ultimately can be re-integrated under the terms that the novel has set up: like Rhys's Antoinette, she must die. However, Clare's death does not signify the impossibility of the fact of whiteness within a transformed, liberated Caribbean. Rather, it suggests the necessity for a transformation of the *meaning* of whiteness into something that is ultimately indistinguishable from Caribbeanness itself.

6

RETURN OF THE NATIVE:

IMMIGRANT WOMEN'S WRITING AND

THE NARRATIVE OF EXILE

[O]ne of the things that was talked a lot about among the women was the nostalgic memory of home as they called it, home. It was very early on that I had a sense of a distinct difference between home, *which had to do with the West Indies, and* this country, *which had to do with the United States . . . I think it began then an interest in this place that was so important to these women and that I began to sense it was important in whomever I was going to discover myself to be.* — Paule Marshall

There was such a crowd of immigrant-type West Indians on the boat-train platform at Waterloo that I was glad I was travelling first class to the West Indies. — V. S. Naipaul, opening sentence, *The Middle Passage*

Naipaul's comment on his return to the West Indies might easily be mistaken for that of a somewhat xenophobic European traveling to the West Indies who eschews contact — bodily or otherwise — with the distasteful, "immigrant-type" natives. But no: Naipaul is both a native of the West Indies and an immigrant to England himself. His authorial positioning belies his origins, as surely it is meant to do, even as he explains later that he "had never wanted to stay in Trinidad," that even after he had emigrated to England he had been "awakened by the nightmare that [he] was back in tropical Trinidad." Now, as a newly minted upper-class member of the First World, with all the weight of metropolitan approbation to arm him, Naipaul is indeed traveling "first class," in more ways than one.

Across the other side of the Atlantic, Paule Marshall contemplates a "return" to a "home" she has never seen because of the powerful reflections on home by her mother and the women who congregated in her kitchen. For the young Marshall, the West Indies is a place to discover not simply her origins but who she *will* be: the key to her future self is tied up in the mystery of this unseen home. Unlike Naipaul, who though *associated* with the First World is not *native* to it, Marshall *is* in fact a native of the First World, a second-generation West Indian child of immigrants born in the United States. The native status of either means very little, ultimately, in the way they are interpreted, both by themselves and by the reader. Naipaul's and Marshall's strikingly different relationship to the idea of the native land and a "return" to that land is tied to the currency of two key words in the Caribbean author's lexicon: "exile" and "immigrant."

These two related yet opposed terms of national subjectivity carry a weight of meaning in the literary history of the anglophone Caribbean. As we have seen, a first generation of Caribbean writers wrote "in exile," usually in London or, in the case of the French Caribbean, Paris. Naipaul is the most famous of these Caribbean writers in self-imposed "exile," yet Naipaul is certainly not the only West Indian who has positioned himself thus or indeed the first to gain currency from this particular relationship to the Caribbean. There are scores of books on West Indian narrative which feature the term "exile" prominently, and one can scarcely find a text on Caribbean literature that does not refer to the canonical figures as "writing in exile."[1] The exile referred to is conceived of as a kind of double exile. On the one hand, there is the internal exile of the intellectual from society as an alienated or inauthentic West Indian subject (a concession to Lamming's vision of the peasantry as the authentic West Indian subject). On the other, there is the exile of self-imposed physical displacement from the Caribbean from which the author can now "objectively" view his society and his relation to it. The premise undergirding the latter view is that physical distance in the metropole is necessary for eventual reintegration into the Caribbean landscape, such as what Bita Plant must undergo in *Banana Bottom*.

McKay and writers in exile such as Lamming and James conceive of this kind of exile then as a necessary component of *nationalism*, and indeed Edward Said contends that "the interplay between nationalism and exile is like Hegel's dialectic of servant and master, oppositions informing and constituting each other. All nationalisms in their early stages develop from a condition of estrangement."[2] However, the fact that exile for West Indian writers means choosing to live in the country of the colonizer from whom he seeks relief at home causes, as Lamming delicately puts it, "certain complications."[3] Certainly, Lamming's choice of England is made easy because his generation owned British passports at the time of leaving. But it is of key importance that our literary symbol of nationalist in exile, Bita, travels to England to be *educated* and thus cannot be confused with a mere immigrant who goes there to work.

Unlike exile and nationalism, *immigration* and nationalism are not perceived to have any relationship to each other. The immigrant's motives are to make money (often, in the case of West Indian women — who constitute the largest portion of West Indian immigrants to the United States[4] — to support families "back home"); her focus is on "making it" in the metropole, as opposed to the apparently loftier aims of the exile, who remains preoccupied with the *meaning* of the native land in one way (Naipaul) or another (Lamming). (This is not to say that menial labor was not a part of the experiences of the Caribbean male writers who migrated to England. It would not be unlikely that these men had at some point to do some such work or perhaps even be supported by women who did. At any rate, this possibility does not negate the way in which their migrant experiences are translated and/or transformed into the trope of exile, both in their fiction and nonfiction.)

The *reasons* for traveling to the metropole, then, the conditions of that journey, are by far of more importance than the fact of actually being there, because the capacity in which the West Indian travels to that society will dictate how that society will "read" her. Consequently, the writer in exile is likely to have a different sort of experience of the First World because of her ability to illustrate a privileged relation to the signifiers of the professional educated class of the West.

Unlike the exile, the immigrant author brings no cultural capital to bear in her invocation of literary authority. In contrast to the glamoured image of the educated — if tortured — exile, thinking and writing in a "cultured" cosmopolitan center where he can finally be understood, the image of the immigrant calls to mind very different scenarios: depressing urban sweatshops and low-status jobs; physical, not intellectual, labor.

The question of commercial and cultural value undergirds the importance of these signifiers, and their value is predicated on their *power* to
invoke authority. As such, my intent in this chapter is to illustrate how
these terms have acquired gendered connotations in anglophone Caribbean narrative through their status as signifiers of commercial or cultural power elsewhere. These connotations affect the author's construction of both the authorial self and that self's relation to the nation
which is being written into existence. Despite his distinctly antinationalist views of the West Indies, the example of V. S. Naipaul is important to
our discussion because his positioning among the categories of "exile,"
"West Indian," and "modernist" is paradigmatic of that of the male
West Indian writers of exile generally. Since I argue that these structuring categories operate *beyond* the more narrowly political aims of the
writers themselves, the choice of Naipaul as one who does *not* seek "reintegration" with the homeland is a strategic one.

V. S. Naipaul and the Genealogy of Exile

In 1986 V. S. Naipaul received the T. S. Eliot Award, which honors authors "of abiding importance whose works affirm the moral principles
of Western Civilization"; in 1990 he was knighted by the queen of
England. Not surprising, in the words of one Indian writer, because Naipaul is "England's favourite nineteenth-century Englishman."[5] The link
between Eliot, the high priest of modernism, and the model of the Victorian gentleman scholar, inform the interpretations of Naipaul's literary
importance at every turn. It would indeed seem that exile, for Naipaul,
has effectively *made* him an Englishman, as it did the American-born
Eliot. (Eliot's modernism, like Naipaul's, ultimately affirms the ideology
of empire, if only in the nostalgia he exhibits for lost — or, in Naipaul's
case, inaccessible — traditions.) Naipaul's pivotal status as a canonical
figure within Western literature (a position he covets) and as a central
inhabitant of the West Indian canon (a position he rejects)[6] is the result
of Naipaul's paradoxical embrace of both modernist and Victorian
sensibilities.

   In his excellent study on Naipaul, Rob Nixon identifies Naipaul's
continuing appeal to the West as his ability to place himself as the
quintessential neutral observer to world events, a position he has ex-
acted by strategically manipulating the terms of exile, nationality, and

Third World status.[7] Certainly Naipaul's description of exile — "one's lack of representation in the world; one's lack of status"[8] — smacks of a certain disingenuousness, given the mileage he has extracted from this condition (as have most writers in exile). The First World also has an investment in "reading" Naipaul in this fashion, according to Nixon:

If critical opinion in Britain and the United States hymns Naipaul as the consummately neutral observer he purports to be, and shares his personal preoccupation with his checkered provenance, this state of affairs is evidently to the advantage of both parties. As a racial East Indian and a natal West Indian, and . . . as one of the wretched of the South exiled in the North, he is treated as qualified to speak as "universal man" in whom all the vectors of geographical bias are perfectly canceled. Unencumbered by the embarrassment of a white skin, born in and associated with the globe's margins, Naipaul can be strategically invoked as a Third World counterweight to opinions that prove discomfiting to the Western hegemony.[9]

The reification of the Naipaulian vision as one of objective detachment is in fact an expression of a *geographic* space, the "nowhereness" that implies "everywhereness" and gives Naipaul both the moral and the *spatial* advantage in critique. The Somewhere Elseness that has been the obstacle to West Indian literary agency becomes, under these conditions, an arena of authority precisely by its negation of place. That is, if the invocation of the Victorian gentleman becomes the "capital" to replace the (nonexistent) ownership of the land under one's feet for the first generation of West Indian writers, the value of that capital is made manifest by the erasure of the *desire* for material land interests.

The ideological corollary to this camouflaging of national connections is the ideal of objectivity, which Naipaul claims for himself: "I think that one reason why my journalism can last is because I never had any such ideas about Left or Right. One just looked at what had happened. There are no principles involved in one's vision."[10] Naipaul's belief in his own objectivity is repeated by First World critics, who refuse to connect him to the vulgarities of political ideology. Their iconizing of Naipaul as a representative of modern objectivity is reminiscent of the central role that English literature as a discipline played in early twentieth-century England, where it was deemed to be a sort of transcendent Truth, above the narrowness of class and political concerns (see my discussion in chapter 2). The erection of this vision of literature coincides with the rise of modernism as the articulation of a transcendent vision of Culture that is both egalitarian and politically nonpartisan. Given that it is modernism and modernist writers such as Eliot who bestowed upon the term "exile" such exalted cultural status, the relationship of modernism to West Indian exile writing assumes crucial dimensions in the assessment of the latter's literary value.

Exile implies, as we have seen, a distance from and therefore an understood "objectivity" toward the place of origin, the "homeland." It also implies enforced banishment, the condition of political enemies of a nation—dethroned monarchs, writers whose novels inspire dissent, and so forth. "Exile" is usually *defined* in terms of ex*patria*tion, the state of being driven away by some "law" or "edict" from one's native land, explains Shari Benstock. Thus, "exile" is "etymologically conjoined with the law of the father/ruler whose law effects and enforces expatriating."[11] However, Nixon contends that

exile, in the domain of literary history, possesses a very specific genealogy that by this stage has less to do with banishment and ostracism than with a powerful current of twentieth-century literary expectations in the West. Writers domiciled overseas . . . commonly imagine and describe themselves as living in exile because it is a term privileged by high modernism and associated with the emergence of the metropolis as a crucible for a more international, though still European- or American-based culture.[12]

Simon Gikandi challenges this reading in the Caribbean context, arguing that, unlike the European literary experience, "exile is not a subjective quest by the Caribbean avant-garde to escape their fixed and fetishized places in the colonial culture." He goes on to quote Jean D'Costa and Barbara Lalla, editors of a collection of eighteenth- and nineteenth-century Jamaican texts: " 'The experience of exile is central to Jamaican history and to the making of language in a Jamaica which spelled banishment for most of its people.' "[13]

D'Costa and Lalla are referring to both the exile of the black Jamaican slaves from their native Africa, and that of the English landowners and overseers who would rather be home in England. What Gikandi's example does not address, however, is the question of the *consequences* of this ancient exile for the black West Indian subject. An eighteenth-century black slave speaking in the banished African mother tongue is in danger of colonial retribution; a twentieth-century black West Indian intellectual writing novels in English, hardly. The relationship of the anglophone Caribbean writer "in exile" to the state is distinctly different from that of, say, African writers in exile, who have often received swift and severe punishment for their literary critiques of the state.[14] The difference between the two finds its basis in the originary relationship of the English-speaking Caribbean to Victorian England, where, as I discuss in chapter 1, the aims of the latter to produce "gentlemen" in the former is tied to England's vision of the Caribbean as a crossroads of civilization and savagery. If authorship is a gentlemanly attribute, then the very act of literary production in the Caribbean necessarily has a very different — more benign — relation to the state's conception of itself. Exile may well be necessary for the Caribbean writer but not necessarily under the same conditions as for African or other Third World writers.

Therefore, I would like to suggest an alternative reading of Caribbean "exile" that takes into account both Benstock's and Nixon's formulations. I wish to gain from the former the gendered connotations it reveals within the term, and in the latter, the classed connotations therein ("class" referring here to global hierarchies that position the "developed" countries of the West at the top of the global social ladder). The clarification of these meanings of exile should illuminate my reading of the return of Naipaul and Marshall to the Caribbean homeland.

If exile for Benstock is predicated on the banishment of the writer by patriarchal authority, the place "he" is banished *from*, the native land, the "matria," is maternalized. Similarly, Freud equates exile from one's native land with exile from the mother: the nostalgia for the home country is in actuality a nostalgia for the mother's body.[15] The land-as-mother thus plays the "object" to the exile's "subject" status. A return of the exile to the "motherland" is then a reappropriation of it. The *matria* is the "internal exclusion" of *patria*, "the other by and through which patria is defined." Its exclusion or "exile" therefore is the very condition of patriarchy's existence, since "*matria* is always ex*patriated*."[16] Benstock's argument builds upon Luce Irigaray's assertion that Western patriarchal culture is founded on a "symbolic matricide." This symbolic function of women leads to women's exile *as women* within patriarchal culture. Irigaray believes that because the woman-mother constitutes the foundation of patriarchy, the nation itself, she cannot exist as a subject *within* the patriarchal nation: "And so woman will not yet have taken [a] place . . . Experienced as all-powerful where 'she' is most radically powerless in her indifferentiation. Never here and now because she is that everywhere elsewhere from whence the 'subject' continues to draw his reserves, his re-sources, yet unable to recognize them/her."[17] This reading suggests that, contrary to the public association of exile with masculine status, its hidden, real meaning is to be found in the female role, which is always/already exiled from national subject status that it yet constructs.

However, the limitation of this reading is that it cannot account for Naipaul — or indeed other writers in self-imposed exile — for whom the primary emotion elicited by the motherland is not nostalgia but ambivalence or even repulsion, unless we reconsider that colonialism is, like Irigaray's "woman," a state of perpetual exile in, of, and *from* itself.[18] Read this way, Naipaul is exiled from *two* nations in a sense: from the Caribbean homeland, which he believes not to exist in a historical sense and therefore which could never have, figuratively speaking, "birthed" him as a latter-day Victorian writer. More importantly, he is psychically exiled from *England*, the homeland of his literary ancestors, with its "real" traditions and history. Naipaul's longing for a literary and cultural tradition within which to place himself could then be read as a displaced desire for the *father*'s body, which would confer masculine origins on the writer. However, if the father is always the subject, and never the object, and the body is always already objectified, then in a symbolic sense the father's body can never be found, since it can never exist. And so the difference in Naipaul's exile lies precisely in the illusion of its bodilessness; that is, in its apparent *lack* of material, geographic, or even biological origins.

Furthermore, the desire for origins sketched in the accounts of Irigaray and Freud seems to belong more precisely to Marshall's female-centered perspective of the unseen home, which is linked very explicitly to the real mothers who congregated in her family kitchen. The "elsewhereness" that Irigaray invokes as the place to which the silenced maternal subject is figuratively exiled reappears in Nixon's description of Naipaul's ontological "nowhereness" which, far from silencing and objectifying him, is instrumental in assigning to him literary authority and *power*. "Nowhereness" can confer authority or obscurity, depending on the historical conditions of writing, of which gender is a key component. What has become a useful space for Naipaul, Lamming, and James, then, is a liability for Rhys. The feminizing of the *condition* of exile found here—as opposed to the (masculinized) social meaning of it—is thus useful in explaining Jean Rhys's outsider status within traditional Caribbean discourse.

Exile and Caribbean Modernism

As the first internationally acclaimed female writer from the anglophone Caribbean, Jean Rhys provides a significant link in our discussion of exile and its relationship to the discourse of modernism. A member—albeit a marginalized one—of the influential modernist writers who congregated in Paris and London after World War One, Rhys nevertheless had initial trouble gaining acceptance because of her ambiguous national status. The interpretations of her works are noticeably tied to critical perception of her relation to the Caribbean.[19] Rhys's status as a modernist writer was problematic in two registers. Women writers even within modernist circles were often left out of critical discussions of modernism, their works often deemed "old-fashioned or of merely anecdotal interest" since modernism was "unconsciously gendered masculine," according to Bonnie Kime Scott.[20] Further, Rhys's exile status—in the sense that she lived and wrote in London— far from gaining her acceptance as an author of Caribbean literature, seemed to actually work *against* her. Naipaul himself notes that Rhys's problem is, like his own, one of audience: she has no "home audience to play to; she was outside that tradition of imperial-expatriate writing in which the metropolitan outsider is thrown into relief against an alien background."[21] Rhys herself believed that the status of her work was determined by irrational editorial policies that revealed an obsession with her national status: "I thought, Am I an expatriate? Expatriate from where? So began several months of writing short stories and having them torn to pieces or praised for reasons I did not understand."[22]

Naipaul's observation on Rhys contains a certain amount of irony for contemporary readers, as we note his own location within the "imperial-expatriate" literary tradition. Naipaul's ability to write like a Victorian about the very non-Victorian subject of the displaced East Indian West Indian has proved the winning combination in gaining him admittance to the West Indian canon (see my discussion in chapter 3).

By contrast, Rhys's detailing of the ambivalent and compromised relationship of the white creole female to West Indian society in *Wide Sargasso Sea*, written in high modernist style, is effectively rejected not only because of the author's whiteness — though that is a key issue — but because her narrative is one of racial and gender dislocation, embodied *within* the modernist structuring of her narrative (multiple points of views, nonlinear time frame, and so forth). Rhys is *not* writing like a West Indian, which means she has not utilized modernism to recover West Indian identity per se but rather to articulate the fragmentation of that identity. Naipaul, whose subject is also the fragmention of West Indian identity, is nevertheless perceived to be writing within a literary tradition. Tradition, in and of itself, is part of a national literary imperative.

Rhys's problems in an earlier Caribbean discourse stem from the idea that the modernist project has become, within the West Indian canon, associated specifically with the recovery of *black* (or, in the case of Wilson Harris, indigenous peoples')[23] identity. Modernism and becoming modernized here are made out to be the same project, though of course these are not particularly so in European narrative, where the suspicion of modernization has given rise to modernism. Modernism's rethematization in anglophone Caribbean narrative as a means to recover rather than to destabilize the idea of the nation is linked to an ongoing discussion within black diaspora discourse on the specifically *modern* meaning of blackness. It is part of the paradox of modernism in Caribbean discourse that the ideas of modernism lead so many writers (Lamming, Marson, and McKay, for instance) not to the avant-garde form but rather to the folk pastoral (see my discussion in chapter 3). However, the problem inherent to modernism's Caribbean rethematization is in its race politics. For Rhys and Naipaul, as nonblack West Indian writers, modernism can never reveal a utopian folk community, since the genesis of the folk pastoral is so clearly about black desire for an identifiably black West Indian historical tradition. It is, ironically enough, their ties to Englishness that finally link them to blackness as it is thus framed in the West Indian literary context.

Paul Gilroy and Manthia Diawara, among others, cite blackness, in its originary moment within the slave trade, as a specifically modern condition.[24] Similarly, because the advent of blackness also meant the advent of slavery and imperialism, the *historical* meaning of modernity has always presented problems for the West Indian author. Modernism became useful as a way of recuperating blackness in modernity because of its critique of bourgeois nineteenth-century cultural models. Indeed, in the heyday of modernism European artists, writers, and intellectuals plumbed the depths of African and African American life and art for a rejuvenating alternative to what they perceived as the sterility of the "civilized" white world.[25] As such, it will be useful here to briefly survey the origins of modernism itself.

Edward Said has argued that the literary purveyors of modernism, the New Critics, tried to dissociate themselves from the "filiations" of the great Western literary tradition by replacing the hegemony of filiation with that of "affiliation." That is, the ideology of modern Western Culture itself, symbolized by the ideas of the progenitors of Culture (namely, Sigmund Freud, Northrop Frye, and other modernist icons), became the central force of interpretation. These ideas were deemed to be part of the international New World Order, so to speak, and not the inheritance of particular national legacies.[26] Literary meaning thus was produced not by private filiative systems which linked the individual to family, class, and country, but rather through immersion into the larger, transcendent values of Culture itself. This system was supposed to democratically reorganize the indices of what constitutes Culture and Meaning by doing away with the old feudal system of attachments so that the individual gained primacy and could articulate dissent and alienation within the New Order.

This supposed democratization of the canon is probably why so many West Indian writers — and critics of West Indian writing — interpret their work within the frame of the modernist tradition.[27] Thus it was that modernism became linked to the modernity of *modernization*, and this version of modernity meant independence, cultural as well as political. This being said, I am well aware that there are different registers to the meaning of "modernity" in historical, philosophical, and literary discourses. The advent of Columbus and the European "discoverers" in the New World is usually the starting point for the modern period in historical terms; the Enlightenment period of the eighteenth century is the beginning of the philosophies that we associate with modernity; but the rapid industrialization and cultural changes in twentieth-century Western society that are associated with contemporary notions of modernity and *modernization*, and from which modernism originated, is the version of modernity with which my discussion here is concerned.

Roberto González Echevarría has observed that "Latin America as a concept and as a political reality was created at the outset of modernity ... at the historical juncture that also brought into being the question of cultural existence, both as a question and as a conceptual need."[28] This statement applies equally to the Caribbean. If we extrapolate from its implications, then we can link the meaning of modernism in the Caribbean context to modernity itself, since the very *creation* of the Caribbean as a Western, geopolitical artifact has its origins in Europe's "discovery" of the region. Modernism brings with it, for the Caribbean writer, not simply the destruction of Old World conventions and ideas, but the *un*covery of the origins of the nation itself in modernity.

Wilson Harris has argued for the liberating potential of modernism in the Caribbean context. He believes that the term implies "an ongoing and unceasing revisionary and innovative strategy that has its roots in the deepest layers of that past that still address us."[29] Yet because the relations between the Caribbean and England were fixed within Victorian discourse, there is always slippage between the modernist trajectory of interpretation and the Victorian ethos from which springs the oppositional nature of the Caribbean narrative; for, as Said points out, the modernist vision of Culture was utilized to effectively differentiate what *is* Culture from what is *not* — and for our purposes to define what constitutes the Great Novel against a plethora of narrative from all quarters of democratized society.

Naipaul's positioning as modernist writer with Victorian sensibilities gains from this tension between modernist and Victorian appropriations precisely because of his status as Third World subject — and therefore the recipient of modernist egalitarian munificence — and First World visionary. He provides the link whereby the project of imperial dominance established by the Victorian gentleman scholar of letters can be continued, albeit in rerouted form; paradoxically, his location between the two systems of discourse provides the rationale for the relegation of the Third World to the periphery of First World discourse. From the vantage point of the metropole, exile has managed to purge Naipaul of his racial and cultural signifiers even as it allows him to invoke precisely those qualities as a means of showing that, in the new global literary order, they do not matter.

From the vantage point of the Caribbean, however, Naipaul's sojourn in London is also "raced" in particular ways as a Caribbean writer abroad. C. L. R. James articulates race as the critical criterion for the Caribbean writer who writes from England. Though he was a part of the influential Beacon literary circle in Trinidad during the 1930s, he realized that while the white writers in the group could stay in the West Indies and hone their talents, "we were black and the only way we could do anything along the lines we were interested in was by going abroad; that's how I grew up."[30] He compares his options to those of white Trinidadian writers such as Albert Gomes and Alfred Mendes, who "went the other way"; that is, who stayed in Trinidad or went to the United States:

Albert Gomes told me the other day: "You know the difference between all of you and me? you all went away; I stayed." I didn't tell him what I could have told him: "You stayed . . . because your skin was white; there was a chance for you, but for us there wasn't — except to be a civil servant and hand papers, take them from the men downstairs and hand them to the man upstairs." We *had* to go, whereas Mendes could go to the United States and learn to practise his writing, because he was white and had money.[31]

James recognizes that, as a nonwhite West Indian, he was effectively dispossessed from his own homeland such that he could only reclaim his space and therefore his national identity by going abroad to a space outside of the Manichean allegory that filled all the possibilities of the West Indian space. (Naipaul himself links his metropolitan desires to James's, noting with bemusement that they have both "charmed [them]selves away from Trinidad.")[32] Yet there is an implicit *class* imperative here; in order for James to write about himself and his nation he cannot be the civil servant running errands up and down the stairs, but presumably must occupy a position similar to Mendes's where he does not have to work at such belittling jobs but can "practise writing." Also significant is the connection of Mendes as a writer within the United States; why is Mendes's residence in the United States not a reflection of exile? Why is the United States not an option for James and his cohorts?

I submit that it was not possible for the West Indian writer to be "exiled" in the United States at that time, given the implications and resonances that the term carries. The relationship of the Caribbean peoples to the United States, particularly during the 1930s, was one of heavily economic immigration. For Gomes to write in America is for Gomes to continue to be white; that is, he joins other white immigrants in the United States who effectively use whiteness as a class option by establishing their difference from American blacks, regardless of socioeconomic background. For James to go to the United States would be for James to lose even the class privilege he possesses in the Caribbean by submergence into the underside of the monolithic American racial equation. By contrast, England contained a history whereby black middle-class men from the Caribbean and Africa could be granted privileged status there as gentlemen.

The paradox for this generation of early West Indian writers was that in order to write as a West Indian one had to, in essence, "make the case" for West Indian literary authority by appealing to an audience established elsewhere. Lamming's and McKay's depiction of the peasantry is meant to argue its merits as a reflection of "authentic" West Indian society. However, their arguments are aimed, not at the peasant, but rather at the metropolitan reader who, understanding modernism's critique of the bankruptcy of Western metropolitan civilization, would be open to an idea that has already been promulgated by such canonical luminaries as D. H. Lawrence.[33] (Though McKay writes from within the United States, his constructed audience is similar to Lamming's in the sense that his fiction gestures to the understanding of literary primitivism found in the global metropoles of London and New York, as opposed to the homeland, to make its claims.) Therefore, when Naipaul expresses anxiety about his audience for *The Middle Passage*, he nevertheless has an idea that, though the book has been commissioned by the Caribbean (through then Prime Minister of Trinidad Eric Williams), because he writes from the vantage point of a "travel writer," its readership *should not* be Caribbean but instead, the First World: "Especially I was aware of not having a metropolitan audience to 'report back' to. The fight between my idea of the glamour of the travel-writer and the rawness of my nerves as a colonial traveling among colonials made for difficult writing."[34] His anxiety stems from his assumption that the writer writes for his own nation; Naipaul wishes to rid himself of his West Indian identity, and that is a large part of the problem, but his conflict in measure obtains for the others. The exiled West Indian writer is in a double bind, since he is attempting to establish a national identity for his region through an oppositional relationship to the metropole, which yet constitutes his residential base and primary audience.

Wilson Harris has argued that the West Indian novel needs to be dissociated from its moorings in the Victorian novel so that it can articulate the specificity of the Caribbean experience.[35] The use of the conventions of the Victorian "novel of persuasion" to convey a revolutionary agenda was paradoxical and inconsistent, he argued. Yet Harris's own narrative experiments rely on — indeed are based on — an intimate knowledge of modernist narrative theories, such that his reading public is, as C. L. R. James complained in an introduction to one of Harris's essays, "confined to London."[36] Therefore, for this generation of West Indian writers, the meaning of their texts is critically mediated by this tension between their construction of nation, interpretive community or reading public, and their self-creation as authors. The nation that is the focus of the oppositional narrative, its central subject, becomes the object around which the West Indian author negotiates the terms of his inclusion into the internationally framed modernist canon. However, the narrative moment in which the nation is invoked is also the moment at which the nation figuratively disappears from the story, displaced by the meaning of nationlessness (and therefore, universality) that the exile carries within himself *as* exile. The Caribbean is displaced from the margins of metropolitan discourse only to be (mis?)placed at its center, positioned there in the newfound celebrity of the Caribbean writer in exile.

Immigrants and Authorship: The Case of Women Writers

Whether the neoconservative Naipaul or the left-leaning Walcott, Lamming, or James, Caribbean male writers in exile have been acclaimed by the critics of England. Derek Walcott has been called "as noble, stern and grand as Milton"; Naipaul, "the most gifted novelist writing in English today"; and James, the "Black Plato of our generation."[37] The comparisons to the canonical figures of European literature are noteworthy not simply because they signify a willingness to accept these writers into the Western canonical tradition but because they signify their *exoticism* in Western literary discourse. These writers represent a new tradition of letters; as West Indian authors, they are *firsts*.

Jean Rhys, acclaimed as she is in contemporary English discourse, is not likely to be called "the West Indian Plato" or compared to Milton. Writing as a woman places Rhys into a more uncertain tradition of letters. There can be no invocation of the Victorian *gentleman* of letters to make her case as a West Indian; unlike the male writers, at the time of writing she was not presumed to be engaged in the project of writing the Caribbean into existence, "simply" writing as she did about women.[38] Hence she cannot draw on the cultural power of exile status. Furthermore, according to Rhys herself, women writers in England in the early twentieth century, far from being accorded the same level of respect as their male counterparts, were often perceived as "freaks."[39] Neither is there a tradition of West Indian women's literature at the time of her writing, so she cannot draw from that either.[40] The difficulty of her position as a West Indian woman writer without a West Indian female reading audience finds an echo in her short story, "The Day They Burned the Books."[41]

The hero of the story is a mulatto boy called Eddie Sawyer, whose father is a white Englishman, his mother a "coloured" West Indian woman. We are told that he is a rebel who "first infected [the narrator] with doubts about 'home', meaning England" (153). The father hates the West Indies — perhaps, we are made to understand, because "he wasn't a gentleman" like the other Englishmen — and insults his wife when he is drunk, saying, "Look at the nigger showing off" (152). After his death Mrs. Sawyer divides the father's books into the ones that she can sell and the less valuable ones, which she intends to burn.

One of the "saved" books is Froude's *English in the West Indies*, further underscoring the metaphorical parallel of Mr. Sawyer's relationship to his wife and Froude's relationship to the West Indies. The boy resists the destruction of his father's books, crying "Now I've got to hate you too," but Mrs. Sawyer persists. The narrator, a young white West Indian girl, notes that Mrs. Sawyer holds a particular hatred for the books by women: "by a flicker of Mrs. Sawyer's eyes I knew that worse than men who wrote books were women who wrote books. . . . Men could be mercifully shot; women must be tortured" (46).

Mrs. Sawyer, though she is a "nicely educated coloured woman," has been placed outside the realm of intellectual labor. It is her apparently uneducated English husband — "who hadn't an 'h' in his composition" — who is the consumer of literary knowledge, and she hates him for it. Mrs. Sawyer, who has been educated *like* a gentleman, can never *be* one, but her husband, who has not been, as an Englishman can invoke the authority of one. The books represent a tradition of Englishness of which she — black, female, alien — can have no part, a tradition of racism which has given her husband the authority to abuse both her blackness and education as insignificant (the "nigger" is merely "showing off"). If "home" in her world is inverted to mean England, a place she has never seen, Mrs. Sawyer is doubly displaced. She is made an exile within her West Indian home, as well as made *immigrant* in the illusory "home" of England since, as a black woman, she cannot claim a filial relation to England in the manner that the white West Indians do. Nor can she claim a relation based on her "purchase" of the literary authority of the Victorian gentleman, as do her black male counterparts (see my discussion of Rhys's "Again the Antilles" in chapter 2).

Significantly, her hatred extends particularly to women writers. The burning of the books signals her act of rebellion against the meaning of those books as symbolic artifacts of English superiority. Yet in the burning of the books Mrs. Sawyer also symbolically destroys the possibility that she, too, might be able to write books in opposition to this totalizing discourse. Eddie says of his mother, "She can't make up a story to save her life." What she does do, he says, is "tell lies." The difference between "story" and "lie" echoes the "raced" difference between "history" and "myth" that has traditionally consigned the unwritten history of the black and nonwhite Caribbean to the status of "myth." If written history is "truth," then what is not written is a "lie."[42] Since the reader understands that Eddie's anger at his mother stems from the fact that he cannot face the knowledge of his father's abuse of his mother, then the reader must also recognize that Mrs. Sawyer's "lies" are, in fact, the truth.

Eddie, as the "inheritor" of his father's books — the "stories" (or "lies") of English culture — understands that his mother is destroying the literary tradition which is meant for him and to which he can gain access as a man. The mother's decision to save the books which have commercial value underscores her outsider status to literary production: she must make money, she must survive, and the books can only have value as they can maintain her survival. We are made to understand that her actions are philistine, if understandable. Thus, while Eddie represents the potential for West Indian male appropriation of the canon, Mrs. Sawyer, resentful at her exclusion from the world of letters, represents the impossibility of a Caribbean female writing or reading community.

Rhys's pessimistic view of a possible West Indian female reading public provides a useful contrast to Cliff's image of Clare Savage in *No Telephone to Heaven*, who as an immigrant West Indian female student in the United States is similarly excluded from the possibility of "owning" the tradition of letters (see my discussion of Clare Savage in chapter 5). Cliff, like Marshall or Kincaid, must also negotiate the gap between the idea of the "author," in its received West Indian/English context, and the "female." Like Rhys, they do not reside in the Caribbean, but unlike Rhys, they are residents of the United States rather than England.

The shifting of the London/Caribbean axis to the United States is clearly linked to the shift in migration patterns after the independence of the British colonies, when North America, not Britain, became the mecca for Caribbean peoples seeking economic prosperity. As I have already discussed, this emigration out of the Caribbean, particularly in the last twenty-five years, has been of a heavily female nature, owing particularly to the burgeoning market in domestic work. Many social scientists have noted that the large influx of Caribbean women who have migrated to metropolitan centers such as New York since the 1970s have been attracted by the chance of employment in a range of domestic services, especially with the huge expansion of the service sector in the 1970s. Further, metropolitan domestic services, rather than radically revise or reduce the gender divide of homebound work as more women in the United States visibly entered the public work force, "crossed, class, race, and national lines" to use West Indian migrant women instead.[43]

Although these writers came to the United States in different capacities, domestic labor figures prominently in their personal narratives and in their fictions. Jamaica Kincaid emigrated from Antigua as a young adult to be an *au pair* girl in the United States, much as does the central character in *Lucy*. Michelle Cliff spent her early childhood in New York and returned later for graduate school. However, the figure of the black female domestic laborer — as nanny, maid, or mother — plays a critical part in the Clare Savage novels, as Clare's silent "other" half. Paule Marshall was born and raised in Brooklyn of Barbadian parents, her mother a domestic laborer. She has paid continuous tribute to the

influence of her mother and the other domestic laborers of her childhood on her work who, as she has often said, were the first "poets" that
she knew.[44] Despite their status as American residents, their writings
reveal a central concern with the meaning of their West Indian identity,
often effected through the figure of the female laborer. The centrality of
the female domestic laborer in these Caribbean-American women's
texts, despite the authors' varying relations to actual female migrant
labor, suggests that the trope of the female laborer functions allegori-
cally. It fuses the image of woman as worker with the contending image
of woman as creator, such that immigrant labor is transformed into a
symbol with literary possibilities.

In contrast to Rhys, the disjuncture between "author" and "immigrant" did not have the same repercussions for these writers. Writing
from within the United States, West Indian women had access to an
already established tradition of black authorship through the African
American women's writing tradition, currently enjoying a second renaissance.[45] If emigrating to the United States meant that American-
style racism would not allow them to appropriate the Western canon, it
also opened up the possibility of joining an established tradition of
black and/or Caribbean female authorship that was not available for
either Jean Rhys or Una Marson.[46]

Accordingly, their negotiation of the West Indian literary subject is
filtered through their relationship to North America and their status as
American subjects. The critical nexus of Caribbean and American engenders a different notion of nation and readership from that implicit
in the writings of the male writers. Specifically, the women writers do
not construct themselves as writers *in exile* from the Caribbean; nor are
they interpreted as such by literary critics. Their *immigrant* status in the
United States immediately refigures their status as authorial subjects
and the interpretation of the subject in their texts.

For Naipaul and Rhys, whose narratives were generated by their
displacement from the national audience, the return to the homeland is
a literary "death" of sorts; Naipaul's chronicle of his return to the
Caribbean in *The Middle Passage* suggests a final parting of the ways,
while the conclusion of Rhys's *Wide Sargasso Sea* with the death of
Antoinette when she kills herself in an hallucinatory attempt to rejoin
her black Caribbean childhood friend suggests, along with Rhys's personal writings, that writing in the native land is an impossibility.[47] For

Marshall, Cliff, and Kincaid, the theme of a return to the West Indies is also present in their narratives. Similarly, the return to the homeland is problematized, as is the possibility of writing "at home." However, the question of audience has been reconfigured in part to articulate the Caribbean female subject within an (African) American subject status that allows for a doubled meaning of "home."

As we have seen, Cliff's protagonist Clare Savage returns to Jamaica to "bury" her mother, who has been dead for a year. The return is linked to a budding revolutionary consciousness which her mother's dead body has come to symbolize. In Jamaica Kincaid's novel, *Lucy*,[48] the protagonist Lucy, an immigrant *au pair* in New York, associates a return to her native Antigua as a regression to her mother's life, which she despises yet cherishes. Like Clare Savage's mother, Lucy's mother represses her anger, her intelligence, and dissent in deference to her husband and a wider social taboo that silences women's voices. In Marshall's *Praisesong for the Widow*, the African American protagonist must recover her cultural legacy through a journey to the Caribbean, which I interpret as a return motif. I will elaborate my argument on the meaning of the immigrant woman's return to the Caribbean in the following readings of *Lucy* and *Praisesong for the Widow*.

Return of the Native: Refiguring the Folk Narrative

At the very beginning of *Lucy* the reader is introduced to the narrator's obsession with the idea of a return to her homeland:

In books I had read . . . someone would suffer from homesickness. A person would leave a not very nice situation and go somewhere else, somewhere a lot better, and then long to go back where it was not very nice. How impatient I would become with such a person, for I would feel that I was in a not very nice situation myself, and how I wanted to go somewhere else. But now I, too, felt that I wanted to be back where I came from. I knew where I stood there. If I had had to draw a picture of my future then, it would have been a large gray patch surrounded by black, blacker, blackest. (6)

Confused by the "gray patches" of her new life in the United States, Lucy yearns for the certainties of Antiguan society, even as she despises its narrowness, its stifling atmosphere for women who want to be something different than that for which they are bred. In Antigua Lucy was weaned on the classics of English education: the Bible, Shake-speare, *Paradise Lost*. (If in some ways *Lucy* is the sequel to *Annie John*, the *Paradise Lost* reference has other meaning, signifying that Antigua itself is the "paradise lost" from which Lucy — a.k.a. Annie John — has been cast out for not abiding by the laws of colonial confor-mity. If her conflicts with her mother, who was once her most beloved companion, have caused her to be cast out, then it would appear that Annie's mother is God, and Annie is Lucifer, as we find out, literally, in *Lucy*.)

Hating her name ("it seemed slight, without substance"), Lucy calls herself by the names of her favorite authors, the Brontë sisters: Emily, Charlotte, Jane (149). Despite this, as Lucy tells her mother, "my whole upbringing had been devoted to preventing me from becoming a slut" (127). The mother comes to symbolize the failure of Antiguan society to give her a creative voice from which to write and speak. The canoni-cal tradition of Shakespeare, Milton, and the Brontës provides no out-let for this young black woman; her mission in life has already been defined for her. She must *not* become the stereotype of black woman-hood which is always already present in Caribbean society: the slut. The meaning of "slut" here takes on defiant connotations, not simply sexual but also a social defiance of the role of deferential womanhood. It is this role which "decent," "respectable" black West Indian women — as opposed to the loud, "masculine" black viragoes of the popular press — must continuously be performing in relation to West Indian men, and in the service of which Lucy's mother has spent a lifetime.[49]

For her mother's failure, Lucy distances herself from the mother-(land). She refuses to reply to her mother's constant letters and rational-izes her behavior by pointing to their oppositeness: "She and I are not alike. She should not have married my father. She should not have had children. She should not have thrown away her intelligence. She should not have paid so little attention to mine" (123).

It is only the discovery that her mother, in anger, named her after Satan — "Lucifer" — that Lucy is able to accept her name. The shift in the name's meaning implies that only radical and total opposition to her society is sufficient to give Lucy a sense of self-definition. The nov-el's central thesis then becomes how Lucy can learn to integrate her love for her mother(land) when her selfhood is defined and maintained through an absolute opposition to what that mother(land) has intended for her to be. Benstock's formulation of the *matria* becomes useful here. If the "law of the father" can be defined as the authority of colonial society represented in the books of Lucy's childhood, then it is the *patria* that has situated black women outside the realm of literary authority. However, it is the *matria* that has produced Lucy's psychic alienation, since it is through her mother, the image of herself, that Lucy learns her "place" as a woman. To be a "respectable" woman in Antigua, she must repress her other, wild, writing self; she is thus exiled from herself, within her own body and within the "body" of the nation. If social mobility for the West Indian intellectual is to write and speak through the Western canonical tradition, then the position of intellectual is not available for Lucy in the Caribbean. Like James and Naipaul, she can only leave.

Still, leaving has not provided the solutions Lucy wants, other than to make her the "slut" of her mother's imagination. She finds a new kind of subjugation in the literary authority of her liberal white American employers, who constantly refer to *their* master texts — they speak of Freud and current Euro-American feminist theory — to explain *her*. (For example, Mariah, Lucy's employer, is described as an adherent of feminist philosophies: "Mariah wanted to rescue me. She spoke of women in society, women in history, women in culture, women everywhere. But I couldn't speak, so I couldn't tell her that my mother was my mother and that society and history and culture and other women in general were something else together" [131–32]. Elsewhere, Lucy relates her dream to Mariah, who then prescribes Freud for Lucy's "problem" [15].)

There is no currency to be gained for Lucy here in intellectual terms, though America has brought other freedoms. Lucy writes her mother, finally, telling her mother that her efforts have failed: she is enjoying life as a "slut" and will never come home again. The mother, "the saint," replies that she will always love Lucy, and Lucy's home will never be anywhere but with her. The novel concludes with Lucy writing her full name upon a page, along with the lines, "I wish I could love someone so much that I would die from it." After this, a "great wave of shame" comes over her and she cries over the page.

Clearly, Lucy wishes she could love herself, but loving herself is tied hopelessly to loving her mother. The mother is Lucy's doppelgänger; by consciously making herself at every point her mother's opposite, Lucy has managed only to bind what her mother is so closely to what she is that she cannot now separate the two. Her mother is herself: to hate her mother is to hate herself. Lucifer needs God to be Lucifer, and, as Lucy reflects, "I often thought of her [the mother] as god-like, and are not the children of gods devils?" (153)

Lucy's obsession with return to the mother/land, to which she has vowed never to return, reflects the psychic split for the immigrant woman writer — similar to that of the exile writer — where writing can only occur "away" from home, but for whom home always means a figurative burial of the voice. Lucy's mother understands what Lucy as yet does not: that Lucy's home *will* always be with her mother/land. Since Lucy's mother can read Lucy in this fashion, the mother symbolizes the West Indian female reading public which does not yet understand what it has itself produced. Thus Home and Away must become the same place to make the author/reader whole. As I have indicated in chapter 4, Lucy's final act on the written page suggests a redeployment and *recuperation* of the writing Caribbean subject that is illuminated by an African American feminist paradigm of subjectivity; that is, the obliteration of the words on the page by the tears of the body fuses the competing claims of body and word, Home and Away. *Praisesong for the Widow* picks up on this theme but completes the return, though not necessarily in the ways one might expect.

Perhaps Marshall's most popular novel, *Praisesong* describes the journey of Avey Johnson, a middle-aged, middle-class African American widow, on a cruise ship to the Caribbean. Avey lives in New York City but was born on Tatem Island, a place which is evidently modeled on the Sea Islands off the coast of South Carolina. The residents of Tatem keep alive the memory of their African ancestors through stories and rituals. As a "successful" African American, Avey has purged all traces of her rural upbringing in her modern lifestyle, which culminates in that ultimate act of First World privilege, the Cruise. The cruise is a pivotal motif in the narrative; it symbolizes Avey's dislocation from her black heritage because of its enactment of a colonizing role toward the Third World region through which it passes. The travelers are First World consumers, who consume the product of the Caribbean and then leave. Avey is a participant in this act perpetrated on black and non-white Caribbean peoples and as such has consolidated her "success" by "evolving" — as she might see it — from being one of the black peoples acted upon in such ways (that is, the Tatem Island community) to being one of the actors.

As a result, the cruise functions as an ironic parody of the journey across the Middle Passage which Avey's forebears were forced to undertake and which their descendant willingly reenacts from the other side, in literal as well as in spiritual terms: as a child, Avey's grandmother witnessed the arrival of the Ibos onto Tatem Island in chains and, as her Great Aunt Cuney tells it, their return to Africa by walking over the water. However, while on board the cruise ship Avey is made ill by a recurring nightmare in which Great Aunt Cuney urges Avey to follow her and reconstitute Avey's own link with her African heritage. Avey, herself now a grandmother, refuses, and the two trade blows until Avey awakens, feeling sore and bruised. She is wrenchingly seasick and momentarily experiences the agony of the slaves on the original Middle Passage:

She was alone in the deckhouse. That much she was certain of. Yet she had the impression as her mind flickered on briefly of other bodies lying crowded in with her in the hot, airless dark. A multitude it felt like lay packed around her in the filth and stench of themselves, just as she was. Their moans, rising and falling with each rise and plunge of the schooner, enlarged upon the one filling her own head. Their suffering — the depth of it, the weight of it, in the cramped space — made hers of no consequence. (209)

Disturbed by her dreams, Avey refuses to rejoin the ship, and stays on Grenada to take a flight back to New York. While there she loses her luggage, her coiffure is ruined — in fact, she loses all vestiges of her middle-class Americanness. When she finally agrees to accompany a chance acquaintance to Carriacou (a small isle off the coast of Grenada), she has been essentially stripped bare of the literal trappings of her success which have obscured her connection to her cultural identity. In this state she is now open to participating in the African-derived rituals which take place on Carriacou every year. These principally take the form of dances, which are an amalgam of the dances of the various ethnic groups from which the slave ancestors came: Yoruba, Ashanti, Koromantee, and so forth. However, when asked "What is Your Nation?" by one of the inhabitants who cannot decide in which dance Avey should participate, Avey cannot answer.

Lest we take this to mean that the Caribbean peoples are the repository of a whole African culture, Avey recognizes that the participants themselves do not actually know their own nations:

It was the essence of something rather than the thing itself she was witnessing. . . . All that was left were a few names of what they called nations which they could no longer even pronounce properly, the fragments of a dozen or so songs, the shadowy forms of long-ago dances and rum kegs for drums. The bare bones. The burnt-out ends. And they clung to them with a tenacity she loved in them and longed for in herself. (240)

The ritual of recalling nation thus points the reader to understanding that such a task is not possible, but it is the *act* of recollection, the ritual of remembrance and reassamblage which is, in the final analysis, the essence of black Western identity. The novel closes with Avey returning to the United States, a spiritually healthy and complete woman who can now recall her Tatem Island childhood. It is significant that Avey wishes to tell the younger generation not about Carriacou or indeed Tatem Island, but rather "about the floor in Halsey Street" (255), the place in Brooklyn where she and her husband lived as struggling, fighting, loving working-class African Americans.

It is tempting to read this novel as a rather simple narrative about an African American's recovery of an African identity, but that is not my aim here. Rather, I view the narrative as a meditation on the irrevocable *loss* of the African/Caribbean identity. This, however, is not a bad thing, since Marshall has reenvisioned the importance of Africa to lie in its reformulation in New World memory. The principal movement of the narrative is from America to the Caribbean, not from America to Africa. Furthermore, if the movement is from First to Third World, it is also, as Avey's status signifies, from one coordinate of the black diaspora to the other: the two become contrasting possibilities to each other.

The Caribbean space functions in two ways: first, as the referent for the "authentic" Avey, in the form of Tatem Island, and second, as the intermediary link with the "authentic" homeland of Africa. In this way, existing not so much in geographical reality as in displaced historical memory, the Caribbean is constituted as a psychic space in which Avey renegotiates the terms of her national identity. It is in fact during the actual Middle Passage, both in fact and in discursive practice, between two distinct continental and national powers, being Western and yet not First World, African derived and yet not African, where the terms of nationhood are renegotiated and transformed. The Caribbean is, in this arrangement, Not-Africa and Not-Black America, but both entities are present in its construction. It must be emphasized that Avey returns to *America*, after all. She has utilized the Caribbean experience to effect her completion as an *African American*. Her concerns are, finally, local ones.

Likewise, the American space is depicted as having alternating realities, from Avey's Tatem Island upbringing to her New York lifestyle. There is on one hand "the American Dream" in the form of the material wealth her husband killed himself to accumulate, and on the other "the American Dream" in the form of Avey's nightmare of her fight with Aunt Cuney, which is associated with her grandmother's vision ("dream") wherein the Ibos return to Africa.

The gender associations are important here. Avey inherits her middle-class status from her husband's position; it is also her husband who is responsible for their mutual rejection of their black cultural habits and black circle of friends. The American Dream is linked in this way to a masculine quest for power and status and *modernity*. If, for one generation of West Indians, access to modernity was acquired through the manners and habits of the English gentry, then for another, it is through the material possessions and habits of the white American middle class. Either way, agency in the guise of social mobility is signified as male. In contrast, the impulses for African traditions are transmitted through female characters: Aunt Cuney and Avey's grandmother. Therefore, the quest to salvage blackness also becomes a journey to reconnect to a feminine identity that has been distorted by First World, masculine-associated modernity.[50] The journey to the Caribbean is effectively a "return" to the womb; the islands, surrounded by water, inhabiting nowhere in particular, imitate the conditions of the child's (pre)historic memory and the formative possibilities of identity.

Why an African American woman should find the mother/land in a "return" to the Caribbean is a question that may be resolved in part by re-introducing Irigaray's thesis that "woman" is always in exile from "nation." Though American herself, Avey is in a metaphorical "exile" from herself, both in terms of the physical place of Tatem and in her very "un-American" desires for Tatem/elsewhereness. When Avey finds that she cannot recognize herself, *literally*, when she looks in store windows or her bathroom mirror, her doctor tells her that this is "a sure sign of money in the bank" (49). "America" means commerce and the ownership of material possessions, but Avey discovers that *acquisition* is not *citizenship*. The "real" nation to which she owes allegiance is not to be found in America, therefore, but somehow in "foreign" Carriacou. National identity, then, is deflected into a maternalized black space that must, of necessity, be found outside the borders of America. When Avey is unable to tell them to which "nation" she belongs, the people of Carriacou finally figure it out themselves and assign her one. What is important is not so much whether or not they are historically correct but the fact that they are able to "read" her in this fashion. The maternalized space of the Caribbean can be interpreted as a metaphor for the reading public with the critical, hidden knowledge that can "translate" — and thereby transform — the immigrant into a national subject. Like Lucy, Avey must "make whole" her American and non-American/Caribbean/African selves by recreating the latter in the former, as she finally does in her plans to retire to Tatem.

The text's ambivalent characterization of the American space easily lends itself to a reading of it as an allegory of the author's anxieties about her own relationship to the United States as a second-generation Caribbean immigrant, now an African *American*, where the pursuit of Americanness in the form of American economic wealth means the loss of Caribbeanness. It also means that subsequent journeys to the Caribbean region inevitably suffer a "sea change," such that the Caribbean immigrant can never travel back across the sea as the same person she was at the beginning of the immigrant journey since she now has the "baggage" (Avey's luggage) of First World economic and social status. Tatem Island, therefore, arguably figures as the simultaneous presence and loss of the *Caribbean* in the *American* historical memory. In this way Marshall has constructed a Caribbean national arena which inhabits American spaces as well as the Caribbean basin and is accessible to both the African American and the Caribbean subject.

This realignment of the Caribbean space also rearranges the conflated notions of modernism, *modernization*, and masculinity associated with the First World. Read within the traditions of the folk narrative that I outline in chapter 3. Marshall's narrative revisits McKay's nostalgia for pastoral black life in its apparent rejection of the fruits of modernization. *Praisesong* similarly attempts to define the terms of modernization at the level of its association with both individual alienation and societal "progress" in the globalization of Culture, incorporating both the philosophical and economic manifestations of the word. The narrative is meant to illustrate that it is modernity that has had detrimental results for the black diasporic national body. The violence done to the black body is manifested in Avey's body — she literally vomits up the signs of material wealth that she has consumed — and in the abandonment of the national bodies of Tatem and Carriacou, two black rural islands which have been abandoned for the modern world, which here is implicitly "raced" as white.

Marshall's renunciation of modernity finds its theoretical model in Paul Ricoeur's dictum that "in order to take part in modern civilization, it is necessary at the same time to take part in scientific, technical, and political rationality, something which very often requires the pure and simple abandonment of a whole cultural past."[51] However, *unlike* McKay's *Banana Bottom*, in *Praisesong* the "whole" cultural past can never be quite whole, and thus the cultural remnants of Africa and Tatem, while they become fundamental to Avey's life in the modern world, are never shown to *displace* modernity. Therefore, while Marshall's text traverses the route first established by Bita Plant in McKay's folk romance, she does not finally renounce modernity altogether. Instead, the folk and the modern become mutually constituting categories. The ideal of modernization is effectively deconstructed as a masculine act and reconstructed as something that can encompass a black, female, immigrant experience without a corollary rejection of folk origins.

Avey's return to the metropolitan United States is particularly important to this reading, because it suggests a closure to the split between dueling homes and audiences. If the metropole must be reconciled to the original home, then Avey's folk self *becomes* the home community *within* the metropole. This folk self must not only be written into the narrative but be able to "read" that narrative, much as the islanders are able to "read" Avey. Avey, finally, can be both folk and modern with impunity. Thus, the exile anxieties of Naipaul, James, et al. on the difficulties of a home readership for a modern, metropolitan novel find an answer in Marshall's refiguration of modernity, nationality, and ultimately, the fiction of exile itself.

In critiquing Fredric Jameson's claim that Third World literature is characterized by the national allegory, Jean Franco posits that not only is "nation" a complex and contested term in itself but that theoretical approaches such as Jameson's — which designate as instantly postmodern the conflations of historical narrative, myth, and personal voice so often found in Latin American literature — fail to comprehend the "simultaneous dissolution of the idea of the nation and the continuous persistence of national concerns."[52] Franco's observation holds true for analyses of contemporary Caribbean women's literature as well, which reflects a desire to dissolve the construction of Caribbean nationhood that has been predicated on such stringently masculinist and European definitions even as it seeks to revalue the genre of the national allegory to include the displaced Caribbean female subject. Literary projects such as the ones discussed herein revise the imperative of the West Indian literary canon, which establishes itself in dialectical relationship to the English canon. By reconceptualizing traditional ideas of what constitutes the West Indian space, West Indian literature, and *who* can be a West Indian author, these female-authored texts have forced a reexamination of key structures in Caribbean discourse and, in the process, expanded the contours of postcolonial Caribbean national identity.

NOTES

Writing the Caribbean: Gender and Literary Authority

1   See C. L. R. James, *Beyond A Boundary* (London: Hutchinson, 1963/1966), 47.

2   A few examples include George Lamming, *Water with Berries* and *The Pleasures of Exile*, a collection of essays which attempts, among other things, to read the Haitian revolution in terms of the Caliban/Prospero/Miranda dyad; Aimé Césaire, *A Tempest*, in *The Collected Poetry of Aimé Césaire*, trans. Clayton Eshleman and Annette Smith (Berkeley: University of California Press, 1983); Edward Kamau Brathwaite, "Caliban," in *Islands* (London: Oxford University Press, 1969).

3   For examples of African American feminist critical approaches to West Indian works, see Mari Evans, "Trajectories of Self-Definition: Placing Contemporary Afro-American Women's Fiction," in *Conjuring: Black Women, Fiction and Literary Tradition*, ed. Marjorie Pryse and Hortense Spillers (Bloomington, Ind.: Indiana University Press, 1985), 233–48.

4   See Carole Boyce Davies, "Writing Home: Gender and Heritage in the Works of Afro-Caribbean/American Women Writers," in *Out of the Kumbla: Caribbean Women and Literature*, ed. Carole Boyce Davies and Elaine Savory Fido (Trenton, N.J.: Africa World Press, 1990), 53–79.

5   See Jamaica Kincaid, *Annie John* (New York: New American Library, 1983), 75–78.

6   Wordsworth's poem, "Daffodils," is clearly a trope of Englishness in Caribbean narrative. It appears variously in the work of Jean Rhys ("The Day They Burned the Books"), Jamaica Kincaid (*Lucy*), Michelle Cliff (*Abeng*), and V. S. Naipaul (*Miguel Street*), as Veronica Gregg has noted; see Veronica Gregg, *Jean Rhys's Historical Imagination* (Chapel Hill: University of North Carolina Press, 1995), 206.

7   See Paule Marshall, *The Chosen Place, the Timeless People* (New York: Vintage, 1969).

8   Examples of mainstream feminist approaches to Rhys's work that tend to exclude discussions of her Caribbean cultural context include Nancy Rebecca Harrison, *Jean Rhys and the Novel as Women's Text* (Chapel Hill: University of North Carolina Press, 1988) and Deborah Kelly Kloepfer, *The Unspeakable Mother: Forbidden Discourse in Jean Rhys and H.D.* (Ithaca: Cornell University Press, 1989).

9   See Alice Walker, "One Child of One's Own — An Essay on Creativity," *Ms.*

(August 1979): 50, quoted in Deborah McDowell, "New Directions in Black Feminist Criticism," in *New Directions in Feminist Criticism*, ed. Elaine Showalter (New York: Pantheon, 1985), 187.

10 See Judith Kegan Gardiner, "The Exhilaration of Exile," in *Women's Writing in Exile*, ed. Mary Lynn Broe and Angela Ingram (Chapel Hill: University of North Carolina Press, 1989), 140.

11 Jean D'Costa points out that the concept of "the lady" haunts West Indian women writers as varied as Jean Rhys, in novels such as *Voyage in the Dark* ("I tried to teach you to talk like a lady and behave like a lady and not like a nigger and of course I couldn't do it. . . ."), and Jamaica Kincaid, in *Annie John* and *Lucy*, which I discuss at length in chapter 6 and which Jean D'Costa has pointed out to me. However, I think there is an important distinction to be made in the desires for gentlemanliness that I have been discussing here and the desires for gentlewomanliness, if you will. Being a lady is associated with race, class, and all of the other host attributes of gentlemanliness, yes, but *not* with intellectual labor. It is precisely this exclusion that vexes the quest for literary authority in the female-authored texts of the women writers in question. For a detailed discussion of the concept of the "proper lady" as it relates to the writer, see Mary Poovey, *The Proper Lady and the Woman Writer: Ideology as Style in the Works of Mary Wollstonecraft, Mary Shelley, and Jane Austen* (Chicago: University of Chicago Press, 1984).

12 See Manuel Moreno Fraginals, "Cultural Contributions and Deculturation," 8, in *Africa in Latin America*, ed. Manuel Moreno Fraginals (New York: Holmes and Meier, 1984), quoted in Vera Kutzinski, *Sugar's Secrets: The Erotics of Cuban Nationalism* (University Press of Virginia, 1994), 216, n. 3, chapter 2.

13 Anthony Trollope describes the black man in Jamaica as capable of "the hardest bodily work," but says that "he is idle, unambitious as to worldly position, sensual, and content with little. Intellectually, he is apparently capable of but little sustained effort; but, singularly enough, here he is ambitious. He burns to be regarded as a scholar, puzzles himself with fine words. . . . delights in aping the little graces of civilization." See Anthony Trollope, *The West Indies and the Spanish Main* (London: Allan Sutton Publishing, 1985/1859). On the other hand, Froude speaks admiringly, if ironically, of black West Indian women's ability to work, and suggests that they were more fit to "rule" the islands than the men. (See my discussion of Froude in chapter 1.) Since the debates on self-rule entailed discussions of *men*, the suggestion is no more than a mocking footnote to the *unfitness* of West Indian men to rule. In another vein, English author Charles Kingsley exhibits horror at what he considers to be the very unfeminine and vulgar behavior of black Trinidadian women during his visit there, documented in his travel narrative, *At Last: A Christmas in the West Indies* (London: Macmillan, 1871, 2 vols.): "I fear that a stranger would feel a

shock — and that not a slight one — at the first sight of the average women of
Port of Spain. . . . Their masculine figures, their ungainly gestures, their loud
and sudden laughter, even when walking alone, and their general coarseness,
shocks, and must shock. . . . The men are civil fellows enough, if you will, as in
duty bound, be civil to them. . . . When you have ceased looking — even staring
— at the black women and their ways, you become aware of the strange variety
of races which people the city." (vol. 1, 138–39) He speculates that if English
men had "intermarried" with the indigenous "Indian" women — whom he perceived to be more docile — instead of with black women, the history of Trinidad
would be very different, presumably much better. I am indebted to Faith Smith
for this observation in her paper, "Transgressive Citizens: 'Woman' and 'Nation' in the 19th Century Caribbean" (Paper presented at the Women's Studies
Colloquium, Johns Hopkins University, October, 1996).

14   See Gauri Viswanathan, "Currying Favour: The Politics of British Educational
and Cultural Policy in India 1813–1854," *Social Text* 19/20 (fall 1988): 103.

15   See Edward Kamau Brathwaite, *Roots* (Havana: Casa de las Americas, 1986/
1971), 54, quoted at length in my discussion of Brathwaite in chapter 3.

16   I am referring to the character of the educated black woman, Bita Plant, in
McKay's *Banana Bottom*, and the educated black protagonist of Marson's
Pocomania. George Lamming also uses a rural, black, educated female protagonist as the vehicle for similar concerns in *Season of Adventure* (London:
Allison and Busby, 1979/1960). However, the protagonist's quest for a way to
reconcile herself as an educated woman within the context of the peasant roots
of the community is undermined by the structuring device of her concomitant
search for her unknown father, who could be either the white man who seduced
her mother, or the black man who raped her. The search for the unknown
father is a metaphor for the quest for national origins; the search for the *patria*
comes to represent tradition itself. The alignment of "authentic" Caribbean
identity with patrilineal descent implicitly conflates identity and masculinity.
My reading challenges that of Simon Gikandi, who posits that the novel is a
"significant critique of nationalist discourse as a system of patriarchal power."
See Gikandi, *Writing in Limbo* (Ithaca: Cornell University Press, 1992), 30.

17   See Bruce King, "Caribbean Conundrum," *Transition* 62 (1993): 148. While I
find King's distinction between local and foreign-based Caribbean writers important, nevertheless I object to his suggestion that it is simply because the
foreign-based writers "remain subject to white-black social divisions" that they
are at all interested in the issues of racial injustice. The "old" racism is alive and
well in the Caribbean, from all accounts. And there is certainly more to anticolonial themes than racial divisions.

18   Of the many, many male West Indian writers who produced their classic work
outside of the Caribbean, some of the most notable are C. L. R. James, V. S.

Naipaul, George Lamming, and Samuel Selvon. James, Naipaul, and Lamming
have written at length about the need for going abroad to write; see my discussion of James, Naipaul, and Lamming in chapter 2.

19 There are a number of studies on the migration of Caribbean women to the
United States which justify the claim that recent West Indian migration is heav-
ily female. For example, see Philip Kasinitz, *Caribbean New York: Black Immi-
grants and the Politics of Race* (Ithaca: Cornell University Press, 1992); Delores
M. Mortimer and Roy S. Bryce-La Porte, "Female Immigrants to the United
States: Caribbean, Latin American and African Experiences" and "Caribbean
Immigration to the United States," RIIES Occasional Papers nos. 1 and 2
(Washington, D.C.: Smithsonian Institution, 1981 and 1983); Olive Senior,
Working Miracles: Women's Lives in the English-Speaking Caribbean (London: James Currey, 1991); Christine Ho, "The Internationalization of Kinship
and the Feminization of Caribbean Migration," *Human Organization* 52, no. 1
(1993); and Shellee Colen, " 'Like a Mother to Them': Stratified Reproduction
and West Indian Childcare Workers and Employers in New York," in *Conceiving the New World Order: The Global Politics of Reproduction*, ed. Faye D.
Ginsburg and Rayna Rapp (Berkeley: University of California Press, 1995). I
discuss some of these studies and their arguments in more detail in chapter 6.

20 Edward Brathwaite and Kenneth Ramchand have rightly noted that Rhys's
work evinces the "terrified consciousness" (Ramchand's phrase) of white West
Indians of black power. See Brathwaite, *Contradictory Omens* (Mona, Jamaica: Savacou Publications, 1978) and Ramchand, *The West Indian Novel
and Its Background* (London: Heinemann, 1983). For a thorough and historicized analysis of Jean Rhys's attitudes toward blacks, see Gregg, *Jean Rhys's
Historical Imagination*, 206.

21 For a discussion of Rhys's character Christophine that reproduces the strong
black matriarch stereotype see, among others, Lucy Wilson, " 'Women Must
Have Spunks': Jean Rhys' West Indian Outcasts," *Modern Fiction Studies* 32,
no. 3 (autumn 1986): 439–48.

22 See Carolyn Cooper's discussion of black female fans of dancehall in *Noises in
the Blood: Orality, Gender and the "Vulgar" Body of Jamaican Popular Culture*
(London: Macmillan, 1993). Cooper's work here, though apparently feminist
in orientation, nevertheless evinces — for me — an uncomfortable similarity to
Orlando Patterson's evocation of "Chaucerian" Jamaican working women who
can ward off sexual harassment with a ready and ribald tongue. Patterson uses
this stereotypical image of strong black Jamaican women as a paradigm for his
claim of the "difference" in black sexual discourse in his editorial defense of
Clarence Thomas in the pages of the *New York Times* during the infamous
Senate hearings. See Orlando Patterson, "Race, Gender and Liberal Fallacies,"
reprinted in *The Black Scholar* 22 (winter 1991/spring 1992): 70–80.

23 Marshall explains in the introduction that the various settings for her short stories, *Soul Clap Hands and Sing* (Chatham, N.J.: Chatham Bookseller, 1961) all begin with "B" — from "Brooklyn to Brazil."

24 I am indebted to Veronica Gregg's excellent study of Jean Rhys for this material. Gregg observes that Rhys's letters and interviews from the late 1950s onward return "obsessively" to the "ingratitude of black people," and she quotes one such letter: "I made up my mind to go back to live [in Dominica], but I was put off, after corresponding, by the turns things have taken there. I grew up with feelings of being surrounded by alien people, but I liked many of them. Now they say that the English are devils, though their culture is derived from English culture; the horrors of slavery are constantly referred to but they leave out all the good." See Thomas Ned, "Meeting Jean Rhys," in *Planet* (Wales) 33 (August 1976): 29–31, quoted in Gregg, *Jean Rhys's Historical Imagination*, 40. However, elsewhere Rhys writes of the mentality of the "average English" in contrast to "us black people." (Unpublished, Jean Rhys Collection, McFarlin Library, University of Tulsa, quoted in Gregg, *Jean Rhys's Historical Imagination*, 45.)

25 Naipaul's discussion of "Negro protest writing" is discussed in chapter 2. The phrase comes from *The Middle Passage* (New York: Vintage Press, 1981/ 1962), 69. His praise of C. L. R. James, also discussed in chapter 2, is chronicled by James himself in *Spheres of Existence: Selected Writings* (Westport, Conn.: Lawrence Hill, 1980), 243.

26 In an interview with Jenny Sharpe, Caryl Phillips discusses the influences of African American narratives on his work, which were particularly important to him in that he felt there was no black British narrative tradition. Interestingly, Phillips does not claim exile writers such as Lamming or James as part of this tradition. He also talks about his interest in telescoping West Indian history through the eyes of white English woman narrators such as the one in his novel *Cambridge*. See Jenny Sharpe, "Of this Time, of that Place: A Conversation with Caryl Phillips," *Transition* 68 (1995): 154–61.

27 Carole Boyce Davies chronicles the accusations of critics who adhere to a belief in the nontheoretical nature of black feminist critique in *Black Women, Writing and Identity: Migrations of the Subject* (New York: Routledge, 1996), in chapter 2, "Negotiating Theories," 39.

Chapter 1 "Race-ing" the Nation: Englishness, Blackness, and the Discourse of Victorian Manhood

1 My focus is on English-speaking Caribbean discourse, so I use "West Indian" interchangeably with "Caribbean."

2 José Martí, "Our America," *La Revista Illustrada* (1891), quoted in Hortense

Spillers, "Introduction: Who Cuts the Border?" in *Comparative American Identities: Race, Sex, and Nationality in the Modern Text*, ed. Hortense Spillers (New York: Routledge, 1991), 1.

3   See Spillers, "Introduction: Who Cuts the Border?" in *Comparative American Identities*, 1–25.

4   See Margarita Zamora, "Abreast of Columbus: Gender and Discovery," *Cultural Critique* 17 (winter 1991): 128.

5   I am using creole in its original sense here—someone of pure European ancestry born in the Americas.

6   See Benedict Anderson, *Imagined Communities* (New York: Verso Press, 1991), 62.

7   See Anderson, *Imagined Communities*, chapter 4.

8   My contention here is debatable; in his definitive study, Orlando Patterson makes the point that many white Jamaicans of the late seventeenth century resented Englishness and called themselves Jamaicans. See Orlando Patterson, *The Sociology of Slavery: An Analysis of the Origins, Development, and Structure of Negro Slave Society* (Kingston, Jamaica: Sangster's Book Stores, 1973/1967), 35, quoted in "Introduction," in *Language in Exile*, ed. Jean D'Costa and Barbara Lalla (Tuscaloosa: University of Alabama Press, 1990), 23. Since Patterson's research is based on the analysis of wills as well as on other public documents, this would suggest that West Indian whites were a good deal more conflicted about their relationship to English national identity than I am positing here. This may have something to do with the numbers of white, non-English people on the island—primarily Scottish and Welsh—that Patterson details. Regardless of these private resentments, however, I believe their *political* Englishness—that is, their public positions on various social and political matters—is the measure of national identity in this context. For instance, the white West Indian claims to Englishness proved pivotal in the massacre of the blacks in the Morant Bay massacre of 1865 in Jamaica, as I discuss later in this chapter. Moreover, the extraordinarily high rate of English planter absenteeism from their own plantations in the Caribbean that Patterson also recounts in his study illustrates, for me, the primarily economic relationship that anglophone whites had to the region.

9   This may have more to do with the sheer population size than to anything else, since the white creoles in English-speaking regions have always been a very small minority among a large black population: their struggle to maintain their English identity may have been aided by this "siege mentality."

10 Zamora, "Abreast of Columbus," 140.

11 Much of West Indian exile writing, such as that of V. S. Naipaul, George Lamming, and Samuel Selvon, attempts to deconstruct this familial relationship to the "Motherland"; as I shall argue later, West Indian women writers writing from outside of the region have a different way of confronting the idea

of the familial relationship between hegemonic "First" World and the "Third," and indeed the notion of exile itself is treated differently.

12 Antoinette Burton notes that in nineteenth-century Britain, " 'national character' was thought to demand the subjugation of 'lesser races' well into the 20th century." See Antoinette Burton citing Thane and Mackay, "The English Woman," in *Burdens of History: British Feminists, Indian Women, and Imperial Culture, 1865–1915* (Chapel Hill: University of North Carolina Press, 1994), 38. This characteristic nineteenth-century conflation of race and nation is hardly unfamiliar to us in the late twentieth century as recent debates in the United States and Europe over which ethnicities of immigrants are more assimilable to the national culture reveal.

13 See Patrick Bryan, *The Jamaican People 1880–1902: Race, Class and Social Control* (London: Macmillan Caribbean, 1991), 69.

14 See Ileana Rodríguez, *House, Garden, Nation: Space, Gender and Ethnicity in Post-Colonial Latin American Literatures by Women*, trans. Robert Carr with author (Durham: Duke University Press, 1994), 3–4. She writes, "in the island nations . . . Progress, Civilization, and the social world order hinge on questions of Independence and the modernization of old plantocracies. . . ."

   ". . . Underlining the theses of my book is that without the primitive accumulation of capital — and hence the formation of a national bourgeoisie — the nation, a sovereign, independent territoriality governed by its own internal laws, is a contradiction in terms. . . . Thus, in all writings on 'nation', there is a truth which some locate in the strict terrain of language and words, in the narrative of the end of narratives, as Jameson has it, and which others like myself, situate in the discussion of land, territory, and land tenure. . . ."

   The question of ownership was also a problem for the Spaniards in their quest to appropriate the Americas as the national property of Spain. Anthony Pagden recounts the tautological argument made in 1550 by Juan Gines de Sepulvéda to justify the Spanish plundering of the land: "since no Indian society had a monetary economy, no Indian could be said to have exercised any rights over any precious metal." See Anthony Pagden, "Dispossessing the Barbarian: the Language of Spanish Thomism and the Debate over the Property Rights of the American Indian," in *The Languages of Political Theory in Early-Modern Europe*, ed. Anthony Pagden (Cambridge: Cambridge University Press, 1987), 81.

15 See Peter Hulme, "Hurricanes in the Caribbees: the Constitution of the Discourse of English Colonialism," in *1642: Literature and Power in the Seventeenth Century* (London: University of Essex Press, 1981), 75.

16 These and other details of Governor Eyre's life are in the biography by Geoffrey Dutton, *The Hero as Murderer: The Life of Edward John Eyre, Australian Explorer and Governor of Jamaica, 1815–1901* (London: William Collins, 1967). My thanks to Jean D'Costa for referring me to this source of informa-

tion. For other historical accounts of the Eyre controversy, see Philip D. Curtin, *Two Jamaicas: The Role of Ideas in a Tropical Colony, 1830–1865* (Cambridge: Harvard University Press, 1955); and Douglas Lorimer, *Colour, Class and the Victorians: English Attitudes of the Negroes in the Mid-Nineteenth Century* (Leicester: Leicester University Press, 1978).

17 See Catherine Hall, "The Economy of Intellectual Prestige: Thomas Carlyle, John Stuart Mill, and the Case of Governor Eyre," *Cultural Critique* 12 (spring 1989): 184. Much of my argument which follows here rehearses Hall's excellent analysis of manliness and individualism in the Carlyle debate, an analysis to which I am indebted. Another excellent analysis of race in the Carlyle/Mill debate is to be found in chapter 2 of Simon Gikandi's book, *Maps of Englishness: Writing Identity in the Culture of Colonialism* (New York: Columbia University Press, 1996).

18 Catherine Hall claims that Mill's belief in the primacy of the intellectual to make social change stems from his early training to "be a worker for the cause of rational and enlightened enquiry and improvement." Hall, "Economy," 175. She refers to Mill's autobiography; see John Stuart Mill, *Autobiography* (London: Oxford University Press, 1924), 82, quoted in Hall, "Economy," 176. "The Man-of-Letters Hero" is Carlyle's term for the literary intellectual, a concept he develops and expands on in his essay, "The Hero as Man of Letters," which I discuss at more length in chapter 2. See Carlyle, "The Hero as Man of Letters," in *Selected Writings* (London: Penguin, 1988).

19 See Thomas Carlyle and John Stuart Mill, *The Nigger Question & the Negro Question* (Dayton, Ohio: Appleton-Century-Crofts, 1971).

20 See Patrick Brantlinger, *Rule of Darkness: British Literature and Imperialism 1830–1914* (Ithaca: Cornell University Press, 1988), 23. Brantlinger goes on to quote Cecil Rhodes ("The Empire . . . is a bread and butter question. If you want to avoid civil war, you must become imperialists.") to support his contention that inasmuch as the ideology of British imperialism involved not simply military conquest and economic exploitation but also "the enactment of often idealistic although nonetheless authoritarian schemes of cultural domination," the guiding logic of British imperialist discourse is "always to weld these seeming opposites together or to disguise their contradiction" (34). It is this seeming contradiction which I believe is evident in the Carlyle/Mill debate.

21 Brantlinger, *Rule of Darkness*, 8.

22 In *Propaganda and Empire: The Manipulation of British Public Opinion 1880–1960* (Manchester: Manchester University Press, 1984), John Mackenzie argues that imperialism effectively combined "national purpose" with "high moral content" to produce relatively peaceful class coexistence. He also argues that it was a "core ideology" in modern Britain because as an essentially middle-class ethos it was transferred to other social classes through media, pageant, photography, and spectacle (quoted in Burton, *Burdens of History*, 40).

23 Thomas Babington Macaulay, arguing for the anglicization of India, in "Speech on the Government of India" (1833), quoted in Brantlinger, *Rule of Darkness*, 30. Eric Williams also quoted in Brantlinger, *Rule of Darkness*, 30.

24 This position was taken earlier by the Spaniards over the legal riddle of whether they actually *owned* the islands. The argument for possession was that the Indians were peripatetic, and hence did not really "settle" the islands at all. See Zamora, "Abreast of Columbus."

25 Thomas Carlyle, "Occasional Discourse on the Nigger Question," in *English and Other Critical Essays* (London: J. M. Dent and Sons, 1964), 327, quoted in Hall, "The Economy of Intellectual Prestige," 179.

26 J. A. Froude, *The English in the West Indies* (New York: Charles Scribner's Sons, 1888), 71.

27 Carlyle, "Occasional Discourse," 327, quoted in Hall, "Economy," 179.

28 Carlyle, "Occasional Discourse," 311, quoted in Hall, "Economy," 179–80.

29 See Eric Williams, *British Historians and the West Indies* (London: Andre Deutsch, 1966), 139.

30 Hall, "Economy," 192.

31 See the *Times* (London), 29 August 1883, 7. I am indebted to Antoinette Burton for passing along to me this and other magazine clippings on the subject.

32 Zamora, "Abreast of Columbus," 131.

33 See Hall, "Economy," 187.

34 This tension between the different attributes of manliness — physical force versus refined sensibilities — was not peculiar to Victorian England. Gail Bederman notes that similar anxieties over what constituted manliness permeated America in the late nineteenth and early twentieth centuries. See Gail Bederman, "Remaking Manhood through Race and 'Civilization'" in *Manliness & Civilization: A Cultural History of Gender and Race in the United States, 1880–1917* (Chicago: University of Chicago Press, 1995).

35 See Anthony Trollope on the consequences of black self-government in *The West Indies and the Spanish Main* (New York: Hippocrene Books, 1985/1859), 48: ". . . To recede from civilization and become again savage . . . has been to [the black man's] taste. I believe that he would altogether retrograde if left to himself."

36 Quoted in Douglas A. Lorimer, *Colour, Class and the Victorians: English Attitudes to the Negro in the Mid-Nineteenth Century* (Leicester: Leicester University Press, 1978), 86.

37 See Lorimer, *Colour, Class and the Victorians*, 59.

38 See Edward Blyden, *The Selected Letters of Edward Wilmot Blyden*, ed. Hollis R. Lynch (Millwood, N.Y.: Krause-Thomson Organization, 1978), 30.

39 Manthia Diawara, "Englishness and Blackness: Cricket as Discourse on Colonialism," *Callaloo* 13 (1990): 830.

40 As Bryan puts it, "[W]hite society accepted a certain level of equality among

whites, not because they believed that all whites were equal but because being white in the Caribbean means, above all, *not* being black." See Bryan, *The Jamaican People*, 67.

41 See V. S. Naipaul, *Middle Passage* (New York: Vintage, 1981/1962), 68.

42 However, as Edward Said has pointed out in his pathbreaking work, *Orientalism* (New York: Vintage, 1978), despite Western Europe's acknowledgment of the prior existence of African and Indian societies, these regions have also been essentially manufactured in Western discourse.

43 See Anthony Trollope, *The West Indies and the Spanish Main* (Gloucester, U.K.: Allan Sutton Publishing, 1985/1859), 42–43.

44 Diawara, "Englishness and Blackness": 831.

45 See Froude, *The English in the West Indies*, 278.

46 Ibid., 278, 286.

47 John Jacob Thomas, *Froudacity: West Indian Fables Explained* (Philadephia: Gebbie, 1890).

48 Ibid., 18.

49 Ibid., 117–18.

50 Ibid., 234.

51 I am indebted for this particular idea to Faith Smith, who makes the connection between the roles of the African and West Indian intellectual elite of the nineteenth century. The notion of cultural mediation comes from P. F. De Moraes Farias's and K. Barber's characterization of the former's identification with both African and English cultures as "brokerage" in *Self-Assertion and Brokerage: Early Cultural Nationalism in West Africa*, ed. Farias and Barber (Birmingham: Centre of West African Studies, Birmingham University, 1990).

52 See Bryan, *The Jamaican People*, 243.

53 Theophilus Scholes, *Glimpses of the Ages of the "Superior and Inferior" Races So-Called, Discussed in the Light of Science and History* (London: John Long, 1905), 1:82, quoted in Bryan, *The Jamaican People*, 211.

54 John Henderson, *Jamaica* (London: Adam and Charles Black, 1906), 103, quoted in Bryan, *The Jamaican People*, 262.

Chapter 2 Literary Men and the English Canonical Tradition

The first epigraph of this chapter is from Edward Kamau Brathwaite, "Roots," in *Roots* (Havana: Casa de Las Americas, 1981/1971). The second is from C. L. R. James, *Beyond A Boundary* (London: Hutchinson, 1963).

1 See V. S. Naipaul, "I Don't Consider Myself a West Indian," *Guyana Graphic*, (30 November 1968): 3.

2 In regard to my assertion that metropolitan critics emphasize either James's black nationalist status at the expense of his Marxism or vice versa, James says

as much himself in *Spheres of Existence: Selected Writings* (Westport, Conn.: Lawrence Hill, 1980), 242.

3   I note that in his book *The Jamaican People 1880–1902: Race, Class and Social Control* (London: Macmillan Caribbean, 1991), Patrick Bryan makes an argument similar to my own with respect to the relationship of the twentieth-century black West Indian nationalists to nineteenth-century discourse. He emphasizes that the same social forces that shaped the views of the nineteenth-century black intelligentsia of the West Indies are the ones that shaped the views of black nationalist Marcus Garvey, indeed that many of the ideas associated with Garvey—the African role in history, the link of the black West Indian to Africa, the moneymaking ventures—can be traced to earlier black West Indian nationalist scholars (282). Thus, to understand twentieth-century West Indian revolutionaries such as Garvey, it is necessary to understand that they are shaped in the late nineteenth-century period.

4   See, for instance, Patrick Taylor, *The Narrative of Liberation: Perspectives on Afro-Caribbean Literature, Popular Culture, and Politics* (Ithaca: Cornell University Press, 1989); Simon Gikandi, *Writing in Limbo: Modernism and Caribbean Literature* (Ithaca: Cornell University Press, 1992); Edward Kamau Brathwaite, *Roots.*

5   Karl de Schweinitz, Jr., *The Rise and Fall of British India: Imperialism as Inequality* (London: Methuen, 1983), 34n, quoted in Patrick Brantlinger, *Rule of Darkness: British Literature and Imperialism 1830–1914* (Ithaca: Cornell University Press, 1988), 3–4.

My point here refers very specifically to the canonical texts of Victorian England; the works of late-nineteenth-century English writers like Rudyard Kipling certainly had a fascination with the peoples of the colonies, but these are not treated as "serious" literature. Nor is this to say that the subtext of the colonial experience is not present in books like *Vanity Fair* through the figure of the mulatto Kittitian heiress Miss Schwartz, or the mad Jamaican creole wife of Mr. Rochester in *Jane Eyre*. For further discussions of the presence of the colonial experience in Victorian literature see Laura E. Donaldson, *Decolonizing Feminisms: Race, Gender and Empire Building* (Chapel Hill: University of North Carolina Press, 1992); Markman Ellis, *The Politics of Sensibility: Race, Gender and Commerce in the Sentimental Novel* (New York: Cambridge University Press, 1996); Susan Meyer, *Imperialism at Home: Race and Victorian Women's Fiction* (Ithaca: Cornell University Press, 1996); *Romanticism, Race and Imperial Culture, 1780–1834*, ed. Alan Richardson and Sonia Hofkosh (Bloomington: Indiana University Press, 1996); and C. C. Eldridge, *The Imperial Experience: From Carlyle to Forster* (New York: St. Martin's Press, 1996).

6   See Thomas Carlyle, "The Hero as Man of Letters" (1841), in *Selected Writings* (London: Penguin, 1988), 235–56. Hereafter all further references are to this edition.

7   See Nancy Armstrong, *Desire and Domestic Fiction: A Political History of the Novel* (New York: Oxford University Press, 1987), chapter 1, quoted in Mary Poovey, *Uneven Developments: The Ideological Work of Gender in Mid-Victorian England* (Chicago: University of Chicago Press, 1989), 125. Armstrong argues that literary discourse acquired its moral authority by its apparent distance from the masculinized sphere of the commerce and social alienation, and this polarity accounts for the conflation of the moral voice and the feminine voice.

8   See Carlyle, "The Hero as Man of Letters," 235, 245.

9   The religious overtones to Carlyle's vision of the literary profession are not accidental. In fact, according to JoAnne Brown, "the earliest meaning of the term 'profession' was religious, and referred to a proclamation of faith. A great 'professor' was one whose religious devotion was unimpeachable . . ." I thank JoAnne Brown for referring me to her article, "Professional Language: Words That Succeed," *Radical History Review* 31 (January 1986): 34.

10   See Carlyle, "The Hero as Man of Letters," 244.

11   See Poovey, *Uneven Developments*, 107.

12   Ibid., 108.

13   Ibid., 110.

14   Brian Doyle, *English and Englishness* (London: Routledge, 1989), 39.

15   Ibid., 49, 37.

16   *The Newbolt Report*, 11/15, quoted in Doyle, 38.

17   George Lamming, *The Pleasures of Exile* (London: Allison and Busby, 1960), 74.

18   Edward Long, quoted in Kenneth Ramchand, *The West Indian Novel and Its Background* (London: Heinemann, 1983), 82–83.

19   See Jean Rhys, "Again the Antilles," in *Jean Rhys: The Collected Short Stories* (New York: Norton, 1987).

20   Jean D'Costa suggested to me that Papa Dom's name is a cryptogram: "Papa" is "Father," "Dom" signifies "Dominica," implying that the character himself is a symbol of West Indian national identity.

21   Jean Rhys, "Again the Antilles," 40–41.

22   Judith Raiskin, "Jean Rhys: Creole Writing and Strategies of Reading," *Ariel* 22, no. 4 (October 1991): 51–67.

23   See Frantz Fanon, *Black Skins, White Masks*, trans. Charles L. Markmann (New York: Grove, 1967), 18; also, Homi K. Bhabha, "Of Mimicry and Man: the Ambivalence of Colonial Discourse," *October* 28 (1984): 128, quoted in Raiskin, 56. I am indebted to Judith Raiskin for noting the relation between Fanon's formulation and Bhabha's rebuttal.

24   "The white community was never an upper class in the sense that it possessed a

superior speech or taste or attainments; it was envied only for its money and its access to pleasure. Kingsley, in spite of all his affection for his white hosts in Trinidad, observed: 'French civilization signifies, practically, certainly in the New World, little save ballet-girls, billiard-tables, and thin boots: English civilization, little save horse-racing and cricket.' Seventy years later James Pope-Hennessy repeated and extended the observation. 'Educated people of African origin would speak to him of subjects about which he was accustomed to talk in his own country: about books, music or religion. English persons on the other hand spoke mainly of tennis-scores, the country-club, whisky or precedence or oil.' Education was strictly for the poor; and the poor were invariably black." V. S. Naipaul, *The Middle Passage* (New York: Vintage Press, 1981/1962), 57.

25 See James, *Beyond A Boundary*, 32.

26 See Faith Smith, "C. L. R. James and the Dilemma of the West Indian Intellectual," paper presented at the African Literature Association Conference, April 21–23, 1991, New Orleans. I rely heavily on Smith's reading of this particular passage of *Boundary* in my analysis here.

27 C. L. R. James, "The Artist in the Caribbean," lecture first given in 1959, reprinted in *Radical America* (Detroit: Detroit Printing Co-op, 1970/1959), 62–63.

28 See C. L. R. James, "Introduction," in *Spheres of Existence*.

29 James, *Spheres*, 243.

30 One of the more scathing indictments of Naipaul's apparent anglophilia and supposed "objective observer" status in the First World is Rob Nixon's *London Calling: V. S. Naipaul, Postcolonial Mandarin* (New York: Oxford University Press, 1992).

31 V. S. Naipaul, *The Middle Passage*, 69.

32 James, *Spheres*, 243.

33 See V. S. Naipaul, "I Don't Consider Myself a West Indian," 3.

34 In *The Middle Passage*, for instance, Naipaul frames his discussion of each nation in the Caribbean with a quotation from Trollope, Froude, and other canonical figures in European narrative: Thomas Mann, Tacitus, James Joyce. I would suggest that the structuring purpose that these quotations serve make Naipaul's observations about the emptiness of West Indian societies a *fait accompli*, a state of affairs already predetermined by European narratives.

35 See V. S. Naipaul, "Cricket," *Encounter* (September 1963): 21–22, reproduced in *The Overcrowded Barracoon* (New York: Vintage, 1984/1972). Furthermore, there is a distinctly Jamesian character in Naipaul's recent novel, *A Way in the World*, a black middle-class gentleman Marxist, who belongs to the "first generation of black men in the region." The narrator, a Naipaulian East Indian–West Indian figure, professes admiration and respect for a man he

describes as a "prodigy" of learning, and is "moved by the fact that such a man came from something like my own background" (117). See V. S. Naipaul, *A Way in the World* (New York: Vintage, 1994).

36 Naipaul, "Cricket," 22.

37 Naipaul describes his early desire to be a writer in the "Forward" to the recent edition of *A House for Mr. Biswas*. See V. S. Naipaul, *A House for Mr. Biswas* (New York: Vintage, 1984/1961), 2.

38 Naipaul, "Jasmine," in *The Overcrowded Barracoon*, 24.

39 Ibid., 25, 26.

40 See Mary Louise Pratt, *Imperial Eyes: Travel Writing and Transculturation* (New York: Routledge, 1992) and Antoinette Burton, *The Burdens of History*, for discussions on the attitudes and assumptions of colonial travel narratives.

41 V. S. Naipaul, *The Enigma of Arrival* (New York: Alfred Knopf, 1987), 153, quoted in Rob Nixon, *London Calling: V. S. Naipaul, Postcolonial Mandarin* (New York: Oxford University Press, 1992), 49. I am indebted to Nixon's reading for clarifying my ideas here.

42 V. S. Naipaul, *The Mimic Men* (Middlesex: Penguin, 1981) and *Guerrillas* (New York: Vintage, 1975). Hereafter all further references to both novels will be to these editions.

43 For a longer discussion of Brontëan references in *Guerillas*, see John Thieme, "'Apparitions of Disaster': Brontëan Parallels in *Wide Sargasso Sea* and *Guerillas*," *Journal of Commonwealth Literature* 14, no. 1 (1979), 116–32.

Chapter 3 Representing the Folk: The Crisis of Literary Authenticity

The epigraph that opens this chapter is from George Lamming, *The Pleasures of Exile* (London: Allison and Busby, 1984/1960), 38–39. All further references to the text are taken from this edition.

1 Edward Brathwaite describes this episode in *History of the Voice: The Development of Nation Language in Anglophone Caribbean Poetry* (London: New Beacon Books, 1984). Judith Raiskin has suggested that white creole women writers in various nonwhite countries suffer the same sense of delusion; her book title alludes to Brathwaite's observation. See Judith Raiskin, *Snow on the Canefields: Women's Writing and Creole Subjectivity* (Minneapolis: University of Minnesota Press, 1996).

C. L. R. James recounts a similar problem with one of his first efforts at writing, which turned out to be an imitation of an English author simply transferred to the context of Trinidad. See C. L. R. James, "The Making of a Literary Life," interview with Paul Buhle, in *C. L. R. James's Caribbean* (Durham: Duke University Press, 1992), 57.

2 Fanon describes the evolution of oppositional consciousnesss in the colonized

as beginning with a period where the educated "native" tries to outdo the colonizer in his own customs, followed by his discovery of the "value" of "native" culture, culminating in a revolutionary consciousness and a "fighting" or oppositional literature. See Frantz Fanon, "On National Culture," in *The Wretched of the Earth* (New York: Grove, 1963), 206–48.

3   An example of folk literature in anglophone Caribbean narrative would be, among others, George Lamming's *Season of Adventure*; Claude McKay's *Banana Bottom*; Vic Reid's *New Day*; Sylvia Wynter's *The Hills of Hebron*; and C. L. R. James's first novel *Minty Alley*. *Minty Alley* is the story of an educated black man who comes to live in a tenement yard in Trinidad. If we read the protagonist as a Jamesian figure himself, a member of the alienated, anglicized black middle class having to "discover" the "real" West Indian cultural experience, the novel is actually an argument for an indigenous West Indian culture worthy of literary analysis, more so than a novel.

4   See, for instance, Aimé Césaire, *A Tempest* (1969), in *The Collected Poetry of Aimé Césaire*, trans. Clayton Eshleman and Annette Smith (Berkeley: University of California Press, 1983), and *Discours sur le colonialisme* (New York: MR, 1972/1955); Fernando Retamar, "Caliban: Notes Toward a Discussion of Culture in Our America," trans. Lynn Garafola, David Arthur McMurray, and Robert Marquez, *Massachusetts Review* 15 (winter/spring 1974): 3–45; George Lamming, *The Pleasures of Exile* (London: Allison and Busby, 1984/1960), and *Water with Berries* (New York: Holt, Rinehart and Winston, 1971); Frantz Fanon's *Black Skins, White Masks*, trans. Charles L. Markmann (New York: Grove, 1967/1952); and Edward Brathwaite, "Caliban," in *Islands* (London: Oxford University Press, 1969).

5   See Bruce King, *The New English Literatures* (London: Macmillan, 1980), 42.

6   See Timothy Brennan, "The National Longing for Form," in *Nation and Narration*, ed. Homi K. Bhabha (London: Routledge, 1990/1993), 48.

7   For an example of this strand of Caribbeanist thinking, see Amon Saakana, *The Colonial Legacy in Caribbean Literature* (Trenton, N.J.: Africa World Press, 1987). Saakana argues against the idea that West Indian culture is inherently fragmented, positing that there is an essential West Indian culture, rooted in an African-based past, over which European customs and systems have been imposed. Any theory of West Indian literature, he concludes, must start from this assumption.

8   Wilson Harris criticizes West Indian novels for their reliance on the nineteenth-century "novel of persuasion," as he terms it, for their model. See Harris, *Tradition, The Writer & Society* (London: New Beacon Press, 1967), 29.

9   Edward Brathwaite, "The Love Axe (1): Developing a Caribbean Aesthetic 1962–1974," in *Reading Black: Essays in the Criticism of African, Caribbean,*

and Black American Literature, ed. Houston A. Baker, Jr. (Ithaca: Cornell University Africana Studies and Research Center Monograph Series 4, 1976), 27.

10   Edward Brathwaite, "Contradictory Omens," *Savacou Publications* (Mona, Jamaica: University of the West Indies, 1978).

11   See Edward Brathwaite, "Roots," in *Roots* (Havana: Casa de las Americas, 1985/1971), 209.

12   See George Lamming, *The Pleasures of Exile* (Ann Arbor: University of Michigan Press, 1992/1960), 45. Hereafter all further references to Lamming's discussion on this topic are taken from this edition. Lamming also discusses the peasantry as the basis of all West Indian narrative in "The Peasant Roots of the West Indian Novel," in *Critics of West Indian Literature*, ed. Edward Baugh (London: Macmillan, 1978).

13   See George Lamming, "Interview with George Lamming," interview with George E. Kent, *Black World* (March 22, 1973): 91. I discuss the issue of violence in Lamming's work at more length in chapter 5.

14   Richard Halpern explores this idea with regard to the use of Shakespeare in "Shakespeare in the Tropics: From High Modernism to New Historicism" (colloquium manuscript, Johns Hopkins University, spring 1994). Halpern points out that in later centuries Shakespeare came to signify English society to the point where his head was studied as a complete embodiment of the nation itself (60). Since it was the Victorian era that produced the particular brand of nationalism that iconized its writers for export in this way, this supports my contention that Shakespeare in some sense is a product of the Victorian age, hence later West Indian fascination with his plays, particularly *The Tempest*.

15   I use the quotation marks to denote that "white" here refers to a West Indian of *mostly* white ancestry. He might also be called "red," in common Jamaican parlance.

16   See Lamming, "The Peasant Roots of the West Indian Novel," 46.

17   This is not to say that black people did not—and do not—actually *own* land; there has been a land-owning class of the peasantry in the English-speaking Caribbean since the 1800s. According to Catherine Hall, English missionaries as early as the 1830s bought land from planters who did not want to sell to blacks, and then resold the land to the blacks themselves. See Catherine Hall, *White, Male and Middle-Class: Explorations in Feminism and History* (Cambridge, U.K.: Polity Press, 1992), 243. My argument here is predicated on the total ownership of the national space, as opposed to individual land spaces: the emphasis is on land as power in the governance of the society, in other words.

18   Rex Nettleford, "European Melodies, African Rhythms," in *Mirror Mirror* (Kingston, Jamaica: Collins and Sangster, 1970).

19   Ibid., 117.

20   Ibid., 117.

21 As Rhys herself writes in her autobiography, "I seem to be brought up willy-nilly against the two sides of the question. Sometimes I ask myself if I am the only one who is; for after all, who knows or cares if there are two sides?" See Jean Rhys, *Smile Please* (New York: Harper and Row, 1979), 51.

22 See Edward Kamau Brathwaite, "Jazz and the West Indian Novel," in *Roots* (Havana: Casa de las Americas, 1985/1971). All further references to this essay are taken from this edition.

23 Ibid., 77.

24 See Brathwaite, "Roots," 51, emphasis added. Interestingly, another West Indian critic who defines Caribbean literary aesthetics as a "resisting" practice, Selwyn Cudjoe, also cites *A House for Mr. Biswas* as well as *The Mimic Men* as Naipaul's greatest works in his study, *V. S. Naipaul: A Materialist Reading* (Amherst: University of Massachusetts Press, 1988), 227.

25 Jean D'Costa suggested to me that the apparent rejection of American writers in evidence here might have something to do with the fact that American literature as a category was rejected for many years at the University of the West Indies, there being only one American literature course in the undergraduate curriculum until the early 1970s. According to her, the English department's view was that major American authors should be taught as part of nineteenth- and twentieth-century English literature, and American culture did not deserve a course of its own: "The subliminal message which came through was that 'these Americans have nothing useful to say to *us*. Our fight is with the British.' "

26 See Brathwaite, "Roots," 54.

27 See Derek Walcott, "The Garden Path," *The New Republic* (April 13, 1987): 30.

28 See V. S. Naipaul, "I Don't Consider Myself a West Indian," 3.

29 Brathwaite, "Roots," 72.

30 See Claude McKay, *Home to Harlem* (New York: Harper and Brothers, 1928) and *Banjo* (New York: Harper and Brothers, 1929).

31 See Claude McKay, *Banana Bottom* (New York: Harcourt Brace Jovanovich, 1961/1933), 212. All further references to the novel are taken from this edition.

32 It has been suggested by several authors that Squire Gensir is a literary depiction of McKay's mentor and friend, Walter Jekyll, an eccentric member of the English upper class who lived in Jamaica and encouraged McKay to write in creole. McKay dedicates his novel to "Pacjo," the Jamaican peasants' nickname for Jekyll (Cobham, 57). Both Rhonda Cobham and Wayne Cooper have suggested that the character of Bita is actually McKay himself; see *The Passion of Claude McKay: Selected Poetry and Prose, 1912–1948*, ed. Wayne F. Cooper (New York: Schocken Books, 1973) and Rhonda Cobham, "Jekyll and Claude: The Erotics of Patronage in Claude McKay's *Banana Bottom*," *Caribbean Quarterly* 38, no. 1 (March 1992): 55–78. Cobham goes further in arguing

that McKay displaces a possibly homoerotic attachment to Jekyll—Jekyll was apparently homosexual, McKay bisexual—onto the heterosexualized relation between Bita and Gensir.

33 McKay, *Banana Bottom*, 124–25.

34 See Gauri Viswanathan, "Currying Favor: The Politics of British Educational and Cultural Policy in India, 1813–1954," *Social Text* 19/20 (fall 1988), 103.

35 See Carolyn Cooper, " 'Only a Nigger Gal!': Race, Gender and the Politics of Education in Claude McKay's *Banana Bottom*," *Caribbean Quarterly* 38, no. 1 (March 1992): 53, 48.

36 In an argument similar to the one I make here, Michael North asserts that the vaunted return to "true" Jamaican values in *Banana Bottom* is a false distinction, since Squire Gensire gives Bita the social sanction to go to tea rooms, speak in dialect, and so forth. However, North goes further by asserting that the essential contest in the novel is not between Bita and the Craigs (the puritanical Scottish missionaries who educate her), Jamaica and England, but rather it is between the Craigs and Squire Gensir, England and *England's* Jamaica. The dichotomy made between English Christian mores and "life-affirming" Jamaican paganism is false because both sides are actually defined by the English. I would differ only in respect to North's argument that because Gensir sanctions "real" Jamaican culture, therefore it only exists because of him. Bita is actually the real focus of this story, and how she negotiates Gensir's views with her own selfhood—which we understand to exist, even if unrecognized—is, ultimately, the real contest. See Michael North, *The Dialect of Modernism: Race, Language and Twentieth-Century Literature* (New York: Oxford University Press, 1994).

37 See Cobham, "Jekyll and Claude," 71, 75.

38 Claude McKay, *A Long Way from Home*, quoted in Rhonda Cobham, "Jekyll and Claude," 62.

39 See Cooper, *The Passion of Claude McKay*, 8.

40 Ibid., 15.

41 See C. S. Chauhan, "Rereading Claude McKay," *CLA Journal* 34, no. 1 (September 1990): 69, 80.

42 See Erika Smilowitz, "Una Marson: Woman Before Her Time," *Jamaica Journal* 16, no. 2 (May 1983): 62–68.

43 Poet Amy Bailey believed that Una Marson was a less authentic Jamaican writer than herself because she had lived abroad for years: "Una Marson? She went away to raise money and never came back. I stayed." See "The Value of an Angry Woman: The Importance of Una Marson," Honor Ford-Smith (manuscript, Kingston Jamaica, 1992), 21.

44 The versions of *Pocomania* and *London Calling* that I use here are the drafts kept in the archives at the Institute of Jamaica.

45 See Ford-Smith, "The Value of an Angry Woman," 11.

46 See Una Marson, "The America I have Discovered" (manuscript, Institute of Jamaica, ca. 1930).

Chapter 4 Theorizing Caribbean Feminist Aesthetics

The second and third quotes that open this chapter are from, respectively, Jamaica Kincaid, interviewed by Selwyn R. Cudjoe, "Jamaica Kincaid and the Modernist Project," in *Caribbean Women Writers: Essays from the First International Conference*, ed. Selwyn R. Cudjoe (Wellesley, Mass.: Calaloux Publications, 1990), 217–18; and Marlene Nourbese Philip, "The Absence of Writing or How I Almost Became a Spy," in *Out of the Kumbla: Caribbean Women and Literature*, ed. Carole Boyce Davies and Elaine Savory Fido (Trenton, N.J.: Africa World Press, 1990), 271.

1 Kincaid asserts ignorance of a West Indian literary tradition in "Jamaica Kincaid and the Modernist Project," 220: "I didn't know about West Indian literature before I came to this country."

2 Jamaica Kincaid, "Jamaica Kincaid and the Modernist Project," 217–18.

3 See "Jamaica Kincaid and the Modernist Project," 215, where Kincaid describes her first years in the United States as an au pair girl.

4 For a more detailed analysis of Jamaica Kincaid's *Lucy* and its use of "home" and "away" thematics, see my discussion in chapter 6.

5 See Helen Tiffin, "Cold Hearts and (Foreign) Tongues: Recitation and the Reclamation of the Female Body in the Works of Erna Brodber and Jamaica Kincaid," *Callaloo* 16, no. 4 (fall 1993), 920.

6 See Helen Tiffin, "Cold Hearts," 918–19, for a discussion of Lucy's recitation of Wordsworth and its use as a trope of the master text in *Lucy*.

7 Mariah, Lucy's employer, is described as an adherent of feminist philosophies: "Mariah wanted to rescue me. She spoke of women in society, women in history, women in culture, women everywhere. But I couldn't speak, so I couldn't tell her that my mother was my mother and that society and history and culture and other women in general were something else together." See *Lucy* (New York: Penguin, 1991), 131–32. (Hereafter all quotations from the novel are taken from the Penguin edition, 1991.) Also, Mariah prescribes Freud for Lucy's "problem" when Lucy describes her dream to Mariah and her husband (15).

8 See Paul Gilroy, *The Black Atlantic: Modernity and Double Consciousness* (Cambridge: Harvard University Press, 1993), 33.

9 See Sandra Harding, "Other 'Others' and Fractured Identities: Issues for Epistemologists," *The Science Question in Feminism* (Ithaca: Cornell University Press, 1986).

10 See Barbara Smith, "Toward a Black Feminist Criticism," in *The New Feminist Criticism: Essays on Women, Literature and Theory*, ed. Elaine Showalter (New York: Pantheon Books, 1985), 168.

11 In his essay "The Uncompleted Argument: Du Bois and the Illusion of Race," Appiah contends that Du Bois is held in thrall by two equally intractable principles of the Other's discourse:

> The thesis in this dialectic — which Du Bois reports as the American Negro's attempt to "minimize race distinctions" — is the denial of difference. Du Bois' antithesis is the acceptance of difference, along with a claim that each group has its part to play; that the white race and its racial Other are related not as superior but as complementaries; that the Negro message is, with the white one, part of the message of humankind.
>
> I call this pattern the classic dialectic for a simple reason: we find it in feminism also — on the one hand, a simple claim to equality, a denial of substantial difference; on the other, a claim to a special message, revaluing the feminine Other not as the helpmeet of sexism, but as the New Woman.

See Anthony Appiah, "The Uncompleted Argument," in *"Race", Writing and Difference*, ed. Henry Louis Gates, Jr. (Chicago: University of Chicago Press, 1985), 25.

12 Léopold Senghor, *Liberté I: Negritude et humanisme* (Paris: Seuil, 1964), 136, 141; this point is summarized in Patrick Taylor, *The Narrative of Liberation: Perspectives on Afro-Caribbean Literature, Popular Culture, and Politics* (Ithaca: Cornell University Press, 1989), 172.

13 See Aimé Césaire, introduction to "Que signifie pour nous l'Afrique?" by Leo Frobenius, *Tropiques* 5 (April 1942); issue reprinted in *Tropiques*, trans. Patrick Taylor (Paris: Jean Michel Place, 1978), 62; quoted in Taylor, *The Narrative of Liberation*, 173. However, there is some dissent about Senghor's and Césaire's beliefs in a biological blackness; in *The Collected Poetry of Aimé Césaire*, trans. Clayton Eshleman and Annette Smith (Berkeley: University of California Press, 1983), Eshleman and Smith write, "Senghor was understood — perhaps wrongly — to consider black culture as the product of a black nature. . . . Césaire seems to have shared Senghor's view in the early part of his career . . . In an interview with Jacqueline Leiner in 1978, however, he maintained that for him black culture had never had anything to do with biology and everything to do with a combination of geography and history: identity in suffering, not in genetic material, determined the bond among black people of different origins" (6).

14 See bell hooks, "An Aesthetic of Blackness," *Yearning: Race, Gender, and Cultural Politics* (Boston: South End Press, 1990), 106.

15 See Kenneth W. Warren, "Delimiting America: The Legacy of Du Bois," *American Literary History* (spring 1989): 178–80.

16   See J. Saunders Redding, "Afro-American Culture and the Black Aesthetic: Notes Toward a Re-Evaluation," in *Reading Black: Essays in the Criticism of African, Caribbean, and Black American Literature,* ed. Houston Baker Jr. (Ithaca: Cornell University Africana Studies and Research Center Monograph Series 4, 1976), 46.

17   See Wole Soyinka, "Aesthetic Illusions," in *Reading Black,* 11.

18   For example, these tenets are explicitly delineated by Bonnie J. Barthold in *Black Time: Fiction of Africa, the Caribbean, and the United States* (New Haven: Yale University Press, 1981), parts one and two. Also, see George Lamming, "Caribbean Literature: the Black Rock of Africa," *African Forum* 1 (spring 1966): 32–52; and Chinweizu, Onwuchekwu Jemie, Ihechukwu Madubuike, *Toward the Decolonization of African Literature,* vol. 1 (Washington, D.C.: Howard University Press, 1983), particularly chapter 4, "Issues and Tasks in the Decolonization of African Literature."

19   *Making a Difference: Feminist Literary Criticism,* ed. Gayle Greene and Coppelia Kahn (London: Methuen, 1985), 22.

20   See Hélène Cixous's contributions in *The Newly Born Woman* (Minneapolis: University of Minnesota Press, 1986); and Luce Irigaray's *This Sex Which Is Not One* (Ithaca: Cornell University Press, 1985), 34; both positions are summarized in Diana Fuss, *Essentially Speaking: Feminism, Nature & Difference* (New York: Routledge, 1990), chapter 1, "The 'Risk' of Essence," 1–21, and chapter 4, "Luce Irigaray's Language of Essence," 55–72.

21   See Evelyn O'Callaghan, "Engineering the Female Subject: Erna Brodber's *Myal*" (paper presented at the Caribbean Women Writers Conference, St. Augustine, Trinidad, April 24–27, 1990), 2. (Later published in another version; see Evelyn O'Callaghan, "Engineering Female Subjectivity," in *Woman Version: Theoretical Approaches to West Indian Fiction by Women* [London: Macmillan, 1993].)

22   See "Preface: Talking It Over," in *Out of the Kumbla,* ed. Carole Boyce Davies and Elaine Savory Fido, 12.

23   See Toril Moi's *Sexual/Textual Politics* (New York: Methuen, 1985) 139, 147–48; and Monique Plaza, "'Phallomorphic Power' and the Psychology of 'Woman'," *Ideology and Consciousness* 4 (autumn 1981): 57–76, for some of the more well-known criticisms leveled at Irigaray in particular. These charges are summarized by Fuss, chapter 4, "Luce Irigaray's Language of Essence," 56–57.

24   Angela Davis, *Women, Race and Class* (New York: Random House, 1981), 33. Antoinette Burton notes that British feminists in the nineteenth century also used the slavery analogy as a way to gain rights for women. See Antoinette Burton, *Burdens of History: British Feminists, Indian Women, and Imperial Culture, 1865–1915* (Chapel Hill: University of North Carolina Press, 1994), 10.

25   See Selwyn Cudjoe, "Maya Angelou and the Autobiographical Statement," in *Black Women Writers (1950–1980)*, ed. Mari Evans (New York: Anchor Books/Doubleday 1984), 6, 9.

26   See Rita Felski, *Beyond Feminist Aesthetics* (Cambridge: Harvard University Press, 1989), 94.

27   See Henry Louis Gates, Jr. *The Signifying Monkey* (Oxford: Oxford University Press, 1988) and "State of Florida vs. Luther Campbell," reprinted in *Passages: A Chronicle of the Humanities* 1 (1991): 3.

28   See Elaine Showalter, "Feminist Criticism in the Wilderness," in *The New Feminist Criticism*, 263.

29   See Rachel Blau DuPlessis, "For the Etruscans," in *The New Feminist Criticism*, 278.

30   DuPlessis, "For the Etruscans," 286 (emphasis added).

31   Felski, *Beyond Feminist Aesthetics*, 161.

32   Ibid., 175, 177.

33   Ibid., 68.

34   Ibid., 78.

35   Ibid., 75.

36   See Jürgen Habermas, *Die Strukturwandel der Öffentlichkeit: Untersuchungen zu einer Kategorie der bürgerlichen Gesellschaft* (*Structural Changes in the Public Sphere*) (1962, reprint Darmstadt: Luchterhand, 1984), quoted in Felski, 165.

37   Felski, *Beyond Feminist Aesthetics*, 166–67.

38   See Hazel Carby, *Reconstructing Womanhood: The Emergence of the Afro-American Woman Novelist* (New York: Oxford University Press, 1987), 39.

39   Carby, *Reconstructing Womanhood*, 35.

40   For an analysis of the role of gender in the division of plantation labor, see Jacqueline Jones, chapter 1, " 'My Mother Was Much of a Woman': Slavery," *Labor of Love, Labor of Sorrow* (New York: Vintage, 1986).

41   Felski, *Beyond Feminist Aesthetics*, 168–69.

42   See interview with Toni Morrison, in *Black Women Writers at Work*, ed. Claudia Tate (New York: Continuum, 1983), 122–23. For a more detailed discussion of Morrison's position on feminism see Paula Giddings, "The Women's Movement and Black Discontent," *When and Where I Enter: The Impact of Black Women on Race and Sex in America* (New York: Bantam, 1985), 299–324.

43   See Kincaid, "Jamaica Kincaid and the Modernist Project," 221.

44   See Diana Fuss, "By our lips we are women," *Essentially Speaking: Feminism, Nature and Difference* (New York: Routledge, 1989), 58–66. Fuss quotes Irigaray at length on the principle of autonomous female pleasure: "Woman's autoeroticism is very different from man's. In order to touch himself, man needs an instrument: his hand, a woman's body, language . . . And this self-

caressing requires at least a minimum of activity. As for woman, she touches herself in and of herself without any need for mediation, and before there is any way to distinguish activity from passivity. Woman 'touches herself' all the time, and moreover no one can forbid her to do so, for her genitals are formed of two lips in continuous contact. Thus, within herself, she is already two—but not divisible into one(s)—that caress each other." (*This Sex Which Is Not One*, 24, quoted in Fuss, 58.)

45 See Andree Nicola McLaughlin, "Introduction," in *Wild Women in the Whirlwind: Afra-American Culture and the Contemporary Literary Renaissance*, ed. Nicole Braxton and Andree Nicola McLaughlin (New Brunswick, N.J.: Rutgers University Press, 1990).

46 See Andree Nicola McLaughlin, *Wild Women in the Whirlwind*, xlii, 175.

47 "The 'Negro Family' has no Father to speak of—his Name, his Symbolic function mark the impressive missing agencies in the essential life of the black community," according to the now-infamous Moynihan Report of 1960, quoted in Spillers, "Mama's Baby, Papa's Maybe: An American Grammar Book," *Diacritics* 4, no. 17 (summer 1987): 65–81.

48 Spillers, "Mama's Baby," 80.

49 See Madhu Dubey, *Black Women Novelists and the Nationalist Aesthetic* (Bloomington: Indiana University Press, 1994), 20.

50 See Davies, "Preface: Talking It Over," in *Out of the Kumbla*, xvi (emphasis added).

51 See, for instance, the centrality of mother/daughter relationships and the accompanying critiques of traditional gender roles in Jamaica Kincaid's *Annie John*, *Lucy*, and *An Autobiography of My Mother*.

52 Kincaid, "Jamaica Kincaid and the Modernist Project," 221, 222.

53 See Morrison, "Interview with Toni Morrison," in *Black Women Writers*, 342, 127, 344.

54 See Lloyd Brown, "Introduction: Regional Writers, Regional Critics," in *Critical Issues in West Indian Literature*, ed. Lloyd Brown (Parkersburg, Iowa: Caribbean Books, 1984), 3.

55 See Alice Walker, *In Search of Our Mothers' Gardens* (San Diego: Harcourt Brace Jovanovich, 1983), xi.

56 Chikenyemi Ogunyemi, "Womanism: The Dynamics of the Contemporary Black Female Novel in English," *Signs* 11, no. 1 (1985): 63–80.

57 See Davies and Fido, "Preface," in *Out of the Kumbla*, xii.

58 See Davies and Fido, "Preface," in *Out of the Kumbla*.

59 See Michelle Cliff (interviewed by Opal Palmer Adisa), "A Journey Into Speech—A Writer Between Two Worlds: An Interview with Michelle Cliff," *African American Review* 28, no. 2 (1994), 279.

60 See Davies, "Preface," in *Out of the Kumbla*, xvii.

61 See Burton, *Burdens of History*, 40.

Chapter 5 The Novel of Revolution and the Unrepresentable Black Woman

1 While Lamming's critical essays in *Pleasures* are based on the characters of Shakespeare's *The Tempest*, Naipaul's novel is explicitly connected to the actual events in Trinidad, during the Black Power revolts of the early 1970s, which he chronicles in his nonfiction essay, "Michael X and the Black Power Killings in Trinidad," in *The Return of Eva Peron with the Killings in Trinidad* (New York: Vintage, 1974). Similarly, Lovelace's more fictive rendering of a failed black ghetto revolt in *Dragon* can be tied to a concern with the historical meaning of the failed Black Power revolts of the 1970s.

2 Stuart Hall asserts that *The Black Jacobins* is the first Caribbean account of the Haitian revolution in "C. L. R. James: A Portrait," in *C. L. R. James's Caribbean*, ed. Paget Henry and Paul Buhle (Durham: Duke University Press, 1992), 8.

3 See Derek Walcott, "The Quarrel with History," in *Is Massa Day Dead? Black Moods in the Caribbean*, ed. Orde Coombs (Kingston, Jamaica: Carifesta Forum, 1976).

4 As Jamaican sociologist and writer Erna Brodber observes of West Indian society, "[The literate] tended to see booklearning not simply as a tool for making a livelihood but as the ultimate truth. . . . The unlettered lowerclass, depending on the oral tradition for its information, was kept in touch with its past of Africa and slavery and with its African identity." The conflation of story and history in the West Indian context is therefore particularly important as a way of empowering the entire spectrum of people and providing a democratic means of shaping Caribbean historical discourse. See Erna Brodber, *Caribbean Quarterly* 31, no. 2 (June 1985): 53.

5 See C. L. R. James, *The Black Jacobins: Toussaint L'Ouverture and the San Domingo Revolution* (New York: Vintage, 1963/1938), 91.

6 James, *The Black Jacobins*, 159.

7 See V. S. Naipaul, *The Middle Passage* (New York: Vintage, 1981/1962), 29.

8 See my discussion of Hortense Spillers's essay, "Mama's Baby, Papa's Maybe" in chapter 4.

9 See Lynda E. Boose, " 'The Getting of a Lawful Race': Racial Discourse in Early Modern England and the Unrepresentable Black Woman," in *Women, "Race," and Writing in the Early Period*, ed. Margo Hendricks and Patricia Parker (London: Routledge, 1994), 45. Similarly, Mary Louise Pratt presents a table from W. B. Stevenson's *Narratives of Twenty Years Residence in South America* (1825), which depicts the "mixture of different castes," and quotes Stevenson's rationale for the different categorizing of the offspring of whites and nonwhites depending on the race of the father: " 'I have classed colours according to their appearance, not according to the mixture of the castes, because I have always remarked, that *a child receives more of the colour of the father than of the*

mother" (vol. 1, 286; emphasis added), quoted in Pratt, *Imperial Eyes: Travel Writing and Transculturation* (New York: Routledge, 1992), 152. Therefore, he continues, "a white father and a negro mother produces a mulatto that is 7/8 white, 1/8 negro, described as 'often fair'. However: A negro father and a white mother produces a 'zambo'; that is 4/8 white, 4/8 negro, and 'dark copper' in complexion."

10 Vera Kutzinski argues that in his poem "El Abuelo," black nationalist Cuban poet Nicholas Guillen similarly conceives of a new, raceless Cuban utopia predicated on the erasure of a black woman, "the one in whose violated body the two races actually met. A masculine consciousness has clearly usurped that site." See Kutzinski, *Sugar's Secrets: Race and the Erotics of Cuban Nationalism* (Charlottesville: University Press of Virginia, 1993), 168.

11 See Jonathan Goldberg, " 'Bradford's 'Ancient Members' and 'A Case of Buggery . . . Amongst Them'," in *Nationalisms and Sexualities*, ed. Andrew Parker, Mary Russo, Doris Sommer, and Patricia Yaeger (London: Routledge, 1992), 63.

12 Among others see Aimé Césaire, *A Tempest* (Paris: Seuil, 1969) and *Discours sur le colonialisme*, 5th ed. (Paris: Présence Africaines, 1970); Roberto Fernández Retamar, "Caliban: Notes Toward a Discussion of Culture in Our America," trans. Lynn Garafola, David Arthur McMurray, and Robert Marquez, *Massachusetts Review* 15 (winter/spring 1974): 3–45; George Lamming, *The Pleasures of Exile* (London: Allison and Busby, 1984) and *Water with Berries* (New York: Holt, Rinehart and Winston, 1971); Frantz Fanon's *Black Skins, White Masks* (New York: Grove, 1967/1952); and Edward Brathwaite, "Caliban," in *Islands* (London: Oxford University Press, 1969). For a thematic survey of Caliban in Third World writing, see Charlotte H. Bruner, "The Meaning of Caliban in Black Literature Today," *Comparative Literature Studies* 13 (September 1976): 240–53. A very useful discussion of Caliban's role in Caribbean and African discourses is Rob Nixon's "Caribbean and African Appropriations of *The Tempest*," in *Politics and Poetic Value*, ed. Robert von Hallberg (Chicago: University of Chicago Press, 1987). Among other things, Nixon notes the "declining significance of Caliban in the age of technocracy."

13 See Laura Donaldson, "The Miranda Complex: Colonialism and the Question of Feminist Reading," *Diacritics* 6 (fall 1988), 68.

14 Gayatri Spivak, "Three Women's Texts and A Critique of Imperialism," *Critical Inquiry* 12 (1985): 243–61, quoted in Donaldson, "The Miranda Complex," 76.

15 The "hermeneutics of suspicion" is a term coined by Paul Ricoeur and used by Gilbert and Gubar to describe the methodology necessary to uncover a distinctively female literary tradition hidden within the masculinist literary traditions within which female writers have had to work.

16 See Donaldson, "The Miranda Complex," 70–71.

17 See bell hooks (Gloria Watson), *Ain't I a Woman: Black Women and Feminism* (Boston: South End Press, 1981), 38.

18 Donaldson is not the first to make this analogy. As I note in chapter 4, Sandra Harding argues that white women and blacks have been constructed as having the same "worldview." See my discussion of Sandra Harding, "Other 'Others' and Fractured Identities," *The Science Question in Feminism*, in chapter 4.

19 See Retamar, "Caliban," 4. "The Prospero complex" is a phrase coined by O. Mannoni in his reading of the psychological impact of colonization through the metaphor of *The Tempest* in *Prospero and Caliban: The Psychology of Colonization* (New York: Praeger, 1956). Mannoni was castigated by Caribbean and African intellectuals for his theory that the colonized person suffers from a "Prospero complex" which causes him to anticipate, even require, the presence of the colonizer. (My use of the masculine pronoun here is deliberate.)

20 See Retamar, "Caliban," 14, 16.

21 See Rob Nixon, "Caribbean and African Appropriations of *The Tempest*," 204.

22 See George Lamming, *The Pleasures of Exile* (London: Allison and Busby 1984/1960). Hereafter all quotations in the text are taken from this edition.

23 For nineteenth-century newspaper accounts of Haitian society, see Douglas Lorimer, *Colour, Class and the Victorians: English Attitudes to the Negro in the Mid-Nineteenth Century* (Leicester: Leicester University Press, 1978). Also, Froude discusses Haiti at length in *The English in the West Indies* (New York: Negro University Press, 1969/1888).

24 See Lamming, *Pleasures of Exile*, 111.

25 I refer to the debate, detailed in chapter 1, among English intellectuals on whether black West Indian men would revert to their natural African barbarism or, with proper English guidance, whether they would be transformed into the British gentleman. It is to these contrasting arguments that I refer when I say that Caliban is perceived to be the very crossroads of possibility itself — the possibilities of savagery or civilization.

26 Lamming, *Pleasures of Exile*, 110.

27 Ibid., 111.

28 For a discussion of Sycorax as a symbol of black motherhood, see Abena Busia, "But Caliban and Ariel Are Still Both Male: On African Colonial Discourse and the Unvoiced Female," in *Crisscrossing Boundaries in African Literatures 1988*, ed. Kenneth Harrow (Washington, D.C.: Three Continents Press, 1991), 129–40.

29 Lamming, *Pleasures of Exile*, 112, 15, 115.

30 See Sylvia Wynter, "Beyond Miranda's Meanings: Un/Silencing the 'Demonic Ground' of Caliban's Woman," in *Out of the Kumbla: Caribbean Women and Literature*, ed. Carole Boyce Davies and Elaine Savory Fido (Trenton, N.J.: Africa World Press, 1990), 355–73.

31 Lamming, *Pleasures of Exile*, 102.

32 For examples of inter-racial rape constructed as a nationalist metaphor, see V. S. Naipaul's *Guerrillas*, where the black revolutionary Jimmy Ahmed rapes and allows the murder of Jane, the liberal white Englishwoman, in order to effect a reconciliation with his disillusioned follower, a mentally disturbed black ghetto boy. Also, Makak, the main character in Derek Walcott's *Dream on Monkey Mountain*, is instructed to kill his white muse because she is "the mother of civilization and the confounder of blackness." See *Dream on Monkey Mountain and Other Plays* (New York: Farrar, Straus and Giroux, 1970), 318–19.

    Further, in *An Island Is a World* Trinidadian writer Samuel Selvon wrote a chapter — deleted by the English publisher — in which his male character sheds his feelings of racial inferiority through sexual domination of the white woman. Selvon describes the character's feelings thus: "[Y]ou know, saying 'I'll *fuck* it all out of you, you white *bitch!*'" Quoted in Daryl Cumber Dance, "Matriarchs, Doves, and Nymphos: Prevalent Images of Black, Indian, and White Women in Caribbean Literature," *Studies in the Literary Imagination* 26, no. 2 (fall 1993), 21–43, esp. 29.

    In African American literature, there are also potent examples of the white female body as a site of black nationalist struggle. One is to be found in Ralph Ellison's depiction of the white female body as the site of conflict in the Battle Royale scene in *Invisible Man*, as well as in Bigger Thomas's desire for the woman he murders in Richard Wright's *Native Son*.

    Interestingly, in Lamming's *Season of Adventure* the metaphor of rape as a colonizing act is effected on the body of a *black* woman, who is first *seduced* by a *white* man and, immediately afterwords, *raped* by a *black* man. Lamming's arrangement of the rape-versus-seduction motif can be interpreted in many different ways, but it seems plausible to suggest that inasmuch as the metaphor of the black man as rapist is still maintained while the original colonial "rapist," if you will, in the symbolic figure of the white man, is (re)constructed as a seducer, rape is still being posited by Lamming as a nationalistic act — albeit a problematic one — against the "seductions" of the colonialist enterprise. For a more thorough account of Lamming's rape thematics as they pertain to *Season of Adventure* in particular, see Supriya Nair, *Caliban's Curse: George Lamming and the Revisioning of History* (Ann Arbor: University of Michigan Press, 1996).

33 See Dance, "Matriarchs, Doves, and Nymphos." Dance notes that images of black women in male-authored fiction tend toward matriarchal figures who dominate the household yet are selfless in their concern for their children.

34 In her excellent analysis of the connection between sexuality and history in Caribbean narrative, Susan Andrade similarly points to male writers' "unproblematized, 'natural' relation between women and colonialism, between

history/geography and sexuality" (218), which she then connects to the black (Caribbean) male perception of the black woman as sexual/racial betrayer contained in Fanon's discussion of interracial sex in *Black Skin, White Masks*. While I do not disagree with the latter argument, I would distinguish that particular strain of black female representation in Caribbean intellectual discourse from the fictional representation of black femaleness in Caribbean narrative, which, as I have said, is remarkable mostly for its absence in terms of historical interracial rape, or indeed of any kind of interracial sex between white men and black women. See Susan Andrade, "The Nigger of the Narcissist: History, Sexuality and Intertextuality in Maryse Conde's *Heremakhonon*," *Callaloo* 16, no. 1 (1993): 213–26.

35   See Jürgen Habermas, *Structural Changes in the Public Sphere* (Darmstandt: Luchterhand, 1984/1962). See discussion of the public sphere and divisions in the feminist movement in chapter 4.

36   The title comes from Caliban's speech to Prospero:

Caliban: I must eat my dinner.
This island's mine, by Sycorax my mother,
Which thou tak'st from me. When thou cam'st first,
Thou strok'st me, and made much of me; wouldst give me
Water with berries in't; and teach me how
To name the bigger light, and how the less,
That burn by day and night: and then I lov'd thee, . . .
. . . Curs'd be I that did so! . . .

37   In a personal discussion of this passage, Paul Breslin has suggested that the name Fernando is meant to remind us of Ferdinand, Miranda's virtuous suitor and the legitimate heir to the King of Naples, and that Fernando may well be a conflation of the two characters. This conflation would then function to illustrate that Shakespeare's virtuous "true" heir — with all the implications of Europe's "natural" legitimacy to rule that such a character holds — is in actuality a usurper and man of violence. I find this reading to be a very persuasive one.

38   See George Kent, "A Conversation with George Lamming," *Black World* 22 (March 1973): 90–91.

39   See my discussion of Lamming in chapter 3, where I quote Lamming in an interview with George Kent, discussing the necessity for violence as a liberatory strategy under colonialism.

40   See Richard Halpern, " 'The Picture of Nobody' White Cannibalism in *The Tempest*," *Shakespeare Among the Moderns* (Ithaca: Cornell University Press, 1997).

41   Lamming is not the only West Indian author who portrays this unassimilability of white femaleness to the new, decolonized Caribbean. See my discussion of

Edward Kamau Brathwaite's critique of Jean Rhys's *Wide Sargasso Sea* in chapter 3.

42 Rob Nixon, "Caribbean and African Appropriations of *The Tempest*," 205.

43 Marshall, "Brazil," in *Soul Clap Hands and Sing* (Chatham, N.J.: Chatham Bookseller, 1961), 135. Hereafter all references in the text are to this edition.

44 Marshall, "Brazil," 140–41.

45 Ibid., 169.

46 Ibid., 171.

47 See Michelle Cliff, *No Telephone to Heaven* (New York: Dutton, 1988), 127. Hereafter all references to the novel in the text are to this edition.

48 The placement of Ruth First, as a white female South African revolutionary, into this pantheon of black male revolutionaries, suggests that Cliff is rewriting the idea of Third World revolutionary subjectivity to be more inclusive, gender- and race-wise.

49 The character of Jimmy Ahmed is a fictive rendering of the historical figure Michael X, whose rise as a Black Power leader and subsequent imprisonment for the murder of his white mistress Gail Benson is chronicled in Naipaul's essay "Michael X and the Black Power Killings in Trinidad." See V. S. Naipaul, *The Return of Eva Peron with the Black Power Killings in Trinidad* (New York: Vintage, 1974/1981).

50 See V. S. Naipaul, *Guerrillas* (New York: Vintage, 1990), 233–38. Hereafter all quotations in the text are taken from this edition.

51 Rob Nixon speculates that Naipaul had Lamming in mind in his short story, *A Flag on the Island*, where the narrator parodies Caribbean celebrations of Caliban by citing a local autobiography, *I Hate You: One Man's Search for Identity*, which begins: "I am a man without identity. Hate has consumed my identity. My personality has been distorted by hate. My hymns have not been hymns of praise, but of hate. How terrible to be Caliban, you say. But I say, how tremendous. Tremendousness is therefore my unlikely subject." See V. S. Naipaul, *A Flag on the Island* (London: Andre Deutsch, 1967), 154, quoted in Nixon, "Caribbean and African Appropriations of *The Tempest*," 195, n. 20.

52 See Mary Lou Emery, *Jean Rhys At World's End: Novels of Colonial and Sexual Exile* (Austin: University of Texas Press, 1990), xii.

53 For a more detailed account of the role of white creole women in Caribbean narrative, see Belinda Edmondson, "Race, Privilege, and the Politics of (Re)-Writing History: An Analysis of the Novels of Michelle Cliff," *Callaloo* 16, no. 1 (1993): 180–91.

54 See Peter Stallybrass and Allon White, *The Politics and Poetics of Transgression* (Ithaca: Cornell University Press, 1986), 83.

55 See Barbara Harlowe, *Resistance Literature* (New York: Methuen, 1987), 189.

56 See Wilson Harris, *Tradition, the Writer & Society* (London: New Beacon, 1967), 64.

57 See Selwyn Cudjoe, *Resistance and Caribbean Literature* (Athens: Ohio University Press, 1990), 56. Alejo Carpentier's definition of magical realism is also quoted here.

58 V. S. Naipaul, *The Mimic Men* (N.Y.: Penguin, 1967).

Chapter 6 Return of the Native: Immigrant Women's Writing and the Narrative of Exile

The opening quotation is from Paule Marshall, "A MELUS Interview: Paule Marshall," with Joyce Pettis, *MELUS* 17, no. 4 (winter 1991–92): 117.

1 For discussions of exile in anglophone Caribbean narrative see, for instance. George Lamming, *The Pleasures of Exile* (London: Allison and Busby, 1984/ 1960); Gareth Griffiths, *A Double Exile* (London: Calder, 1978); Mary Lou Emery, *Jean Rhys at World's End: Novels of Colonial and Sexual Exile* (Austin: University of Texas Press, 1990); and Simon Gikandi, chapters 1 and 2 of *Writing in Limbo: Modernism and Caribbean Literature* (Ithaca: Cornell University Press, 1992).

2 See Edward Said, "Reflections on Exile," *Granta* 13 (autumn 1984): 162, quoted in Simon Gikandi, *Writing in Limbo*, 71. I owe much of my material here on exile in anglophone Caribbean narrative to Simon Gikandi's very thorough analysis.

3 See Lamming, *The Pleasures of Exile*, 24.

4 The phenomenon of a largely female emigration from the Caribbean to the United States has been documented by several sources; see, among others, Philip Kasinitz, *Caribbean New York: Black Immigrants and the Politics of Race* (Ithaca: Cornell University Press, 1992); Delores M. Mortimer and Roy S. Bryce-La Porte, "Female Immigrants to the United States: Caribbean, Latin American and African Experiences" and "Caribbean Immigration to the United States," RIIES Occasional Papers nos. 1 and 2 (Washington, D.C.: Smithsonian Institution, 1981 and 1983); Olive Senior, *Working Miracles: Women's Lives in the English-Speaking Caribbean* (London: James Currey, 1991); Christine Ho, "The Internationalization of Kinship and the Feminization of Caribbean Migration," *Human Organization* 52, no. 1 (1993); and Shellee Colen, "'Like a Mother to Them': Stratified Reproduction and West Indian Childcare Workers and Employers in New York," in *Conceiving the New World Order: The Global Politics of Reproduction*, ed. Faye D. Ginsburg and Rayna Rapp (Berkeley: University of California Press, 1995).

The huge numbers of Caribbean women migrating to the United States seems very clearly linked to the burgeoning market in domestic work. Kasinitz states that the large influx of Caribbean women who have migrated to metropolitan centers such as New York since the 1970s have been attracted by the chance of employment in a range of domestic services, especially with the huge expansion of the service sector in the 1970s (70). Further, Colen argues that metropolitan domestic services, rather than radically revise or reduce the gender divide of homebound work as more women in the United States visibly entered the public work force, "crossed, class, race, and national lines" (83) to use West Indian migrant women instead. My thanks to Supriya Nair for sharing her essay with me, from which I gleaned the Kasinitz and Colen citations. See Supriya Nair, "Homing Instincts: Immigrant Nostalgia and Gender Politics in *Brown Girl, Brownstones*," in *Caribbean Romances: The Politics of Regional Representation*, ed. Belinda Edmondson (Charlottesville: University Press of Virginia, 1999).

5   See "Naipaul Gets Eliot Award," *New York Times*, 16 September 1986, C20; and Bharati Mukherjee and C. J. Wallia, both quoted in Scott Winokur, "The Unsparing Vision of V. S. Naipaul," *Image* (5 May 1991): 11; which is quoted in Rob Nixon, *London Calling: V. S. Naipaul, Postcolonial Mandarin* (New York: Oxford University Press, 1992), 3–4.

6   See V. S. Naipaul, "I Don't Consider Myself a West Indian," *Guyana Graphic*, 30 Nov. 1968: 3.

7   Nixon notes some examples of what might be termed "Naipaul worship" in American and European literary circles: Eugene Goodheart, "V. S. Naipaul's Mandarin Sensibility," *Partisan Review* 50 (1983): 244–56; Joseph Epstein, "A Cottage for Mr. Naipaul," *New Criterion* (October 1987): 6–15; Conor Cruise O'Brien and John Lukacs's defense of Naipaul from Edward Said's criticism in "The Post-Colonial Intellectual: A Discussion with Conor Cruise O'Brien, Edward Said and John Lukacs," *Salmagundi* 70, no. 1 (spring–summer 1986): 65–81.

8   See V. S. Naipaul, "The Novelist V. S. Naipaul Talks About His Work to Ronald Bryden," *The Listener* (22 March 1973), quoted in Nixon, *London Calling*, 23.

9   Nixon, *London Calling*, 28.

10 See Ronald Bryden, "The Novelist V. S. Naipaul Talks About His Work to Ronald Bryden," *The Listener* (22 March 1973), 367, quoted in Nixon, *London Calling*, 30.

11 See Shari Benstock, "Expatriate Modernism," in *Women's Writing and Exile*, ed. Mary Lynn Broe and Angela Ingram (Chapel Hill: University of North Carolina Press, 1989), 24.

12 Nixon, *London Calling*, 25.

13 See Simon Gikandi, "Introduction," in *Writing in Limbo*, 26. Also, see *Voices in Exile: Jamaican Texts of the 18th and 19th Century*, ed. Jean D'Costa and Barbara Lalla (Tuscaloosa: University of Alabama Press, 1989), 1.

14 I am thinking particularly of Kenyan novelist Ngugi wa Thiong'o, whose *Devil on the Cross* landed him in jail, as did his efforts at establishing a people's open

theater; also, Nigerian playwright and Nobel laureate Wole Soyinka, who, like Ngugi wa Thiong'o, must live in exile in the West for fear of retribution from the Nigerian government. At last report Soyinka has been charged *in absentia* with treason by the Nigerian government.

15 See Sigmund Freud, "The Uncanny" ("Das Unheimliche"), in *Standard Edition of the Complete Psychological Works of Sigmund Freud*, trans. and ed. James Strachey (London: Hogarth Press, 1955), quoted in Samantha Heigh, "The Return of Africa's Daughters: Negritude and the Gendering of Exile," (paper presented at the African Literature Association conference, Guadeloupe, 1993), 13. I am indebted to Samantha Heigh's reading of Irigaray, Benstock, and Freud in my teasing out the meanings of exile and "motherland" here.

16 Benstock, "Expatriate Modernism," 25.

17 See Luce Irigaray, *This Sex Which is Not One* (Ithaca: Cornell University Press, 1985), 168–69.

18 In support of this conclusion, Simon Gikandi points out that a generation of Caribbean writers conceived of colonialism as a state of "perpetual exile," a reference to the psychic alienation of the Caribbean intellectual from his society. See Gikandi, *Writing in Limbo*, 36.

19 A lack of understanding of Rhys's Caribbean concerns and heritage influenced critics of *Wide Sargasso Sea*, and they interpreted it solely in terms of its relation to English literature. Jean D'Costa argues that Rhys's "problems of classification disguise problems of interpretation and acceptance." See Jean D'Costa, "Jean Rhys, 1890–1979," in *Fifty Caribbean Writers*, ed. Daryl Dance (New York: Greenwood Press, 1986), 390–404. When it was first published in 1966, many early critics dismissed *Wide Sargasso Sea* as the "pre-history" of *Jane Eyre*; and, most strikingly, described Antoinette as a victim of her own "predatory temperament." Both quotations are from "A Fairy-Tale Neurotic," *Times Literary Supplement* (London), 17 November 1966, 1039. Others criticized it as no more than a "romantic evocation of the Caribbean scene" (Allan Ross, *London Magazine* [6 November 1966], 42); one *Sunday Times* (London) critic called the novel "enormous fun," but wished that Rhys would return to writing "with an aspect of life she has observed and experienced [that is, stories of white English women] rather than by annotating Charlotte Brontë." (Kay Dick, "Wife to Mr. Rochester," Sunday *Times* (London), 30 October 1966, 50. This comment is particularly ironic, given Rhys's West Indian background. There were other insults: the male critic of the *New York Times Book Review* who declared the novel to be a failure for the simple reason that the character of Mr. Rochester is "too shadowy a figure." (Walter Allen, *New York Times Book Review*, 18 June 1967.)

20 See Bonnie Kime Scott, "Introduction," *The Gender of Modernism: A Critical Anthology* (Bloomington: Indiana University Press, 1990), 2–3. Scott fur-

ther emphasizes that the modernists themselves gendered the viewing of their works, attaching such labels as "virile" and "feminine" to the new writing and attributing different meanings and values to the terms (3).

21   See V. S. Naipaul, "Without a Dog's Chance," in *Critical Perspectives on Jean Rhys*, ed. Pierrette Frickey (Washington, D.C.: Three Continents Press, 1990), 54.

22   Jean Rhys, unpublished letters from the Jean Rhys Collection, University of Tulsa, quoted in Veronica Gregg, *Jean Rhys' Historical Imagination: Reading and Writing the Creole* (Chapel Hill: University of North Carolina Press, 1995), 57.

23   For example, Wilson Harris's novel, *The Palace of the Peacock* (London: Faber and Faber, 1973/1960), excavates the pre-Columbian Caribbean past through the use of modernist structuring techniques.

24   See Paul Gilroy, *The Black Atlantic: Modernity and Double Consciousness* (Cambridge: Harvard University Press, 1994), chapter 1, and Manthia Diawara, "Englishness and Blackness: Cricket as Discourse on Colonialism," *Callaloo* 13 (1990)".

25   David Levering Lewis gives an account of white fascination with black life and art during the Harlem Renaissance in *When Harlem was in Vogue* (New York: Alfred Knopf, 1981). The influence of African art on Picasso and other painters of the early twentieth century is well documented; for one interesting account, see Marianne Torgovnick, *Gone Primitive: Savage Intellects, Modern Lives* (Chicago: University of Chicago Press, 1990).

26   See chapter 1 of Edward Said's book, *The World, the Text and the Critic* (Cambridge: Harvard University Press, 1983).

27   Mary Lou Emery describes the novels of Jean Rhys, Michelle Cliff, and Bessie Head as part of a tradition of "Third World Modernism" at the conclusion of *Jean Rhys At World's End: Novels of Colonial and Sexual Exile* (Austin: University of Texas Press, 1990); Edward Brathwaite connects his poems to the influence of T. S. Eliot in "Roots"; Simon Gikandi reads the Caribbean canon within the modernist frame in *Writing in Limbo: Modernism and Caribbean Literature* (Ithaca: Cornell University Press, 1992); and so forth.

28   Roberto González Echevarría, *Voice of the Masters: Writing and Authority in Modern Latin American Literature* (Austin: University of Texas Press, 1985), 11, quoted in Gikandi, *Writing in Limbo*, 11.

29   Stephen Slemon, "Interview with Wilson Harris," *Ariel: A Review of International English Literature* 19 (July 1988): 48, quoted in Gikandi, *Writing in Limbo*, 4. However, some Caribbean writers and critics explicitly reject the "gift" of modernism, most notably Jamaican scholar Michael Thelwell who argues that modernism has functioned to justify "a general retreat from [a] wide-ranging engagement with social and moral questions." See Michael Thelwell, "Modernist Fallacies and the Responsibility of the Black Writer," in *Du-*

ties, Pleasures, and Conflicts: Essays in Struggle (Amherst: University of Massachusetts Press, 1987), 221, quoted in Gikandi, *Writing in Limbo*, 3.

30   See C. L. R. James, "Discovering Literature in Trinidad: the 1930s," in *Spheres of Existence: Selected Writings* (Westport, Conn.: Lawrence Hill, 1980), 237.

31   James, "Discovering Literature in Trinidad," 238–39.

32   See V. S. Naipaul, "Cricket," *The Overcrowded Barracoon* (New York: Vintage, 1984/1972), 22.

33   D. H. Lawrence is famous for his advocacy of "rude" English peasant culture as a repository of cultural depth and meaning in such novels as *Lady Chatterley's Lover* (1928) and *Sons and Lovers* (1913).

34   See V. S. Naipaul, *The Enigma of Arrival* (New York: Alfred Knopf, 1987), 153.

35   See Wilson Harris, *Tradition, the Writer & Society* (London: New Beacon, 1967).

36   See C. L. R. James, "Introduction," in Harris, *Tradition, the Writer & Society*, 75.

37   See the back cover of Derek Walcott, *The Castaway* (London: Jonathan Cape Poetry Paperbacks, 1969), which features the quote by the Sunday *Times* (London); the back cover of V. S. Naipaul, *A Flag on the Island* (London: Penguin, 1967), featuring a quote from the *London Financial Times*; and the back cover of C. L. R. James, *At the Rendezvous of Victory* (London: Allison and Busby, 1984) featuring a quotation from the *Times* (London). I owe this observation to Faith Smith, who notes this phenomenon in her essay, "Coming Home to the Real Thing: Gender and Intellectual Life in the Anglophone Caribbean," *South Atlantic Quarterly* 93, no. 4 (fall 1994): 918, n. 6.

38   In its review of Jean Rhys's *Wide Sargasso Sea*, the London *Times Literary Supplement* complains that "all her novels are about the injustice done by cruel men to lovely women." See *Times Literary Supplement*, 17 November 1966, 1039. The *Times*'s comment underscores the prevailing view of the time that novels about women's lives were not as profound as those about men.

39   "I think that the Anglo-Saxon idea that you can be rude with impunity to any female who has written a book is utterly *damnable*. You come and have a look out of curiosity and then allow the freak to see what you think of her. It's only done to the more or less unsuccessful and only by Anglo-Saxons. . . ."
     See Jean Rhys, *Jean Rhys: Letters, 1931–1966* (Harmondsworth: Penguin, 1985), 32, quoted in Veronica Gregg, "Jean Rhys on Herself as a Writer," in *Caribbean Women Writers: Essays from the First International Conference*, ed. Selwyn R. Cudjoe (Amherst: Calaloux Publications, 1990), 113.

40   Veronica Gregg notes that Rhys's reading audience was white English women, not black West Indians. See Gregg, *Jean Rhys' Historical Imagination*, 43.

41   See Jean Rhys, "The Day They Burned the Books," (1960) reprinted in *The Collected Short Stories* (New York: W. W. Norton, 1987), 151–57. Hereafter all references in the text are to this edition.

42   The degraded status of myth in the Caribbean probably has American parallels. Zora Neale Hurston observes that the black people of the South refer to the stories they tell not as "stories" but as "lies." See Zora Neale Hurston, *Dust Tracks on a Road*, ed. Robert Hemenway (Urbana: Illinois University Press, 1984/1942).

43   See, for example, Kasinitz, *Caribbean New York: Black Immigrants and the Politics of Race*, 70. The direct quote is from Colen, " 'Like a Mother to Them,' " in *Conceiving the New World Order*, 83.

44   See Paule Marshall, "The Making of a Writer: From the Poets in the Kitchen," in *Reena and Other Stories* (New York: Feminist Press, 1983). Marshall's novel, *Brown Girl, Brownstones* (New York: Feminist Press, 1981/1959), clearly draws on her childhood observations of West Indian female domestic laborers in New York.

45   Clearly, the tradition of African American women's writing has its own troubled history. The earlier literature of nineteenth-century and early twentieth-century writers such as Frances Watkins Harper, Nella Larsen, Jessie Faucet, and Zora Neale Hurston was literally "buried" until the past fifteen years or so, where the second renaissance of black women writers such as Toni Morrison, Alice Walker, and Gloria Naylor has allowed these earlier writers to be "exhumed." I do not mean to suggest that the African American women's literary tradition has been an unbroken line of recognition.

46   There is currently a body of literature emerging in Britain from black women of Caribbean descent — and indeed by all black people of Caribbean descent — which, like the literature produced by their Caribbean-American counterparts, centers specifically around the immigrant experience in the metropole. Some of the more notable Caribbean-British writers include Joan Riley, Grace Nichols, and Janice Shinebourne. Indeed, many of the arguments that I make here regarding Caribbean women and immigrant literature apply to their works, too. However, since the writings of these black British writers are generally less concerned with the issues of literary traditions and authorship than that of the Caribbean-American writers, it is more useful for my purposes to concentrate on the latter as the literary "heirs" to the earlier generation of anglophone Caribbean writers.

For a more extended discussion of black British women writers see Carole Boyce Davies, *Black Women, Writing and Identity: Migrations of the Subject* (London: Routledge, 1994), chapter 4.

47   I am referring here to the conclusion of *Wide Sargasso Sea*, where Antoinette, now Bertha Mason and "mad," jumps from Rochester's mansion after setting it on fire, in an effort to join her old black childhood friend. In chapter 5 I have suggested that the death of Antoinette also suggests the impossibility of living in the newly emancipated Caribbean as a white creole female. Of course, I am not the first to suggest this: Kenneth Ramchand argues that *Wide Sargasso Sea*,

204   NOTES TO CHAPTER 6

as well as other novels like *Orchid House* by white West Indian authors, exhibit a "terrified consciousness" of the fall of the planter class in the wake of decolonization and the political accession to power of the black populations of the English-speaking islands. See Kenneth Ramchand, "Terrified Consciousness," in *The West Indian Novel and Its Background* (London: Faber and Faber, 1974/1970), 223–36.

Similarly, as I have observed earlier, Veronica Gregg has pointed out that in Rhys's letters and interviews from the late 1950s to the 1970s she returns obsessively to the "ingratitude of black people," and gives this as a reason for not returning.

48 Jamaica Kincaid, *Lucy* (New York: Penguin, 1991). Hereafter all references to *Lucy* in the text are taken from this edition.

49 The image of the black virago who must, at all costs, be repressed, resurfaces in Marshall's *Praisesong*, when the protagonist Avey screams at her husband, and he stops short in horror, comparing her to the working-class woman "in the street" who raises her voice nightly in public. The memory of that reprimand with her always, Avey's suppression of the rebellious "primal" woman into the "respectable" accountant's wife ultimately causes her not to recognize herself, literally. See Paule Marshall, *Praisesong for the Widow* (New York: Putnam, 1983), 48.

50 A similar gender binary can be found operating in Paule Marshall's novel, *Daughters*, the plot of which also moves between the United States and the Caribbean and which, as she herself says, is a roman à clef about her relationship with her father and about themes of "seduction, of dependency and of dominance." Marshall makes the point that the theme of patriarchal seduction, dominance, and dependence is also a metaphor for how the United States "seduces" the Third World. See Paule Marshall, "A *MELUS* Interview: Paule Marshall," interview with Joyce Pettis, *MELUS* 17, no. 4 (winter 1991–92): 128.

51 See Paul Ricoeur, "Civilization and National Cultures," in *History and Truth* (Evanston: Northwestern University Press, 1965), 267–77, quoted in Timothy Brennan, "The National Longing for Form," in *Nation and Narration*, ed. Homi K. Bhabha (London: Routledge, 1993/1990), 46.

52 Jean Franco, "The Nation as Imagined Community," *The New Historicism*, ed. H. Aram Veeser (New York: Routledge, 1989), 211.

BIBLIOGRAPHY

Achebe, Chinua. *Things Fall Apart*. New York: Astor-Honor, 1959.

Allen, Walter. "Bertha the Doomed." *New York Times Book Review*, 18 June 1967: 5.

Anderson, Benedict. *Imagined Communities*. New York: Verso, 1991.

Andrade, Susan. "The Nigger of the Narcissist: History, Sexuality and Intertextuality in Maryse Conde's *Heremakhonon*." *Callaloo* 16, no. 1 (1993): 213–26.

Appiah, Kwame Anthony. "The Uncompleted Argument: DuBois and the Illusion of Race." In *"Race," Writing and Difference*, ed. Henry Louis Gates, Jr. Chicago: University of Chicago Press, 1985.

Azim, Firdous. *The Colonial Rise of the Novel*. London: Routledge, 1993.

Baker, Houston A. Jr. "In Dubious Battle." *New Literary History* 18, no. 2 (winter): 363–69.

———, ed. *Reading Black: Essays in the Criticism of African, Caribbean and Black American Literature*. Ithaca: Cornell University Africana Studies and Research Center Monograph Series 4, 1976.

Barber, K., and P. F. De Moraes Farias, eds. *Self-Assertion and Brokerage: Early Cultural Nationalism in West Africa*. Birmingham: Centre of West African Studies, Birmingham University, 1990.

Barber-Williams, Patricia. "Images of the Self: Jean Rhys and Her French West Indian Counterpart." *Journal of West Indian Literature* 3, no. 2 (September 1989): 9–19.

Barthold, Bonnie J. *Black Time: Fiction of Africa, the Caribbean and the United States*. New Haven: Yale University Press, 1981.

Bederman, Gail. *Manliness & Civilization: A Cultural History of Gender and Race in the United States, 1880–1917*. Chicago: University of Chicago Press, 1995.

Benstock, Shari. "Expatriate Modernism." In *Women's Writing and Exile*, ed. Mary Lynn Broe and Angela Ingram. Chapel Hill: University of North Carolina Press, 1989.

Bhabha, Homi K. *The Location of Culture*. London: Routledge, 1994.

———. "Of Mimicry and Man: the Ambivalence of Colonial Discourse." In *The Location of Culture*, 85–92. London: Routledge, 1994.

Blyden, Edward. *The Selected Letters of Edward Wilmot Blyden*, ed. Hollis R. Lynch. Millwood, N.Y.: Krause-Thomson Organization, 1978.

Boose, Lynda E. " 'The Getting of a Lawful Race': Racial Discourse in Early Modern England and the Unrepresentable Black Woman." In *Women, "Race," and*

Writing in the Early Period, ed. Margo Hendricks and Patricia Parker. London: Routledge, 1994.

Brantlinger, Patrick. *Rule of Darkness: British Literature and Imperialism 1830–1914*. Ithaca: Cornell University Press, 1988.

Brathwaite, Edward Kamau. *Contradictory Omens*. Mona, Jamaica: Savacou Publications, 1978.

———. *History of the Voice: The Development of Nation Language in Anglophone Caribbean Poetry*. London: New Beacon Books, 1984.

———. "Jazz and the West Indian Novel." *Roots*. Havana: Casa de las Americas, 1985/1971.

———. "The Love Axe (1): Developing a Caribbean Aesthetic 1962-1974." In *Reading Black: Essays in the Criticism of African, Caribbean and Black American Literature*, ed. Houston A. Baker, Jr. Ithaca: Cornell University Africana Studies and Research Center Monograph Series 4, 1976.

———. "Roots." *Roots*. Havana: Casa de las Americas, 1985/1971.

Braxton, Nicole, and Andree Nicola McLaughlin, eds. *Wild Women in the Whirlwind: Afra-American Culture and the Contemporary Literary Renaissance*. New Brunswick: Rutgers University Press, 1990.

Brennan, Timothy. "The National Longing for Form." In *Nation and Narration*, ed. Homi K. Bhabha, 44–70. London: Routledge, 1993/1990.

Brodber, Erna. "Black Consciousness and Popular Music in Jamaica in the 1960s and 1970s." *Caribbean Quarterly* 31, no. 2 (June 1985): 53–86.

Brown, JoAnne. "Professional Language: Words That Succeed." *Radical History Review* 31 (January 1986): 33–51.

Brown, Lloyd. "Introduction: Regional Writers, Regional Critics." In *Critical Issues in West Indian Literature*, ed. Lloyd Brown. Parkersburg, Iowa: Caribbean Books, 1984.

Bruner, Charlotte H. "The Meaning of Caliban in Black Literature Today." *Comparative Literature Studies* 13 (September 1976): 240–53.

Bryan, Patrick. *The Jamaican People 1880–1902: Race, Class and Social Control*. London: Macmillan Caribbean, 1991.

Bryce-La Porte, Roy S. "Caribbean Immigration to the United States." RIIES Occasional Papers no. 2. Washington, D.C.: Smithsonian Institution, 1983.

Bryden, Ronald. "The Novelist V. S. Naipaul Talks About His Work to Ronald Bryden." *The Listener*, March 22, 1973.

Burton, Antoinette. *Burdens of History: British Feminists, Indian Women, and Imperial Culture, 1865–1915*. Chapel Hill: University of North Carolina Press, 1994.

Busia, Abena. "But Caliban and Ariel Are Still Both Male: On African Colonial Discourse and the Unvoiced Female." In *Crisscrossing Boundaries in African Literatures 1988*, ed. Kenneth Harrow, 129–40. Washington, D.C.: Three Continents Press, 1991.

Carby, Hazel. *Reconstructing Womanhood: The Emergence of the Afro-American Woman Novelist*. New York: Oxford University Press, 1987.

Carlyle, Thomas. "The Hero as Man of Letters." (1841) In *Selected Writings*. London: Penguin, 1988.

———. "Occasional Discourse on the Nigger Question." In *English and Other Critical Essays*. London: J. M. Dent and Sons, 1964.

Carlyle, Thomas, and John Stuart Mill. *The Negro Question and Occasional Discourse on the Nigger Question*, ed. Eugene R. August. Dayton: Appleton-Century-Crofts, 1971.

Césaire, Aimé. *The Collected Poetry of Aimé Césaire*. Trans. Clayton Eshleman and Annette Smith. Berkeley: University of California Press, 1983.

Chauhan, C. S. "Rereading Claude McKay." *CLA Journal* 34, no. 1 (September 1990): 68–80.

Chinweizu, Onwuchekwu Jemie, and Ihechukwu Madubuike. *Toward the Decolonization of African Literature*. Vol. 1. Washington, D.C.: Howard University Press, 1983.

Cixous, Hélène, and Catherine Clement. *The Newly Born Woman*. Trans. Betsy Wing. Minneapolis: University of Minnesota Press, 1986.

Cliff, Michelle. *Abeng*. Trumansberg, N.Y.: Crossing Press, 1984.

———. "A Journey into Speech." In *Multicultural Literacy*, ed. Rick Simonson and Scott Walker. St. Paul, Minn.: Graywolf, 1988.

———. "A Journey into Speech — A Writer Between Two Worlds: An Interview with Michelle Cliff." Interview by Opal Palmer Adisa. *African American Review* 28, no. 2 (1994): 273–82.

———. *No Telephone to Heaven*. New York: Dutton, 1988.

Cobham, Rhonda. "Jekyll and Claude: The Erotics of Patronage in Claude McKay's *Banana Bottom*." *Caribbean Quarterly* 38, no. 1 (March 1992): 55–78.

Colen, Shellee. " 'Like a Mother to Them': Stratified Reproduction and West Indian Childcare Workers and Employers in New York." In *Conceiving the New World Order: The Global Politics of Reproduction*, ed. Faye D. Ginsburg and Rayna Rapp. Berkeley: University of California Press, 1995.

Collins, Merle. *Angel*. Seattle: Seal Press, 1987.

Cooper, Carolyn. *Noises in the Blood: Orality, Gender and the "Vulgar" Body of Jamaican Popular Culture*. London: Macmillan, 1993.

———. " 'Only a Nigger Gal!': Race, Gender and the Politics of Education in Claude McKay's *Banana Bottom*." *Caribbean Quarterly* 38, no. 1 (March 1992): 40–54.

Cooper, Wayne, ed. *The Passion of Claude McKay: Selected Poetry and Prose, 1912–1948*. New York: Schocken Books, 1973.

Cudjoe, Selwyn R. *Resistance and Caribbean Literature*. Athens: Ohio University Press, 1980.

———. *V. S. Naipaul: A Materialist Reading*. Amherst: University of Massachusetts Press, 1988.

Cumber Dance, Daryl. "Matriarchs, Doves, and Nymphos: Prevalent Images of Black, Indian, and White Women in Caribbean Literature." *Studies in the Literary Imagination* 26, no. 2 (fall 1993): 21–43.

Curtin, Philip D. *Two Jamaicas: The Role of Ideas in a Tropical Colony, 1830–1865*. Cambridge: Harvard University Press, 1955.

Davies, Carole Boyce. *Black Women, Writing and Identity: Migrations of the Subject*. New York: Routledge, 1996.

Davies, Carol Boyce, and Elaine Savory Fido. "Preface: Talking It Over." In *Out of the Kumbla: Caribbean Women and Literature*, ed. Carole Boyce Davies and Elaine Savory Fido. Trenton: Africa World Press, 1990.

Davis, Angela. *Women, Race, and Class*. New York: Random House, 1981.

D'Costa, Jean. "Jean Rhys, 1890–1979." In *Fifty Caribbean Writers*, ed. Daryl Dancem, 390–404. New York: Greenwood Press, 1986.

D'Costa, Jean, and Barbara Lalla, eds. *Voices in Exile: Jamaican Texts of the 18th and 19th Century*. Tuscaloosa: University of Alabama Press, 1989.

deSchweinitz, Jr., Karl. *The Rise and Fall of British India: Imperialism as Inequality*. London: Methuen, 1983.

Diawara, Manthia. "Englishness and Blackness: Cricket as Discourse on Colonialism," *Callaloo* 13 (1990): 830–44.

Dick, Kay. "Wife to Mr. Rochester." Sunday *Times* (London), 30 October 1966, 50.

Donaldson, Laura. *Decolonizing Feminisms: Race, Gender and Empire Building*. Chapel Hill: University of North Carolina Press, 1995.

———. "The Miranda Complex: Colonialism and the Question of Feminist Reading." *Diacritics* 6 (fall 1988): 65–77.

Doyle, Brian. *English and Englishness*. London: Routledge, 1989.

Dubey, Madhu. *Black Women Novelists and the Nationalist Aesthetic*. Bloomington: Indiana University Press, 1994.

DuPlessis, Rachel Blau. "For the Etruscans." In *Feminist Criticism: Essays on Women, Literature, Theory*, ed. Elaine Showalter. New York: Pantheon, 1985.

Dutton, Geoffrey. *The Hero as Murderer: The Life of Edward John Eyre, Australian Explorer and Governor of Jamaica, 1815–1901*. London: William Collins, 1967.

Echevarría, Roberto González. *Voice of the Masters: Writing and Authority in Modern Latin American Literature*. Austin: University of Texas Press, 1985.

Edmondson, Belinda. "Race, Privilege, and the Politics of (Re)Writing History: An Analysis of the Novels of Michelle Cliff." *Callaloo* 16, no. 1 (1993): 180–91.

Eldridge, C. C. *The Imperial Experience: From Carlyle to Forster*. New York: St. Martin's Press, 1996.

Ellis, Markman. *The Politics of Sensibility: Race, Gender and Commerce in the Sentimental Novel*. New York: Cambridge University Press, 1996.

Emery, Mary Lou. *Jean Rhys At World's End: Novels of Colonial and Sexual Exile*. Austin: University of Texas Press, 1990.

Epstein, Joseph. "A Cottage for Mr. Naipaul." *New Criterion* (October 1987): 6–15.

Eshleman, Clayton, and Annette Smith, trans. *The Collected Poetry of Aimé Césaire*. Berkeley: University of California Press, 1983.

Evans, Mari, ed. *Black Women Writers (1950–1980)*. New York: Anchor Books/Doubleday, 1984.

Evans, Mari. "Trajectories of Self-Definition: Placing Contemporary Afro-American Women's Fiction." In *Conjuring: Black Women, Fiction, and Literary Tradition*, ed. Hortense Spillers and Marjorie Pryse. Bloomington: Indiana University Press, 1985.

Fanon, Frantz. *Black Skins, White Masks*. Trans. Charles L. Markmann. New York: Grove, 1967.

———. *The Wretched of the Earth*. Trans. Constance Farrington. New York: Grove, 1963.

Felski, Rita. *Beyond Feminist Aesthetics*. Cambridge: Harvard University Press, 1989.

Ferguson, Moira. *Colonialism and Gender Relations from Mary Wollstonecraft to Jamaica Kincaid*. New York: Columbia University Press, 1993.

Ford-Smith, Honor. "The Value of an Angry Woman: The Importance of Una Marson." Manuscript. Kingston, Jamaica (1992): 1–22.

Franco, Jean. "The Nation as Imagined Community." In *The New Historicism*, ed. H. Aram Veeser. New York: Routledge, 1989.

Freud, Sigmund. "The Uncanny" ("Das Unheimliche"). In *Standard Edition of the Complete Psychological Works of Sigmund Freud*, trans. and ed. James Strachey. London: Hogarth Press, 1955.

Froude, James Anthony. *The English in the West Indies*. New York: Negro University Press, 1969/1888.

Fuss, Diana. *Essentially Speaking: Feminism, Nature & Difference*. New York: Routledge, 1989.

Gardiner, Judith Kegan. "The Exhilaration of Exile." In *Women's Writing in Exile*, ed. Mary Lynn Broe and Angela Ingram. Chapel Hill: University of North Carolina Press, 1989.

Gates, Henry Louis Jr. "Racism in the Profession." *African Literature Association Bulletin* 15, no. 1 (1989): 11–21.

———. *The Signifying Monkey*. Oxford: Oxford University Press, 1988.

———. "State of Florida vs. Luther Campbell." Reprinted in *Passages: A Chronicle of the Humanities*, no. 1 (1991): 3.

———. "'What's Love Got to Do With It?' Critical Theory, Integrity, and the Black Idiom." *New Literary History* 18, no. 2 (winter 1987): 345–362.

———, ed. *'Race', Writing and Difference*. Chicago: University of Chicago Press, 1985.

Giddings, Paula. *When and Where I Enter: The Impact of Black Women on Race and Sex in America*. New York: Bantam, 1985.

Gikandi, Simon. *Maps of Englishness: Writing Identity in the Culture of Colonialism*. New York: Columbia University Press, 1996.

———. *Writing in Limbo: Modernism and Caribbean Literature*. Ithaca: Cornell University Press, 1992.

Gilbert, Sandra, and Susan Gubar. *The Mad Woman in the Attic: The Woman Writer and the Nineteenth Century Imagination*. New Haven: Yale University Press, 1984.

Gilroy, Paul. *The Black Atlantic: Modernity and Double Consciousness*. Cambridge: Harvard University Press, 1993.

Goldberg, Jonathan. " 'Bradford's 'Ancient Members' and 'A Case of Buggery . . . Amongst Them.' " In *Nationalisms and Sexualities*, ed. Andrew Parker, Mary Russo, Doris Sommer, Patricia Yaeger. London: Routledge, 1992.

Goodheart, Eugene. "V. S. Naipaul's Mandarin Sensibility." *Partisan Review* 50 (1983): 244–56.

Greene, Gayle, and Coppelia Kahn, eds. *Making a Difference: Feminist Literary Criticism*. London: Methuen, 1985.

Gregg, Veronica. *Jean Rhys' Historical Imagination: Reading and Writing the Creole*. Chapel Hill: University of North Carolina Press, 1995.

———. "Jean Rhys on Herself as a Writer." In *Caribbean Women Writers: Essays from the First International Conference*, ed. Selwyn R. Cudjoe, 109–115. Wellesley, Mass.: Calaloux Publications, 1990.

Griffiths, Gareth. *A Double Exile*. London: Calder, 1978.

Habermas, Jürgen. *Die Strukturwandel der Öffentlichkeit: Untersuchungen zu einer Kategorie der bürgerlichen Gesellschaft. (Structural Changes in the Public Sphere.)* Darmstandt: Luchterhand, 1984/1962.

Hall, Catherine. "The Economy of Intellectual Prestige: Thomas Carlyle, John Stuart Mill, and the Case of Governor Eyre." *Cultural Critique* 12 (spring 1989): 167–96.

———. *White, Male and Middle-Class: Explorations in Feminism and History*. Cambridge, U.K.: Polity Press, 1992.

Hall, Kim. *Things of Darkness: Economies of Race and Gender in Early Modern England*. Ithaca: Cornell University Press, 1995.

Hall, Stuart. "C. L. R. James: A Portrait." In *C. L. R. James's Caribbean*, ed. Paget Henry and Paul Buhle, 3–16. Durham: Duke University Press, 1992.

Halpern, Richard. " 'The Picture of Nobody' White Cannibalism in *The Tempest*." *Shakespeare Among the Moderns*. Ithaca: Cornell University Press, 1997.

———. "Shakespeare in the Tropics: From High Modernism to New Historicism." Colloquium manuscript, Johns Hopkins University, spring 1994.

Harding, Sandra. *The Science Question in Feminism*. Ithaca: Cornell University Press, 1986.

Harlowe, Barbara. *Resistance Literature*. New York: Methuen, 1987.

Harris, Wilson. *The Palace of the Peacock*. London: Faber and Faber, 1973/1960.

——. *Tradition, the Writer & Society*. London: New Beacon, 1967.

Harrison, Nancy Rebecca. *Jean Rhys and the Novel as Women's Text*. Chapel Hill: University of North Carolina Press, 1988.

Heigh, Samantha. "The Return of Africa's Daughters: Negritude and the Gendering of Exile." Paper presented at the African Literature Association Conference, Guadeloupe, 1993.

Henderson, John. *Jamaica*. London: Adam and Charles Black, 1906.

Ho, Christine. "The Internationalization of Kinship and the Feminization of Caribbean Migration." *Human Organization* 52, no. 1 (1993).

Hobsbawm, Eric. *Nations and Nationalism Since 1780*. London: Cambridge University Press, 1990.

hooks, bell. *Yearning: Race, Gender and Cultural Politics*. Boston: South End Press, 1990.

Hulme, Peter. "Hurricanes in the Caribbees: The Constitution of the Discourse of English Colonialism." In *1642: Literature and Power in the Seventeenth Century*, ed. Francis Barker, Jay Bernstein, John Coombes, Peter Hulme, Jennifer Stone, Jon Stratton. Essex: University of Essex Press, 1981.

Hurston, Zora Neale. *Dust Tracks on a Road*. Ed. Robert Hemenway. Urbana: Illinois University Press, 1984/1942.

Irigaray, Luce. *This Sex Which is Not One*. Ithaca: Cornell University Press, 1985.

James, C. L. R. *Beyond a Boundary*. London: Hutchinson, 1963.

——. *The Black Jacobins: Toussaint L'Ouverture and the San Domingo Revolution*. New York: Vintage, 1963/1938.

——. "The Making of a Literary Life." Interview with Paul Buhle, 1987. In *C. L. R. James's Caribbean*, ed. Paget Henry and Paul Buhle, 56–60. Durham: Duke University Press, 1992.

——. *Minty Alley*. London: Secker and Warburg, 1936.

——. *Radical America*. Detroit: Detroit Printing Co-op, May 1970.

——. *Spheres of Existence: Selected Writings*. Westport, Conn.: Lawrence Hill, 1980.

Jameson, Fredric. *The Political Unconscious: Narrative as a Socially Symbolic Act*. Ithaca: Cornell University Press, 1981.

JanMohamed, Abdul. *Manichean Aesthetics: The Politics of Literature in Colonial Africa*. Amherst: University of Massachusetts Press, 1983.

Jones, Jacqueline. *Labor of Love, Labor of Sorrow*. New York: Vintage, 1986.

Joyce, Joyce A. "The Black Canon: Reconstructing Black American Literary Criticism." *New Literary History* 18, no. 2 (winter 1987): 335–44.

Kasinitz, Philip. *Caribbean New York: Black Immigrants and the Politics of Race*. Ithaca: Cornell University Press, 1992.

Kincaid, Jamaica. *Annie John*. New York: New American Library, 1983.

——. *Autobiography of My Mother*. New York: Farrar, Straus and Giroux, 1996.

——. "Jamaica Kincaid and the Modernist Project." Interview with Selwyn R. Cudjoe (1989). In *Caribbean Women Writers: Essays from the First International Conference*, ed. Selwyn R. Cudjoe, 215–32. Wellesley, Mass.: Calaloux Publications, 1990.

——. *Lucy*. New York: Penguin, 1991.

King, Bruce. "Caribbean Conundrum." *Transition* 62 (1993): 140–57.

——. *The New English Literatures*. London: Macmillan, 1980.

Kingsley, Charles. *At Last: A Christmas in the West Indies*. 2 vols. London: Macmillan, 1871.

Kloepfer, Deborah Kelly. *The Unspeakable Mother: Forbidden Discourse in Jean Rhys and H.D.* Ithaca: Cornell University Press, 1989.

Kutzinski, Vera. *Sugar's Secrets: The Erotics of Cuban Nationalism*. Charlottesville: University Press of Virginia, 1994.

Lamming, George. "Caribbean Literature: the Black Rock of Africa." *African Forum* 1 (spring 1966): 32–52.

——. "An Interview with George Lamming." By George E. Kent. *Black World* 22 (March 1973): 4–14, 88–97.

——. "The Peasant Roots of the West Indian Novel." In *Critics of West Indian Literature*, ed. Edward Baugh. London: Macmillan, 1978.

——. *The Pleasures of Exile*. London: Allison and Busby, 1984/1960.

——. *Season of Adventure*. London: Allison and Busby, 1979/1960.

——. *Water with Berries*. New York: Holt, Rinehart and Winston, 1971.

Lewis, David Levering. *When Harlem was in Vogue*. New York: Alfred Knopf, 1981.

Lindfors, Bernth. "The West Indian Conference on Commonwealth Literature." *World Literature Written in English* 19 (1971): 10.

Look Lai, Wally. "The Road to Thornfield Hall." *New Beacon Reviews* (Collection 1, 1968): 38–52.

Lorde, Audre. *Zami: A New Spelling of My Name*. Watertown, Mass.: Persephone, 1982.

Lorimer, Douglas A. *Colour, Class and the Victorians: English Attitudes to the Negro in the Mid-Nineteenth Century*. Leicester: Leicester University Press, 1978.

Lovelace, Earl. *The Dragon Can't Dance*. Essex: Longman, 1979.

Mackenzie, John. *Propaganda and Empire: The Manipulation of British Public Opinion 1880–1960*. Manchester: Manchester University Press, 1984.

Mais, Roger. *Brother Man*. London: Heinemann, 1974.

Mannoni, O. *Prospero and Caliban: The Psychology of Colonization*. New York: Praeger, 1956.

Marshall, Paule. *Brown Girl, Brownstones*. New York: Feminist Press, 1981/1959.

——. *The Chosen Place, the Timeless People*. New York: Harcourt Brace and World, 1969.

——. *Daughters*. New York: Atheneum, 1991.

——. "The Making of a Writer: From the Poets in the Kitchen." In *Reena and Other Stories*. New York: Feminist Press, 1983.

——. "A MELUS Interview: Paule Marshall." Interview with Joyce Pettis. *MELUS* 17, no. 4 (winter 1991–92): 117–30.

——. *Praisesong for the Widow*. New York: Putnam, 1983.

——. *Soul Clap Hands and Sing*. Chatham, N.J.: Chatham Bookseller, 1961.

Marson, Una. "The America I have Discovered." Manuscript, Institute of Jamaica, ca. 1930.

——. *London Calling*. Manuscript, Institute of Jamaica, 1935.

——. *Pocomania*. Manuscript, Institute of Jamaica, 1938.

Martí, José. "Our America." *La Revista Illustrada* (Cuba), 10 January 1891.

McDowell, Deborah. "New Directions in Black Feminist Criticism." In *New Directions in Feminist Criticism*, ed. Elaine Showalter. New York: Pantheon, 1985.

McKay, Claude. *Banjo*. New York: Harper, 1929.

——. *Home to Harlem*. New York: Harper, 1928.

——. *The Passion of Claude McKay: Selected Poetry and Prose, 1912–1948*. Ed. Wayne F. Cooper. New York: Schocken Books, 1973.

McWatt, Mark, ed. *West Indian Literature and Its Social Context: Proceedings of the Fourth Annual Conference on West Indian Literature*. Cave Hill, Barbados: University of the West Indies, 1985.

Memmi, Albert. *The Colonizer and the Colonized*. Boston: Beacon, 1965.

Meyer, Susan. *Imperialism at Home: Race and Victorian Women's Fiction*. Ithaca: Cornell University Press, 1996.

Mill, John Stuart. *Autobiography*. London: Oxford University Press, 1924.

——. *The Subjection of Women*. Cambridge: MIT Press, 1970.

Mill, John Stuart, and Thomas Carlyle. *The Negro Question and Occasional Discourse on the Nigger Question*. Ed. Eugene R. August. Dayton: Appleton-Century-Crofts, 1971.

Mills, Sara. *Discourse of Difference: An Analysis of Women's Travel Writing and Colonialism*. London: Routledge, 1991.

Mohanty, Chandra Talpade. "Under Western Eyes: Colonialism and Feminist Discourse." In *Third World Women and the Politics of Feminism*, ed. Chandra Talpade Mohanty, Ann Russo, and Lourdes Torres, 51–80. Bloomington: Indiana University Press, 1991.

Moi, Toril. *Sexual/Textual Politics: Feminist Literary Theory*. New York: Methuen, 1985.

Mordecai, Pamela, and Elisabeth Wilson, eds. *Her True-True Name: An Anthology of Prose Writing by Caribbean Women*. Kingston: Heinemann, 1989.

Morrison, Toni. *Song of Solomon.* New York: New American Library, 1977.

Mortimer, Delores M. *Female Immigrants to the United States: Caribbean, Latin American and African Experiences.* RIIES Occasional Papers No. 1. Washington, D.C.: Smithsonian Institution, 1981.

Naipaul, V. S. *The Enigma of Arrival.* New York: Alfred Knopf, 1987.

——. *A Flag on the Island.* London: Andre Deutsch, 1967.

——. *Guerrillas.* New York: Vintage, 1990/1975.

——. *A House for Mr. Biswas.* New York: Vintage, 1984/1961.

——. "I Don't Consider Myself a West Indian." *Guyana Graphic,* 30 Nov. 1968: 3.

——. "Michael X and the Black Power Killings in Trinidad." In *The Return of Eva Peron with the Killings in Trinidad.* New York: Vintage, 1974.

——. *The Middle Passage.* New York: Vintage, 1981/1962.

——. *Miguel Street.* New York: Vintage, 1984/1959.

——. *The Mimic Men.* 1967. Middlesex: Penguin, 1981.

——. *The Overcrowded Barracoon.* New York: Vintage, 1984/1972.

——. *A Way in the World.* New York: Vintage, 1994.

——. "Without a Dog's Chance." In *Critical Perspectives on Jean Rhys,* ed. Pierrette Frickey, 54–66. Washington, D.C.: Three Continents Press, 1990.

Nair, Supriya. *Caliban's Curse: George Lamming and the Revisioning of History.* Ann Arbor: University of Michigan Press, 1996.

——. "Homing Instincts: Immigrant Nostalgia and Gender Politics in *Brown Girl, Brownstones.*" In *Caribbean Romances: The Politics of Regional Representation,* ed. Belinda Edmondson. Charlottesville: University Press of Virginia, forthcoming 1999.

Ned, Thomas. "Meeting Jean Rhys." *Planet.* Wales. 33 (August 1976): 29–31.

Nettleford, Rex. *Mirror Mirror: Identity, Race & Protest in Jamaica.* Kingston, Jamaica: Collins and Sangster, 1970.

——. "European Melodies, African Rhythms." In *Mirror Mirror: Identity, Race & Protest in Jamaica.* Kingston, Jamaica: Collins and Sangster, 1970.

Nixon, Rob. "Caribbean and African Appropriations of *The Tempest.*" In *Politics and Poetic Value,* ed. Robert von Hallberg. Chicago: University of Chicago Press, 1987.

——. *London Calling: V. S. Naipaul, Postcolonial Mandarin.* New York: Oxford University Press, 1992.

North, Michael. *The Dialect of Modernism: Race, Language and Twentieth-Century Literature.* New York: Oxford University Press, 1994.

Nourbese, Philip Marlene. "The Absence of Writing or How I Almost Became a Spy." In *Out of the Kumbla: Caribbean Women and Literature,* ed. Carole Boyce Davies and Elaine Savory Fido, 271–88. Trenton: Africa World Press, 1990.

Nunez-Harrell, Elizabeth. "The Paradoxes of Belonging: the White Creole Woman in West Indian Fiction." *Modern Fiction Studies* 31, no. 2 (summer 1985): 281–93.

O'Callaghan, Evelyn. "Engineering the Female Subject: Erna Brodber's *Myal.*" Paper presented at the Caribbean Women Writers Conference, St. Augustine, Trinidad, April 24–27, 1990.

———. "Outsider's Voice: White Creole Women Novelists in the Caribbean Literary Tradition." *Journal of West Indian Literature* 1, no. 1 (Oct. 1986): 75–78.

———. *Woman Version: Theoretical Approaches to West Indian Fiction by Women.* London: Macmillan, 1993.

Ogunyemi, Chikyeni. "Womanism: The Dynamics of the Contemporary Black Female Novel in English." *Signs* 11, no. 1 (1985): 63–80.

Pagden, Anthony. "Dispossessing the Barbarian: the Language of Spanish Thomism and the Debate over the Property Rights of the American Indians." In *The Languages of Political Theory in Early Modern Europe*, ed. Anthony Pagden. Cambridge: Cambridge University Press, 1987.

———. *European Encounters with the New World: From Renaissance to Romanticism.* New Haven: Yale University Press, 1993.

Patterson, Orlando. "Race, Gender and Liberal Fallacies." *The Black Scholar* 22 (winter 1991/spring 1992): 70–80.

———. *The Sociology of Slavery: An Analysis of the Origins, Development, and Structure of Negro Slave Society in Jamaica.* Kingston, Jamaica: Sangster's Book Stores, 1973/1967.

Phillips, Caryl. "Of This Time, of That Place: A Conversation with Caryle Phillips." Interviewed by Jenny Sharpe. *Transition* 68 (1995): 154–61.

Plaza, Monique. " 'Phallomorphic Power' and the Psychology of 'Woman'." *Ideology and Consciousness* 4 (autumn 1981): 57–76.

Poovey, Mary. *Uneven Developments: The Ideological Work of Gender in Mid-Victorian England.* Chicago: University of Chicago Press, 1988.

———. *The Proper Lady and the Woman Writer: Ideology as Style in the Works of Mary Wollstonecraft, Mary Shelley, and Jane Austen.* Chicago: University of Chicago Press, 1984.

Pouchet Paquet, Sandra. *The Novels of George Lamming.* Kingston: Heinemann, 1982.

Pratt, Mary Louise. *Imperial Eyes: Travel Writing and Transculturation.* New York: Routledge, 1992.

Raiskin, Judith. "Jean Rhys: Creole Writing and Strategies of Reading." *Ariel: A Review of International English Literature* 22, no. 4 (October 1991): 51–67.

———. *Snow on the Canefields: Women's Writing and Creole Subjectivity.* Minneapolis: University of Minnesota Press, 1996.

Ramchand, Kenneth. *Introduction to the Study of West Indian Literature.* Middlesex: Thomas Nelson, 1976.

——. *The West Indian Novel and Its Background*. London: Faber and Faber, 1974/1970.

Redding, J. Saunders. "Afro-American Culture and the Black Aesthetic: Notes Toward a Re-Evaluation." In *Reading Black: Essays in the Criticism of African, Caribbean and Black American Literature*, ed. Houston A. Baker, Jr., 41–47. Ithaca: Cornell University Africana Studies and Research Center Monograph Series 4, 1976.

Retamar, Roberto Fernández. "Caliban: Notes Towards a Discussion of Culture in Our America." Trans. Lynn Garafola, David Arthur McMurray, and Robert Marquez. *Massachusetts Review* 15 (winter–spring 1974): 7–72.

Rhys, Jean. *Jean Rhys: The Collected Short Stories*. Ed. Diana Athill. New York: Norton, 1987.

——. *Jean Rhys: Letters, 1931–1966*. Harmondsworth: Penguin, 1985.

——. *Smile Please: An Unfinished Autobiography*. New York: Harper and Row, 1979.

——. *Wide Sargasso Sea*. New York: Popular Library, 1966; Norton, 1982.

Richardson, Alan, and Sonia Hofkosh, eds. *Romanticism, Race, and Imperial Culture, 1780–1834*. Bloomington: Indiana University Press, 1996.

Ricoeur, Paul. *History and Truth*. Evanston: Northwestern University Press, 1965.

Rodríguez, Ileana. *House, Garden, Nation: Space, Gender and Ethnicity in Post-Colonial Latin American Literatures by Women*. Trans. Robert Carr with author. Durham: Duke University Press, 1994.

Rohlehr, Gordon. "The Problem of the Problem of Form: The Idea of an Aesthetic Continuum and Aesthetic Code-Switching in West Indian Literature." *Caribbean Quarterly* 31, no. 1 (March 1985): 1–52.

Saakana, Amon. *The Colonial Legacy in Caribbean Literature*. Trenton, N.J.: Africa World Press, 1987.

Said, Edward. *Orientalism*. New York: Vintage, 1978.

——. "Reflections on Exile." *Granta* 13 (autumn 1984): 162.

——. *The World, the Text, and the Critic*. Cambridge: Harvard University Press, 1983.

Said, Edward, Conor Cruise O'Brien, and John Lukacs. "The Post-Colonial Intellectual: A Discussion with Conor Cruise O'Brien, Edward Said, and John Lukacs." *Salmagundi* 70–71 (spring–summer 1986): 65–81.

Sander, Reinhard W. *The Trinidad Awakening: West Indian Literature of the Nineteen-Thirties*. Westport, Conn.: Greenwood, 1988.

Scholes, Theophilus. "Glimpses of the Ages of the 'Superior and Inferior' Races So-Called, Discussed in the Light of Science and History." Vol. 1. London: John Long, 1905.

Scott, Bonnie Kime. "Introduction." In *The Gender of Modernism: A Critical Anthology*, ed. Bonnie Kime Scott. Bloomington: Indiana University Press, 1990.

Senghor, Léopold. *Liberté I: Negritude et humanisme*. Paris: Seuil, 1964.

Senior, Olive. *Working Miracles: Women's Lives in the English-Speaking Caribbean*. London: James Currey, 1991.

Shand Allfrey, Phyllis. *The Orchid House*. Washington, D.C.: Three Continents, 1985.

Sharpe, Jenny. *Allegories of Empire: The Figure of the Woman in the Colonial Text*. Minneapolis: University of Minnesota Press, 1993.

Showalter, Elaine. "Feminist Criticism in the Wilderness." In *The New Feminist Criticism: Essays on Women, Literature and Theory*, ed. Elaine Showalter. New York: Pantheon, 1985.

Slemon, Stephen. "Interview with Wilson Harris." *Ariel: A Review of International English Literature* 19 (July 1988): 48.

Smilowitz, Erika. "Una Marson: Woman Before Her Time." *Jamaica Journal* 16, no. 2 (May 1983): 62–68.

Smilowitz, Erika Sollish, and Roberta Quarles Knowles, eds. *Critical Issues in West Indian Literature: Selected Papers from West Indian Literature Conferences 1981–1983*. Kingston: Heinemann, 1984.

Smith, Barbara. "Toward a Black Feminist Criticism." In *The New Feminist Criticism: Essays on Women, Literature and Theory*, ed. Elaine Showalter. New York: Pantheon, 1985.

Smith, Faith L. "Coming Home to the Real Thing: Gender and Intellectual Life in the Anglophone Caribbean." *The South Atlantic Quarterly* 93, no. 4 (fall 1994): 895–924.

———. "Resisting Culture: C. L. R. James and the Dilemma of the Colonial Intellectual." Paper presented at the African Literature Association Conference, New Orleans, La., 1991.

———. "Transgressive Citizens: 'Woman' and 'Nation' in the Nineteenth-Century Caribbean." Unpublished paper presented at the Women's Studies Colloquium at Johns Hopkins University, October 1996.

Smith, Paul. *Discerning the Subject*. Minneapolis: University of Minnesota Press, 1988.

Soyinka, Wole. "Aesthetic Illusions." In *Reading Black: Essays in the Criticism of African, Caribbean and Black American Literature*, ed. Houston A. Baker, Jr., 1–12. Ithaca: Cornell University Africana Studies and Research Center Monograph Series 4, 1976.

Spillers, Hortense. "Mama's Baby, Papa's Maybe: An American Grammar Book." *Diacritics* 4, no. 17 (summer 1987): 65–81.

———. "Introduction: Who Cuts the Border?" In *Comparative American Identities: Race, Sex, and Nationality in the Modern Text*, ed. Hortense Spillers, 1–25. New York: Routledge, 1991.

Spivak, Gayatri. *In Other Worlds: Essays in Cultural Politics*. New York: Methuen, 1987.

———. "Three Women's Texts and A Critique of Imperialism." *Critical Inquiry* 12 (1985): 243–61.

Stallybrass, Peter, and Allon White. *The Politics and Poetics of Transgression.* Ithaca: Cornell University Press, 1986.

Tate, Claudia, ed. *Black Women Writers at Work.* New York: Continuum, 1983.

Taylor, Patrick. *The Narrative of Liberation: Perspectives on Afro-Caribbean Literature, Popular Culture, and Politics.* Ithaca: Cornell University Press, 1989.

Thelwell, Michael. *Duties, Pleasures, and Conflicts: Essays in Struggle.* Amherst: University of Massachusetts Press, 1987.

Thieme, John. "'Apparitions of Disaster': Brontëan Parallels in *Wide Sargasso Sea* and *Guerrillas.*" *Journal of Commonwealth Literature* 14, no. 1 (1979): 116–32.

Thomas, John Jacob. *Froudacity: West Indian Fables Explained.* Philadelphia: Gebbie, 1890.

Tiffin, Helen. "Cold Hearts and (Foreign) Tongues: Recitation and the Reclamation of the Female Body in the Works of Erna Brodber and Jamaica Kincaid." *Callaloo* 16, no. 4 (fall 1993): 909–21.

———. "Mirror and Mask: Colonial Motifs in the Novels of Jean Rhys." *World Literature Written in English* 17 (April 1978): 328–41.

Torgovnick, Marianne. *Gone Primitive: Savage Intellects, Modern Lives.* Chicago: University of Chicago Press, 1990.

Trollope, Anthony. *The West Indies and the Spanish Main.* New York: Hippocrene Books, 1985/1859.

Viswanathan, Gauri. "Currying Favour: The Politics of British Educational and Cultural Policy in India 1813–1854." *Social Text* 19/20 (fall 1988).

wa Thiong'o, Ngugi. *Decolonising the Mind: the Politics of Language in African Literature.* London: Heinemann, 1986.

———. *Devil on the Cross.* Trans. by author. London: Heinemann, 1982.

Walcott, Derek. *The Castaway.* London: Jonathan Cape Poetry Paperbacks, 1969.

———. *Dream on Monkey Mountain and Other Plays.* New York: Farrar, Straus and Giroux, 1970.

———. "The Garden Path." *New Republic* (April 13, 1987): 27–31.

———. "The Quarrel with History." In *Is Massa Day Dead? Black Moods in the Caribbean,* ed. Orde Coombs. Kingston, Jamaica: Carifesta Forum, 1976.

Walker, Alice. *In Search of Our Mothers' Gardens: Womanist Prose.* San Diego: Harcourt Brace Jovanovich, 1983.

———. "One Child of One's Own—An Essay in Creativity." *Ms.* (August 1979): 50.

Warren, Kenneth W. "Delimiting America: The Legacy of Du Bois." *American Literary History* (spring 1989): 172–89.

Weixlmann, Joe, and Chester J. Fontenot, eds. *Studies in Black American Literature II.* Greenwood, Fla.: Penkevill, 1986.

Williams, Eric. *British Historians and the West Indies*. London: Andre Deutsch, 1966.

——. *Capitalism and Slavery*. London: Andre Deutsch, 1990/1944.

Willis, Susan. "Caliban as Poet: Reversing the Maps of Domination." *Massachusetts Review* (fall 1989): 615–30.

Wilson, Lucy. " 'Women Must Have Spunks': Jean Rhys' West Indian Outcasts." *Modern Fiction Studies* 32, no. 3 (autumn 1986): 439–48.

Winokur, Scott. "The Unsparing Vision of V. S. Naipaul." *Image* (May 5, 1991): 11.

Wynter, Sylvia. "Beyond Miranda's Meanings: Un/Silencing the 'Demonic Ground' of Caliban's Woman." In *Out of the Kumbla: Caribbean Women and Literature*, ed. Carole Boyce Davies and Elaine Savory Fido. Trenton, N.J.: Africa World Press, 1990.

——. *The Hills of Hebron*. New York: Simon and Schuster, 1962.

Zamora, Margarita. "Abreast of Columbus: Gender and Discovery." *Cultural Critique* 17 (winter 1991): 127–49.

Index

Absenteeism, 174 n.8. *See also* Land; Slavery

Africa, 20, 33; in African American aesthetics, 87; agrarian societies in, 88; art of, 201 n.25; Caribbean history and, 117, 179 n.3, 183 n.7; Caribbean writers on, 46; and England, 32; English perceptions of, 29, 115; in literature, 114, 162–63; modernism and, 149; survivalisms in the Caribbean, 7, 35, 37, 38, 59, 60, 62–63, 65, 112, 144, 162, 192 n.4; in Western discourse, 179 n.42. *See also* Modernism; Religion

African American literature, 83, 84, 103, 203 n.42; autobiography and, 90; female-authored, 2, 12, 101, 157, 203 n.45; influence on Caribbean literature, 173 n.26; male-authored, 15, 195 n.32. *See also* Black feminist theory

African diaspora, 36

African literature, 86, 87, 103

Africans, 24, 30, 32, 56, 87, 161, 178 n.51

Allfrey, Phyllis: *Orchid House,* 66–67, 204 n.47

America: definition of, 20–21. *See also* Latin America; New World; United States

American literature, 185 n.25

Amerindians, 21, 22, 61, 113, 135, 148; English views of, 171 n.13; language of, 23–24; Spanish views of, 175 n.14, 177 n.24

Anderson, Benedict, 21–22, 61

Andrade, Susan, 195 n.34

Antigua: in literature, 158–59

Anti-slavery movement, U.S., 90

Appiah, Anthony, 188 n.11

Austen, Jane, 38, 74

Bailey, Amy, 186 n.43

Baraka, Amiri, 87

Barber, Karin, 178 n.51

Beacon (Trinidad), 151

Bederman, Gail, 177 n.34

Benstock, Shari, 144–45, 160

Beyle, Marie-Henri. *See* Stendhal

Bhabha, Homi, 45, 180 n.23

Black Arts Movement, 87–88

Black British literature, 15, 203 n.46

Black feminist theory, 16, 85, 94–102, 161; and West Indian literature, 169 n.3

Black identity: in the Caribbean, 8, 33, 163, 192 n.4; and Caribbean literature, 103, 148, 161, 165. *See also* Negritude

Black middle class, 23, 46, 70, 152; in literature, 71, 75–76, 161, 181 n.35, 183 n.3; nationalism and, 37; sensibilities of, 39, 51, 69

Black nationalism, 8, 38, 39, 48, 66, 74, 179 n.3, 197 n.49; African American, 67; in literature, 53, 99, 128–32, 193 n.10. *See also* Caribbean nationalism; Pan-Africanism

Black Power. *See* Black nationalism

Blake, William, 71

Bloom, Harold, 47

Blyden, Edward, 30, 51

Bogle, Paul, 31. *See also* Morant Bay Rebellion

Boose, Lynda, 107

Bourgeoisie. *See* Middle classes

Boyce Davies, Carole, 103, 173 n.27

Brantlinger, Patrick, 26, 176 n.20

Brathwaite, Edward Kamau, 9, 13, 59, 76, 182 n.1; and Caribbean aesthetics, 62–64, 66–70, 87; and the folk novel, 61; influences on, 201 n.27; and nation-language, 9, 38; *Roots,* 38, 39; on V. S. Naipaul, 66–69; on white West Indian writers, 66, 172 n.20

Brennan, Timothy, 62

Breslin, Paul, 196 n.37

British feminism. *See* Victorian feminists

Brodber, Erna, 192 n.4

Brontë, Charlotte, Emily, and Jane, 3, 159, 200 n.19; *Jane Eyre,* 2, 109, 132, 179 n.5; *Wuthering Heights,* 54

Brown, JoAnne, 180 n.9

Bryan, Patrick, 37, 177 n.40, 179 n.3

Burton, Antoinette, 175 n.12, 177 n.31, 189 n.24

Caliban: as anticolonial symbol, 61, 109, 111–17, 129, 193 n.12; in Caribbean literature, 2, 4, 117–26, 137, 194 n.25, 197 n.51; relationship to Miranda, 110–11. *See also* Shakespeare, William

Canonical writers, 11, 140, 152, 159, 181 n.34

Canons (literary): criteria for, 89; English, 3–5, 40, 45, 50, 57, 59, 108, 110, 133, 155, 167, 179 n.5; European, 55; modernist, 153; national basis for, 84, 153; national identity and, 103; Western, 157, 160; West Indian, 2, 7, 11, 16, 37, 38, 63, 69, 70, 142, 147–48, 167, 201 n.27

Capitalism, 25

Carby, Hazel, 94

Caribbean identity. *See* West Indian identity

Caribbean independence. *See* Decolonization

Caribbean nationalism. *See* Nationalism

Carlyle, Thomas, 26, 176 n.17; and the "Literary Man," 41, 46, 49, 176 n.18; "Occasional Discourse on the Nigger Question," 25; views on West Indian blacks, 26–29

Carpentier, Alejandro, 135

Césaire, Aimé, 86: *A Tempest,* 112; and negritude, 188 n.13

Cixous, Hélène, 89

Classics. *See* Canons

Class relations: English, 25, 26; Jamaican, 24; and race, 29, 37, 152, 112, 180–81 n.24. *See also* Race relations

Cliff, Michelle, 2, 3, 158; *Abeng,* 3, 4, 126, 131; characters in novels by, 158; influences on, 102–3, 157; and modernism, 201 n.27; *No Telephone to Heaven,* 3–4, 109, 123, 126–38, 156

Cobham, Rhonda, 73, 185 n.32

Colen, Shellee, 198 n.4

Colonialism, 8, 33, 60, 62, 146; gender and, 99, 195 n.34; and government, 9; race and, 26; violence and, 196 n.39

Colonization, 106–7, 115, 135; psychological impact of, 194 n.19. *See also* Colonialism

Columbian texts, 21, 22

Columbus, Christopher, 19–20; in *Annie John,* 3

Conrad, Joseph: *Heart of Darkness,* 2
Cooper, Carolyn, 14, 73, 172 n.22
Cooper, Wayne, 74, 185 n.32
Creole languages, 9, 35, 43, 69, 88; use
 in literature, 75, 185 n.32
Creoles, 43, 113, 174 n.5, 174 n.9;
 blacks as, 32; in English fiction, 179
 n.5; in Latin America, 21, 63, 111.
 See also White West Indians
Creolization, 68
Cricket. *See* James, C. L. R.
Cuba, 7, 112, 193 n.10
Cudjoe, Selwyn, 90, 135, 185 n.24; *Re-
 sistance and Caribbean Literature,*
 105, 107

Dance, Daryl Cumber, 195 n.33
D'Costa, Jean, 144, 170, 175 n.16, 185
 n.25, 200 n.19
Decolonization, 4, 51, 59, 64, 107,
 112, 156; rape and, 121, 125; vio-
 lence and, 129; white fear of, 172
 n.20, 204 n.47
Democracy, 41
De Moraes Farias, P. F., 178 n.51
Diawara, Manthia, 31, 33, 36, 148
Dickens, Charles, 26, 38, 40, 49, 134;
 Great Expectations, 4
Domestic labor, 141, 156, 198–99 n.4;
 in literature, 127–28, 157, 203 n.44
Donaldson, Laura, 109–11
Doyle, Brian, 42
DuBois, W. E. B., 91
DuPlessis, Rachel Blau, 91

East Indians, 24, 32; in the Caribbean,
 52, 65, 67–69, 147; in literature, 181
 n.35
Education: colonial, 9, 30–31, 46, 74,
 82, 192 n.4; English, 10, 42–43, 159;
 in literature, 44, 71, 171 n.16; race
 and, 181 n.24

Eliot, T. S., 40, 47, 142, 144
Ellison, Ralph: *Invisible Man,* 15, 195
 n.32
Emery, Mary Lou, 134, 201 n.27

Fanon, Frantz, 45, 128, 180 n.23; *The
 Wretched of the Earth,* 129, 182–83
 n.2
Felski, Rita, 86, 90–96
Feminist theory, 2, 84–85, 160; and
 black aesthetics, 85; and black
 women, 94; and Caribbeanist dis-
 course, 110–11, 134; French, 96–97.
 See also Black feminist theory;
 Cixous, Hélène; Irigaray, Luce
First, Ruth, 197 n.48
Ford-Smith, Honor, 76
Foucault, Michel, 2
Franco, Jean, 167
Freud, Sigmund, 145, 146, 149, 160; in
 literature, 187 n.7
Froudacity. See Thomas, John Jacob
Froude, James Anthony, 35, 50; *The
 Bow of Ulysses: The English in the
 West Indies,* 1, 4–5, 27, 30, 34; in
 Caribbean literature, 4, 55, 56, 154,
 181; views on blacks, 170 n.13;
 views on Indians, 52
Frye, Northrop, 149
Fuss, Diana, 97

Garvey, Marcus, 74, 128, 179 n.3
Gates, Henry Louis, Jr., 86; *The Sig-
 nifying Monkey,* 91; and double-
 voicedness, 91
Gayle, Addison, 87
Gikandi, Simon, 144, 171 n.16, 176
 n.17, 201 n.27
Gilbert, Sandra, 109, 193 n.15
Gilroy, Paul, 84, 148
Gines de Sepulvéda, Juan, 175 n.14
Goldberg, Jonathan, 108

Gomes, Albert, 151–52
González Echevarría, Roberto, 150
Gordon, George William, 25, 29
Governor Eyre debate, 24–31. *See also*
    Morant Bay Rebellion
Greene, Gayle, 89
Gregg, Veronica, 173 n.24, 202 n.40
Grenada: in literature, 162–63
Gubar, Susan, 109, 193 n.15
Guillen, Nicholas, 193 n.10

Habermas, Jürgen, 94, 117
Haiti: English fears of, 30; Haitian rev-
    olution in, 33, 105–6, 112–13, 169
    n.2
Hall, Catherine, 25, 29, 176 nn.17, 18
Hall, Stuart, 192 n.2
Halpern, Richard, 121, 184 n.14
Harding, Sandra, 85, 194 n.18
Harlem Renaissance, 70, 76, 201 n.25
Harlowe, Barbara, 135
Harris, Wilson, 148; and modernism,
    150; on narrative form, 63, 135, 153,
    183; *Palace of the Peacock,* 2
Head, Bessie, 201 n.27
Hearne, John, 64
Hegel, G. W. F., 140
History: colonial, 60; and gender, 108,
    132–33, 195–96 n.34; in literature,
    3–4, 51–56, 107, 127, 135, 155,
    167, 173 n.26; and memory, 165; as
    myth, 105, 136, 155, 167, 203 n.42;
    oral, 105, 135, 192 n.4; revolution-
    ary, 105–7, 135
Homosexuality, 94; in literature, 131–
    32
hooks, bell, 87, 95, 109
Hulme, Peter, 23–24
Hurston, Zora Neale, 203 nn.42, 45

Immigrants: in Britain, 203 n.46; Ca-
    ribbean men as, 13, 141; Caribbean

women as, 6, 10–12, 13, 134, 139–
    41, 156–57, 165–66, 172 n.19, 198–
    99 n.4; national debates over, 175
    n.12; white, 152
Imperialism, 8, 26, 117, 176 nn.20, 22;
    race and, 103; slavery and, 148. *See
    also* Colonialism
India, 20; relationship to England, 32;
    in Western discourse, 178 n.42
Indians. *See* Amerindians; East Indians
Indigenous peoples. *See* Amerindians
Individualism, 25, 32, 41, 46, 176 n.17
Industrialization, 149
Intellectuals. *See* Middle classes
Irigaray, Luce, 145–46, 164, 190–91
    n.44; and parler femme, 89, 97. *See
    also* Feminist theory

Jamaica: dancehall culture of, 14, 172
    n.22; English views on, 24–31, 34,
    43, 170 n.13; ghettoes in, 66; lan-
    guage in, 144; in literature, 126–28,
    130, 158, 186 n.36; nationalism in,
    174 n.8; race in, 65; rural culture of,
    70. *See also* Morant Bay Rebellion
James, C. L. R., 1, 15, 42, 49, 70, 76,
    122, 133, 137, 153, 173 n.26; on ar-
    tistic production, 47–48; *Beyond a
    Boundary,* 1, 38, 46; *The Black Jac-
    obins,* 38, 105–6, 113, 192 n.2;
    cricket and, 46–47; critics on, 153,
    178 n.2, 202 n.37; in England, 13;
    and exile, 140, 146, 151–52, 160,
    166; and Kincaid, 82; literary influ-
    ence of, 81; Marxism and, 38, 178
    n.2; middle-class sensibilities of, 51;
    Minty Alley, 183 n.3; and national-
    ism, 1, 38, 39, 178 n.2; and pan-
    Africanism, 38, 39; and Thackeray,
    1, 39, 46, 106; and V. S. Naipaul
Jameson, Fredric, 167, 175 n.14
Jekyll, Walter, 185–86 n.32

Kahn, Coppelia, 89
Kasinitz, Philip, 198–99 n.4
Kincaid, Jamaica, 2, 3, 81, 158; *Annie John*, 3, 159, 170 n.11; and feminism, 95, 100–101; *Lucy*, 3, 81–83, 103–4, 158–61, 170 n.11, 187 n.7; views on literature, 82, 187 n.1
King, Bruce, 11, 62, 171 n.16
Kingsley, Charles, 26, 54, 181 n.24; *At Last: A Christmas in the West Indies*, 170–71 n.13
Kipling, Rudyard, 47, 179 n.5
Kutzinski, Vera, 193 n.10

Lalla, Barbara, 144
Lamming, George, 1, 3, 47, 48, 69, 76, 133, 137, 141, 146, 173 n.26, 174 n.11; critics on, 153; on decolonization, 64; and the folk novel, 61–65, 87, 148, 152; literary influence of, 81; parodies of, 197 n.51; and the peasantry, 58–61, 140, 184 n.12; *The Pleasures of Exile*, 43, 58, 105, 112–16, 120, 192 n.1; *Season of Adventure*, 171 n.16, 195 n.32; on Shakespeare, 63–64; *Water with Berries*, 108, 117–22, 129
Land (land ownership, land owners): colonization and, 175 n.14; language of, 144; in literature, 52–53, 130, 134–35; as metaphor, 145; and nationalism, 45, 60–61, 117; peasantry and, 184 n.17; and race, 23, 28, 184 n.17; Spanish debates over, 177 n.24
Language(s): African, 88; African American dialects and, 88; African-based Caribbean; English, 43, 50; national, 62; nation formation and, 175 n.14; as symbol of civilization, 114; as symbol of decolonization, 119, 136–37. *See also* Creoles
Latin America, 20, 21, 50, 112, 121,

123; literature of, 167; and modernity, 150
Lawrence, D. H., 202 n.33
Levering Lewis, David, 201 n.25
Literary traditions. *See* Canons
Long, Edward: *The History of Jamaica*, 43
Lorimer, Douglas, 30, 31
L'Ouverture, Toussaint, 106, 113, 122. *See also* Haiti
Lovelace, Earl: *The Dragon Can't Dance*, 105, 129, 192 n.1

Mais, Roger: *Brother Man*, 66
Maroons, 130–31
Marshall, Paule, 2, 3, 14, 139–40, 145, 146, 156, 158; "Brazil," 4, 108, 123–26; *The Chosen Place, the Timeless People*, 3, 4; *Daughters*, 3, 204 n.50; *Praisesong for the Widow*, 3, 158, 161–67, 204 n.49; *Soul Clap Hands and Sing*, 3
Marson, Una, 10, 57, 75, 77, 127, 157; critics of, 186 n.43; the folk novel and, 61, 148; *Pocomania*, 10, 75–76, 171 n.16
Martí, José, 21, 111–12
Marxism: Caribbean writers and, 1, 39, 74, 106
McKay, Claude, 10, 57, 74, 76, 127, 133; *Banana Bottom*, 10, 70–74, 75, 137, 140, 166, 171 n.16, 186 n.36; *Banjo*, 73; the folk novel and, 61, 148, 152, 166; *Home to Harlem*, 73–74; sexuality of, 186 n.32; use of creole, 185 n.32
McKenzie, John, 176 n.22
Mendes, Alfred, 151
Mestizaje, 111. *See also* Mulattoes
Middle classes: English, 5, 26, 176 n.22; formation of, 175 n.14; Western, 141; West Indian, 37, 45–46,

Middle classes (*cont.*)
58–59, 63, 152, 178 n.51; (white)
American, 164. *See also* Black middle
class
Middle Passage, 51, 56, 137, 162, 164.
See also Slavery
Mill, John Stuart: Governor Eyre de-
bate and, 26–29; "The Negro Ques-
tion," 25; "The Subjection of
Women," 29
Milton, John, 5, 47, 76, 134, 154; *Para-
dise Lost,* 159
Minority literature, 16
Modernism, 40, 91, 143–44, 165; Ca-
ribbean, 147–53; critics of, 201 n.29;
origins of, 149–50; "Third World,"
201 n.27
Modernity, 13, 14, 149; Caribbean na-
tionalism and, 23, 64; race and, 33,
113, 148, 164, 166
Modernization, 23, 148, 149, 165, 166,
175 n.14. *See also* Modernity
Morant Bay Rebellion, 24, 31, 174 n.8.
See also Governor Eyre debate
Morrison, Toni, 203 n.45; and black
aesthetics, 95–96, 100; *Song of Solomon,* 88, 101
Moynihan Report, 191 n.47
Mulattoes, 63, 107–8, 192–93 n.9; in
literature, 3, 44, 112, 154, 179 n.5,
193 n.10
Music: in literature, 66–67, 75
Myth. *See* History

Naipaul, V. S., 1, 9, 32, 39, 42, 57, 133,
140; on black power, 48, 192 n.1;
and blacks, 45; Caribbean history
and, 107, 136; and C. L. R. James,
48–49, 151, 181 n.35; critics and,
153, 185 n.24, 202 n.37; and the English canon, 49–50, 59, 181 n.34; exile and, 141–47, 160, 166, 174 n.11;
and George Lamming, 197 n.51;
Guerrillas, 51, 105, 129–30, 195
n.32; *A House for Mr. Biswas,* 10,
38, 67–68; and Jamaica Kincaid, 82;
The Middle Passage, 1, 50, 139, 152,
157, 181 n.34; *The Mimic Men,* 51–
56; modernism and, 142–43, 148,
150–52; and nationalism, 14–15, 51,
129; *A Way in the World,* 181 n.35;
West Indians' views on, 48, 67, 69,
81; and whites, 180–81 n.24; views
on writing, 50–51, 152, 182 n.37
Nair, Supriya, 199 n.4
Nationalism, 33, 61, 62; Caribbean, 1,
7, 8, 23, 39, 123, 140; English, 42;
European, 62; exile and, 140–41;
Latin American, 21, 111–12, 123.
See also Black nationalism; Imperial-
ism; Pan-Africanism
National liberation. *See* Decolonization
Neal, Larry, 87
Negritude, 62, 85, 91, 188 n.13
Nettleford, Rex, 65–66
New Criticism, 149
New World, 33, 51, 135, 163, 181
n.24; formation of, 20–21, 23, 175
n.14; race discourse of, 111. *See also*
America
Nixon, Rob, 122, 142–43, 146, 193
n.12, 197 n.51
North, Michael, 186 n.36

Obeah. *See* Religion
O'Callaghan, Evelyn, 89
Ogunyemi, Chikwenye, 102
Orality, 63, 88, 192 n.4

Pagden, Anthony, 175 n.14
Pan-Africanism, 8, 9, 35, 36, 38, 39,
48, 67; and black aesthetics, 85–89;
black leaders and, 128
Patterson, Orlando, 172 n.22, 174 n.8

Peasantry, 58–60, 62, 70, 152, 184 n.17; English, 202 n.33
Philip, Marlene Nourbese, 81–82, 103
Phillips, Caryl, 15, 173 n.26
Picasso, Pablo, 201 n.25
Plantocracy. *See* Land
Pocomania. See Religion
Poovey, Mary, 41, 170 n.11
Pope-Hennessy, James, 181 n.24
Postmodernism, 167
Poststructuralism, 93
Primitivism, 33, 70, 113, 152
Professional class. *See* Middle classes
Property. *See* Land
Prospero complex. *See* Shakespeare, William

Race relations, 112, 134, 188 n.11
Racialism. *See* Racism
Racism, 134, 155, 171 n.16; scientific, 31, 34
Raiskin, Judith, 180 n.23, 182 n.1
Ramchand, Kenneth, 172 n.20, 203 n.47
Rape: in literature, 116–19, 129, 132, 171 n.16, 193 n.10, 195 n.32. *See also* Sex, interracial
Redding, J. Saunders, 87
Religion: Obeah, 71, 128, 131, 135; and literary authority, 180 n.9; *Pocomania,* 75
Renaissance, 107, 115
Retamar, Roberto Fernández, 111–12, 121, 123
Revolutionaries, 179 n.3, 195 n.32, 197 n.48. *See also* Black nationalism; Nationalism
Rhodes, Cecil, 176 n.20
Rhys, Jean: "Again the Antilles," 44, 155; critics on, 153, 172 n.20; "The Day They Burned the Books," 4, 154–55; exile and, 147; feminist the-

ory and, 134, 156, 169 n.8; and *Jane Eyre,* 2; modernism and, 148, 201 n.27; and nationalist literature, 14–15; views on blacks, 172 n.20, 173 n.24, 185 n.21; views on the English, 202 n.39; *Voyage in the Dark,* 170 n.11. *See also Wide Sargasso Sea*
Ricoeur, Paul, 166, 193 n.15
Rodo, José Enrique: *Ariel,* 111
Rodríguez, Ileana, 23, 175 n.14
Romanticism, 62, 69
Rousseau, Jean Jacques, 21

Saakana, Amon, 183 n.7
Said, Edward, 140, 150, 178 n.42
Scholes, Theophilus, 37
Scott, Bonnie Kime, 147
Selvon, Samuel: *An Island Is a World,* 195 n.32
Senghor, Léopold, 188 n.13
Sex, interracial, 192–93 n.9; in Caribbean literature, 171 n.16; and colonization, 171 n.13; in nationalist discourse, 196 n.34; in Renaissance literature, 107–8. *See also* Rape
Shakespeare, William, 2, 35, 47, 76, 134; in Caribbean literature and criticism, 44, 63, 69, 72, 159; as symbol of Englishness, 184 n.14. *See also* Caliban; *The Tempest*
Sharpe, Jenny, 173 n.26
Showalter, Elaine, 91
Slavery, 65, 95, 192 n.4; gender divisions in, 190 n.40; and imperialism, 148; in literature, 3, 53, 126–27, 135; and motherhood, 98–99; and women's rights, 189 n.24
Slaves, 87, 94–95, 106, 113, 144; children and, 114; in literature, 52, 162; women as, 109–10, 115. *See also* Africans
Smith, Barbara, 85

Smith, Faith, 46, 178 n.51, 181 n.26, 202 n.37

Soyinka, Wole, 88, 200 n.14

Spillers, Hortense, 21, 98–99, 104, 107

Spivak, Gayatri Chakravorty, 97

Stallybrass, Peter, 134

Stendhal: *The Red and the Black,* 55

Stereotypes: Amerindians and, 21, 171 n.13; of black men, 8, 27–28, 30, 170 n.13; of black women, 8, 14, 28, 30, 159, 170 n.13, 172 n.22

The Tempest, 2, 108–9, 113–26, 184 n.14, 192 n.1, 196 nn.36, 37; Ariel, as anticolonial symbol in, 111–12; Prospero, as symbol of colonialism in, 2, 194 n.19; Sycorax, as symbol in, 115. *See also* Shakespeare, William

Thackeray, William Makepeace, 1; *Vanity Fair,* 46, 106, 179 n.5

Thelwell, Michael, 201 n.29

Thomas, John Jacob, 35, 51; *Froudacity,* 35

Tiffin, Helen, 82–83

Travel writing, 50–51, 60, 152

Trinidad, 59, 68, 151; and Black Power revolts, 192 n.1; in literature, 183 n.2; in travel narratives, 139, 170–71 n.13, 181 n.24

Trollope, Anthony, 40, 49, 55; and views on West Indian blacks, 30, 32–33, 36, 170 n.13, 177 n.35; in West Indian literature, 181 n.34; *The West Indies and the Spanish Main,* 1, 170 n.13

United States, 21, 90; academic scholarship in, 16; art forms, 66–67; blacks in, 149, 152; Caribbean writers in, 2, 13, 139, 151–52, 157, 203 n.46; difference from Britain, 29; hegemony and, 4; and Latin America, 111–12; in literature, 73, 76, 127, 133, 156, 158, 162–65, 204 n.50; manliness in, 177 n.34; migration to, 12, 141, 152, 156, 198 n.4; slavery in, 98, 109–10. *See also* Harlem Renaissance; Immigrants; Slavery

University of the West Indies, 185 n.25

Victorian feminists, 103, 189 n.24. *See also* Feminist theory

Viswanathan, Gauri, 72

Walcott, Derek, 1, 69, 105, 153; critics on, 202 n.37; *Dream on Monkey Mountain,* 195 n.32

Walker, Alice, 101–2

Warren, Kenneth, 87

wa Thiong'o, Ngugi, 199 n.14

West Indian identity, 157, 167. *See also* Black identity

West Indian nationalism. *See* Caribbean nationalism

White, Allon, 134

White West Indians, 21–24, 31–32, 64; and blacks, 177–78 n.40; and class, 180–81 n.24; and decolonization, 172 n.20; definition of, 184 n.15; and England, 174 n.8; in literature, 185 nn.32, 44

White women: and colonialism, 109, 182 n.1; and decolonization, 196 n.39; in literature, 11, 123–30, 132–34, 138, 173 n.26, 195 n.32; as readers, 202 n.40; in revolutionary discourse, 123; worldview of, 194 n.18. *See also* Rape; Sex, interracial; White West Indians

Wide Sargasso Sea, 157, 203 n.47; and Afro-Caribbean discourse, 66; in Caribbean literature, 132; critics on,

200 n.19, 202 n.38; images of black
women in, 14; and modernism, 148;
relationship to *Jane Eyre,* 2, 110. *See
also* Rhys, Jean
Williams, Eric, 50, 152; *Capitalism and
Slavery,* 26
Women's Movement, U.S., 90
Women writers: Caribbean-American,
5, 158; English, 4, 154; West Indian,

170 n.11, 174 n.11. *See also* African
American literature
Wordsworth, William, 76; in literature,
169 n.6; in *Lucy,* 3, 83
Wright, Richard: *Native Son,* 195 n.32
Wynter, Sylvia, 63, 68, 115–16; *The
Hills of Hebron,* 89

Zamora, Margarita, 21–22, 28

*Belinda Edmondson is Assistant Professor of English and African/
African-American Studies at Rutgers University, Newark.*

Library of Congress Cataloging-in-Publication Data
Edmondson, Belinda.
Making men : gender, literary authority, and women's writing in Caribbean
narrative / Belinda Edmondson.
p. cm.
Includes bibliographical references and index.
ISBN 0-8223-2131-9 (acid-free paper). —
ISBN 0-8223-2263-3 (pbk. : acid-free paper)
1. Caribbean literature (English) — Women authors — History and criticism.
2. Caribbean literature (English) — Men authors — History and criticism.
3. Emigration and immigration in literature.   4. Feminism and literature —
Caribbean area.   5. Authorship — Sex differences.
6. Imperialism in literature.   7. Masculinity in literature.
8. Authority in literature.   9. Colonies in literature.
10. Narration (Rhetoric)   I. Title.
PR9205.05E36   1999
810.9'9729 — dc21   98-22005   CIP